Contemporary Perspectives on Social Capital in Educational Contexts

A Volume in:
Contemporary Perspectives on Capital in Educational Contexts

Series Editor

RoSusan D. Bartee

Contemporary Perspectives on Capital in Educational Contexts

Series Editor

RoSusan D. Bartee
University of Central Florida

Contemporary Perspective on Capital in Educational Contexts (2010)
RoSusan D. Bartee

Contemporary Perspectives on Social Capital in Educational Contexts

Edited by

RoSusan D. Bartee
Phillis. L. George

INFORMATION AGE PUBLISHING, INC.
Charlotte, NC • www.infoagepub.com

Library of Congress Cataloging-In-Publication Data

The CIP data for this book can be found on the Library of Congress website (loc.gov).

Paperback: 978-1-64113-638-9
Hardcover: 978-1-64113-639-6
E-book: 978-1-64113-640-2

Printed in the United States of America

CONTENTS

PART II

ACCESS STRATEGIES

FOREWORD

EXTERNAL ACCESS AND INTERNAL ACCOUNTABILITY

The Currency Conduits for Maximizing Social Capital in Public Schools and Higher Education

RoSusan D. Bartee and Phillis L. George

The 21st century, American education landscape is extremely dynamic. Largely shaped by political and economic challenges (Bastedo, Altbach, & Gumport, 2016) both globally and nationally (Altbach, 2016), the landscape is fast-changing and ever responsive to evolving, societal demands. Although attempts are made in earnest to address the educational needs of all societal agents and members, invariably, there are individuals and groups who are perpetually marginalized in K–12 and higher education due to their social standing and access to capital (Bowen & Bok, 1998; Bowen, Kurzweil, & Tobin, 2005; Bowen & McPherson, 2016). Pierre Bourdieu (1986) defines social capital as "the aggregate of the actual or potential resources which are linked to possession of a durable network of more or less institutionalized relationships of mutual acquaintance and recognition—or in other words, to membership in a group" (p. 251). Social capital contains embedded resources as a tool for manifesting opportunities and options among and between individuals and groups. The currency of social capital serves

Contemporary Perspectives on Social Capital in Educational Contexts,
pages ix–xxii.
Copyright © 2019 by Information Age Publishing

as an important function given the capacity to generate external access (*getting to*) and internal accountability (*getting through*). Consequently, external access and internal accountability as currency conduits offer transferable resources to more strategically navigate increasingly complex social and educational attainment pathways within and across groups.

As educational stakeholders, we must consistently challenge ourselves with the question, "How do K–12 schools and colleges and universities accomplish shared, egalitarian goals of achieving access and accountability?" Such goals become fundamental toward ensuring students matriculating through K–12 and higher education, irrespective of background, are provided the caliber of education and schooling experiences to prepare them for economic mobility and social stability. Within the confines of this book, access is broadly defined (i.e., along the educational continuum) as perfected systems, policies, and practices that encourage all students—especially those who are historically minoritized and marginalized—to enroll and persist toward graduation and degree completion. As aptly stated by Engstrom and Tinto (2008), "Access without support is not opportunity" (p. 50). In building upon this qualified notion of access, it is worth noting that educational access is not simply limited to opening up previously restricted doors and channels. Instead, it is defined and operationalized within this body of scholarly work as a responsibility that befalls schools and colleges to create unobstructed, environmental systems of advocacy and support for all students—thereby helping to breed creativity and ingenuity, build critical thinking and analytic skills, promote academic and self-efficacy, plant seeds of intellectual curiosity, and develop and cultivate aspirational desires for learning and advanced educational attainment.

Fullan and Quinn (2016) broadly refers to accountability as "taking responsibility for one's actions" (p. 110). Fullan and Quinn (2016) further states that a "… real accountability system is in the tasks that students are asked to do" (p. 110). Within the current body of work, accountability is expanded to include responsibility from the perspective of individuals and institutions and their corresponding actions. This perspective suggests the need for mutual, shared responsibility (i.e., to ensure student success) that is required from both the individual and institution, alike. Building upon this notion, Fullan and Quinn (2016) specifically articulates internal accountability as "conditions that increase the likelihood that people will be accountable to themselves and to the group... Internal accountability occurs when individuals and groups willingly take on personal, professional, and collective responsibility for continuous improvement and success for all students" (pp. 109–110). Internal accountability flourishes when the cultural context of the respective environment is conducive toward the holistic growth and development of individuals. Thus, it becomes important for institutions of education (i.e., secondary, postsecondary, and continuing) to assume efforts with intentionality and deliberateness to promote access and accountability.

To that end, the volume, *Contemporary Perspectives on Social Capital in Educational Contexts* (2019), as part of the book series, *Contemporary Perspectives on Capital in Educational Contexts*, offers a unique opportunity to explore social capital as a currency conduit for creating external access and internal accountability for K–12 and higher education. The commonalities of social capital emerging within the 12 chapters of the volume include the following: 1) Social Capital as Human Connectedness; 2) Social Capital as Strategic Advocacy; 3) Social Capital as Intentional Engagement; and 4) Social Capital as Culturally-Responsive Leadership. Figure 1 is a graphic to highlight the shared characteristics.

Specifically, Figure 1 shows social capital as currency conduits, given the linkages between access and accountability. Social capital as *culturally responsive leadership* is based upon "the ability of school leaders to create school contexts and curriculum that responds effectively to the educational, social, political, and cultural needs of students...and is relevant to the context (Khalifa, Gooden, & Davis, 2016). Figure 1 also shows how social capital as *strategic advocacy* involves active sponsorship of individuals who demonstrate notable talent and non-cognitive factors of behavior, attitude, and strategies that will transfer into both short and long-term opportunities (Lederman, 2013; Lucero, Maes, & Klingmith, 2014; University of Chicago, 2012).

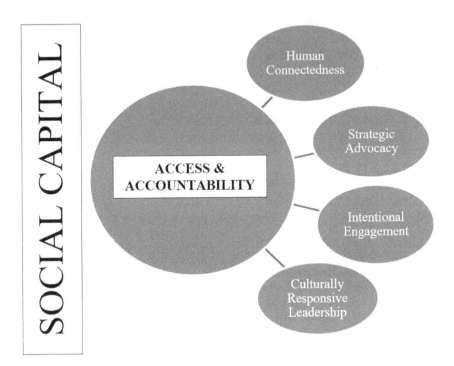

FIGURE 1.   Currency Conduits of Social Capital

Social capital as *intentional engagement* involves the conscious pursuit of selected academic and non-academic endeavors to advance participation in and relationship with social, civic, community, and related networks and organizations (Morimoto & Friedland, 2013; Putnam, 2000). Figure 1 indicates that social capital as *human connectedness* involves the personal and professional trust that naturally prevails or emerges between individuals involved with a shared, collective interest (Ellison, Wohn, & Greenhow, 2014). The caliber of access and accountability acquired becomes a manifestation of how individual students are engaged or engage with the K–12 and/or higher education institution.

SOCIAL CAPITAL AS HUMAN CONNECTEDNESS

As mentioned, social capital as *human connectedness* involves the personal and professional trust that naturally prevails or emerges between individuals involved with a shared, collective interest (Ellison, Wohn, & Greenhow, 2014). Part of the capacity of social capital as *human connectedness* to improve academic outcomes within K–12 and higher education is influenced by fundamental perspectives situated within *Maslow's Hierarchy of Needs*. The duo of university-school-community partnerships and the focus toward generating *connectedness* among diverse stakeholders becomes an important component for responding affectively and socially to human motivation, protecting individual safety, and fostering belonging within an educational continuum context (i.e., K–12 through higher and continuing education). The short- and long-term impact of these internal and external dynamics are critical toward maintaining and forging social relationships and academic rigor necessary to keep students involved and retained (Jensen, 2009; Shultz, 2006). Epstein (2011) further expands upon this work to include family as part of the intricacies of this dynamic and suggests the trio of school-family-community partnerships as being "carried out everywhere that children [or students] learn, including homes, early childhood education programs, schools, after-school programs, faith-based institutions, playgrounds, and community settings" (p. 31). The implication of family as part of this expanded duo-to-trio approach shows the importance of cultivating social capital within the teaching and learning context (Ferrara, 2015; Leana & Pill, 2014; Long, 2016; U. S. Department of Education, 2013). Additionally, Ellison et. al (2014) assert the following:

> In sum, different kinds of social network structures—those that facilitate exposure to diverse, weak ties or those that limit interactions to more insular, homogenous strong ties—provide different kinds of benefits. In the context of young people living in nonurban communities with a population that has low rates of upward mobility and college-going…bridging social capital may be especially important because it is a mechanism for encountering more diverse life paths. (p. 519)

Such an approach demonstrates the importance of fostering the development of social capital between and among people. There are unique linkages between issues of access and accountability regarding the opportunities that may or may not emerge due to the absence or presence of social capital. This volume's inclusion of work by Taylor, Hartman, and Jones titled, "Diversity Mission Statement Inclusion as Social Capital: How the Language of Appeasement Fails Egalitarian Goals in Postsecondary Institutions," highlight these linkages. The particular study employs content analysis by way of grounded theory to analyze institutional diversity mission statements from public flagship institutions. In doing so, the study addresses pressing questions about the value colleges place on different forms of diversity and how and to whom that value is or is not communicated to various stakeholders. Further, its findings articulate which forms of diversity hold institutional value or social capital via their inclusion in diversity mission statements. To complement the work of Taylor, Hartman, and Jones, the current volume includes work done by McNamee—which fosters much needed discussion on rurality, utilizing Bourdieu's (1986) theory of social capital to detail how rural students' current forms of social capital (or lack thereof) in their tight-knit communities affects the educational attainment of rural citizens. McNamee's chapter is titled, "Social Capital in the Rural United States and Its Impact on Educational Attainment." In it, McNamee draws hard lines between issues of access and accountability in rural locales (i.e., especially pertaining to higher education aspirations and opportunities) and argues that citizens residing in these regions are often left out of pertinent discussions due to a historical focus on urban educational spaces rather than rural universities, schools, and communities.

In addition to the aforementioned chapters, this volume's inclusion of Price's work titled, "Social Capital Resources in Schools: Explaining Effective School Community," is critical toward understanding how schools as organizations integrate the structural components of relationships among school faculty that compose the teachers' social capital. This chapter addresses the fundamental research question: What is the extent to which the social resources of teachers in schools explain school community? The study particularly focuses on how two levels of so cial resources, interpersonal teacher and organization-wide faculty relationships, offer processes associated with the aspects of positive school community. Similarly, Farmer-Hinton and Holland's chapter titled, "Embracing the Fullness of Postsecondary Planning: Utilizing Social Capital to Serve Students at the Nexus of Navigational Capital and Care," offers insight into how institutions of higher education need to ready themselves to serve diverse populations. An inordinate need exists toward expanding the manner in which college and career readiness is approached, particularly once students arrive on campus and the sense of belonging that gets or does not get created. Social capital, as comprised of networks of individuals with varying levels of exposure, norms, and support, serve as a viable, yet often, untapped resource for creating communities of care. Farmer-Hinton and Holland's chapter demonstrate how access to those communities of care generates an affective type of response while also serving as a practical (re) source used for navigating issues and instances on campus. Both resources are complimentary and critically important toward preparing students more holistically to achieve success within postsecondary education.

This volume's inclusion of research conducted by Fowler titled, "Social Capital and School Reform: The Role of School Leaders in Fostering Relationships Amongst Stakeholders," builds upon the extant literature related to social capital within the PreK–12 educational context and the implications for school reform. The manner in which school leaders need to promote social capital within the school's ecosystem as a means for improving educational outcomes is examined. Fowler further examines how the importance of relationships between school leaders and their respective stakeholders (i.e., staff, students, parents, community members, and business owners). Such an approach allows for a focused demonstration and discussion of how social capital found within school leaders' relationships can be used as a resourceful tool in school reform.

SOCIAL CAPITAL AS CULTURALLY RESPONSIVE LEADERSHIP

Social capital as *culturally responsive leadership* is based upon "the ability of school [and institutional] leaders to create school [and institutional] contexts and curriculum that respond effectively to the educational, social, political, and cultural needs of students…and is relevant to the context (Khalifa, et al., 2016). As a result, the administration of leadership as culturally or non-culturally responsive becomes an (un)desired reflection of the embedded school and academic culture and climate (Beachum, 2011; Madhlangobe & Gordon, 2012; McCray & Beachum, 2011). Whether or not students choose to enter or are encouraged to pursue co-curricular programmatic activities and/or gifted education are often impacted by the influence of instructors and administrators as well as current school policies and institutional practices (Ford, 2013; Grantham et al., 2011). How students engage informal experiences of schooling and formalized demands of education get crystalized through the quality of peer-to-peer and peer-to-adult interactions within institutions and schools.

Culturally responsive leadership, as a venue to promote access and accountability, has to be undertaken by both administrators and instructors at both macro and micro levels. And why, pray tell, are these areas matters of social capital? Let's use the example of high-stakes tests at the secondary education end of the continuum to help answer the aforementioned question. High-stakes test performance of students is a matter that directly concerns educational administrators. The tests not only affect school and school district ratings but also high school degree completion, high school-to-college transitions, and college matriculation and success rates. The collective perception of students' cognitive ability and/or level of preparation is often influenced by where they attend school (Croft et al., 2017). It is no secret that some schools, because of their affiliate tax base, have more resources than others and are, therefore, less impacted by high-stakes tests. However, it is reasonable to conclude that high-stakes tests carry a great deal of weight for other schools and districts (i.e., with fewer resources), particularly school districts with high numbers of minoritized and socio-economically marginalized students. Attentiveness to such disparities must then become the work of culturally informed and responsive, school leaders. To be clear, the disparities speak directly to issues of access and accountability, regarding social capital.

Beyond the potentially negative impact on historically minoritized and socio-economically marginalized students, culturally responsive leaders must also be attentive to high-stakes test performance requirements and their influence on teacher evaluation ratings (e.g., negatively or positively), particularly because of the value-added model. The value-added model purports that "value" that "a teacher adds to a student's academic progress" can essentially "…be…teased out, by way of a mathematical formula using the test scores" (Straus, 2015). The value-added model becomes useful in establishing accountability, given its focus on growth (i.e., for all students) and not solely on proficiency. The teacher's and/or instructor's ability to deliver pedagogy in a manner to achieve student mastery of content is consistently being assessed. More specifically, concerted efforts can and should be placed on subgroups (e.g., English language learners, historically marginalized and underrepresented minorities, exceptional education students, lowest 25% performing students, etc.) to ensure growth targets are fulfilled on an annual basis. Thus, the culturally responsive leader and/or instructor can utilize the value-added model to address persistent achievement disparities, thereby advancing core principles of access and accountability as tenets of social capital through their teaching, learning, and leading capacities.

To that end, the volume's inclusion of work by Crutchfield, Bailey, and Crutchfield entitled, "The Role of School Leaders Managing Social Capital within urban and Rural School Settings," focuses on the need to assume responsibility for leveraging internal and external resources as well as human and fiscal resources within school settings. Such leveraging serves to ensure equity in education and access to academic and social supports for every student, regardless of a school district's tax base. Crutchfield, Bailey, and Crutchfield particularly highlight the social and institutional resources or rather, social capital, needed by school administrators to educate students served by urban and rural school systems. The chapter offers insights into the commonalities and disparities in the evaluable capital of urban and rural school contexts and how the management of these specified resources need to be pursued.

With *culturally responsive leadership*, the work of Trigosso, Reggio, and McCray, "Closing Achievement Gaps through Parent Involvement: How School Leaders Can Increase the Social Capital of Parents," focuses on how effective school leaders foster critical pathways for parental involvement. The pathways serve to inform parents, develop their capacity to enhance their children's academic progress, and increase social capital in concrete and meaningful ways. Trigosso, Reggio, and McCray further suggest that parents need to make choices toward the investment of their children's growth. The authors purport the need for parents to engage in interactions with their children to encourage their children's development (i.e., language barriers, cultural boundaries, lack of time and access, etc.). Such perspectives encourage shared responsibility between families/parents and the schools regarding issues of access and accountability and the capacity to promote social capital.

In keeping with the arguments of Trigosso, Reggio, and McCray, Keung and Ho offer a chapter titled, "Social Capital and Educational Expectations: Exploring Adolescents' Capabilities to Aspire for Post-Secondary Education," which posits existing research largely built on Bourdieu's *Social Reproduction Theory* often explains the structural constraints for inequality access to higher education, but few studies have applied Amartya Sen's *Capability Approach* addressing the agency of "capability to aspire" for differential post-secondary education transitions. In a sense, the *Capability Approach* much like the value-added model, serves as an alternative but useful tool for culturally responsive leaders of schools, universities, and colleges (alike) to help address persistent issues of limited educational aspirations and lowered educational attainment levels. In this chapter, Keung and Ho review the interplay between structural and agency factors which influence adolescents' postsecondary educational expectations—factors which culturally responsive leaders and instructors should be fully knowledgeable of and responsive to in their work. The authors extend their inquiry by exploring social capital gained from families and schools, on the one hand, shaping adolescents' pursuit of post-secondary education and on the other hand, examining adolescents' own skills and abilities which are formed as important capabilities that influence them in achieving particular educational goals.

SOCIAL CAPITAL AS INTENTIONAL ENGAGEMENT

Social capital as *intentional engagement* involves the conscious pursuit of selected academic and non-academic endeavors to advance participation in and relationship with social, civic, community, and related networks and organizations (Morimoto & Friedland, 2013). In effect, multi-dimensional capacities and implications of social capital for students matriculating within educational contexts generate mutually-beneficial outcomes when there is "…access to social networks and connections; aspirational capital, meaning seeing a vision for the future; familial capital, which is having a shared and connected history; and navigational capital, meaning understanding how to successfully navigate" (Yosso, 2005). The capacity to ensure such access requires intentional and focused engagement by schools, higher education institutions, students, families, and even communities. There is a diverse array of student experiences regarding academic preparation, socioeconomic status, familial experience with college, and racial and ethnic diversity that points to the potential for social capital to positively impact student retention (Greene, Marti, & McClenney, 2008; Lucero, Maes, & Klingsmith, 2014, p. 525). Given such potentiality, *intentional engagement* reflects the extent to which students have the requisite knowledge and experience involving expectations for success within schools and colleges. Ultimately, this speaks to an educational passport to (un)spoken rules of engagement for success. Students with access to social capital experience appropriate ease and have heightened levels of familiarity when participating in certain educational dialogues and pursuits. Further, they see these dialogues and pursuits as strategic means to achieve both short and long-term opportunities (and rightfully so).

Having social capital is a value-added commodity for fostering a sense of belonging, particularly for those who may or may not emanate from a higher socioeconomic status or majority / mainstreamed background. Social capital offers a different kind of currency where non-economic resources (e.g., organizational networks, professional relationships, people circles, association involvement, cultural networks, etc.) are core components for cultivating and/or legitimizing access. According to Kaplan and Ownings (2013):

> Social capital, resilience, and civic capacity—the interest, knowledge, and skills required to participate competently as citizens in a democracy—all focus on assuming that every community has assets that can be used to support children and youth. Unlike the deficit model which looks at nontraditional families, economic decline or the presence of immigrant groups with different traditions as creating cumulative obstacles to community well-being and school success, the cultural asset model looks for the positive features in all children's [and students'] cultures. (p. 179)

Individual and collective empowerment exist within the depth and breadth of social capital to generate access to and for diverse educational opportunities. As a form of academic currency, the purview of social capital as *intentional engagement* offers the appropriate access to human and material resources for establishing cross-relational and multi-layered connections among and across diverse communities. What is learned and/or gained from attending school becomes a proxy for fostering civic engagement as a means to promote the development of intellectual, psychological, emotional, and social outcomes (Winter, 2003). The bi-product of such intentional development has the capacity to create higher, more competent levels of self-efficacy, decision-making skills, and sense of responsibility.

Within the current volume, the work of Mittenfelner Carl addresses how social capital can be misplaced and used to operate from a deficit stance within a school unless deliberate approaches are taken. Aptly titled, "Nyeisha's Mother: An Ethnographic Examination of Urban Schooling and Adopting a Resource Orientation Toward Social Capital," the ethnography uses a case study to discuss the actions of Ms. Crawford—a mother of six, soon to be seven, children—who is described as a 'waste.' Mittenfelner Carl explores how a social capital orientation needs to be inclusive of different funds of knowledge that individuals bring to schools. Such a bilateral approach coupled with the need for intentional engagement legitimates the diversity of experiences that students possess. Building on Mittenfelner Carl's contributions, Morrison's chapter titled, "Nós Por Nós (Us for Us): Black Brazilian University Students and Social Capital," further legitimizes diverse student experiences and backgrounds and the embedded social capital that lies within. Morrison examines the use of social capital theory as a lens to view Afro-Brazilian students' navigation of the university as an elite space. Three examples of social capital in practice are subsequently explored. Morrison concludes with implications for using a social capital perspective to improve the practice of institutions that serve underrepresented students, thereby speaking directly to institutional imperatives regarding *intentional engagement*.

The volume's additional inclusion of Lofton's "Still Chasing the Dream: The Possibilities and Limitations of Social Capital in Dismantling Racialized Tracks," presents a qualitative work highlighting the voices of 26 African American parents whose children attended a racially diverse middle school while living in a poor Black community. The research focuses on ways in which social networks provided a means for a few of the African American parents to receive information about academic success; yet, these same parents were not afforded vital information regarding academic placement. Lofton further explores how a framework of respectability politics was used to explain why many of the African American students were in lower academic track placements. In reviewing Lofton's chapter, *intentional engagement* becomes a targeted approach for redirecting the attitudes and perspectives about the capacity of social capital, as a means of access and accountability, to change the life trajectory of students.

SOCIAL CAPITAL AS STRATEGIC ADVOCACY

Social capital as *strategic advocacy* involves active sponsorship of individuals who demonstrate notable talent and non-cognitive factors of behavior, attitude, and strategies that will transfer into both short and long-term opportunities (Lederman, 2013; Lucero, Maes, Klingmith, 2014; University of Chicago, 2012). The backgrounds of students are often associated with their families' ability (or lack thereof) to reside in neighborhoods or areas with higher tax bases and properties within the local areas. In effect, those families who have higher incomes have access to schools with more adequate resources and more direct pipelines to colleges and universities. Those families with lower incomes have less access to schools with more adequate resources; by extension, they have far less access to college. The questions become as follows: (1) As a measure of accountability, who will advocate for or speak on behalf of those who have not?; (2) Who will sponsor or go to great lengths for those students who do not have access to resources?

To that end, *strategic advocacy* is needed in many of the less-resourced schools (particularly regarding Title I). Within Title I contexts, this federal funding seeks to establish equity and parity by supplementing costs associated with hiring qualified teachers, offering professional development, encouraging parental involvement, and integrating classroom technology. State appropriations are primarily used for teacher and administrative salaries with a limited amount used for instructional supplies. Whatever social capital is or can become is an indication of the status of culture and equity (Kaplan & Owings, 2013; Smith, Frey, Pumpian, & Fisher, 2017). From the types of professional development encouraged by the school administration to the employment policies, the cultural context of the schools informs the practices within the schools. Smith, Frey, Pumpian, and Fisher (2017) particularly describe the role of the school regarding the attainment of social capital:

> Access to human and social capital begins before birth and is affected by access to health care and nutrition, the parents' level of education, and income. While schools have a less direct influence on some of these elements, other gates are entirely erected by schools. These include entry and screening requirements that place young children in remedial groups, tracked courses in secondary schools, and suspension and expulsion practices that result in a disproportionate number of students of color, students with disabilities and students with language differences being excluded from instruction (p. 86).

There are existing arguments that suggest minimal effects of the secondary school's role in generating access to and accountability regarding social capital. Notwithstanding, this volume posits schools (along with colleges and universities) assume a major role in the academic preparation of students and creation of meaningful pathway for success or failure for the life trajectory of students. With such immense power comes intense responsibility to be strong and strategic advocates for all students, most especially those who are historically minoritized and systematically marginalized (i.e., along the educational continuum).

This volume's inclusion of work done by Ryan and Romero titled, "The Past, Present, and Future of Social Capital Measurement Among Youth," focuses on transition-age youth between the ages of 16 and 24 and the need for more valid and reliable tools for measuring social capital. The authors argue that due to a lack of focused, societal resources and (arguably) *strategic advocacy*, there has been a persistent inability to document how inequitable access to resources through social networks result in stratified opportunities and outcomes during the transitionary, life stage known as young-adulthood. Ryan and Romero consider the current challenges and limitations involving social capital measurements (i.e., during this transitional life stage) and the need to pilot an instrument to measure youth social capital in the context of postsecondary transitions. Such instrumentation is poised to respond to the need for more empirical social capital research about youth and disparities that might exist among youth during critical, life transitions.

CONCLUDING REMARKS

The foreword, *External Access and Internal Accountability: The Currency Conduits for Maximizing Social Capital in Public Schools and Higher Education*, has provided useful perspectives about the role of social capital for individuals, schools, institutions. As demonstrated by the chapters in this edited volume, social capital emerges in the following ways: (1) Human Connectedness; (2) Strategic

Advocacy; (3) Intentional Engagement; and (4) Culturally Responsive Leadership. These conduits of social capital provide a meaningful pathway to generate the quality of outcomes and opportunities necessary to achieve success within and outside of the respective cultural context of education. These conduits of social capital also show the importance of having forward thinking administrative leadership within K–12 and higher education to achieve access (*getting to*) and maintain accountability (*getting through*). The extent to which this type of leadership is present and pervasively practiced determines the larger extent to which social capital is maximized (i.e., by all students) as a tool of currency for successfully navigating and negotiating academic pathways.

REFERENCES

Altbach, P. G. (2016). *Global perspectives on higher education.* Baltimore, MD: The Johns Hopkins University Press.

Bastedo, M. N., Altbach, P. G., & Gumport, P. J. (Eds.). (2016). *American higher education in the twenty-first century: Social, political, and economic challenges* (4th ed.). Baltimore, MD: The Johns Hopkins University Press.

Beachum, F. (2011). Culturally relevant leadership for complex 21st–century school contexts. In W. E. Fenwick (Ed.), *The SAGE handbook of educational leadership: Advances in theory, research, and practice* (2d ed., pp. 27–35). Thousand Oaks, CA: SAGE.

Bourdieu, P. (1986). The forms of capital. In J. Richardson (Ed.), *Handbook of theory and research for the sociology of education* (pp. 241–258). New York, NY: Greenwood.

Bowen, W. G., & Bok, D. (1998). *The shape of the river: Long-term consequences of considering race in college and university admissions.* Princeton, NJ: Princeton University Press.

Bowen, W. G., Kurzweil, M. A., & Tobin, E. M. (2005). *Equity and excellence in American higher education.* Charlottesville, VA: University of Virginia Press.

Bowen, W. G., & McPherson, M. S. (2016). *Lesson plan: An agenda for change in American higher education.* Princeton, NJ: Princeton University Press.

Croft, S., Roberts, M. & Stenhouse, V. (2017). *The perfect storm of education reform: High-stakes testing and teacher evaluation.* Retrieved on February 7, 2017 from http://www.socialjusticejournal.org/archive/139_42_1/139_05_Croft_Roberts_Stenhouse.pdf)

Ellison, N. B., Wohn, D. Y., & Greenhow, C. M. (2014). Adolescents' visions of their future careers, educational plans, and life pathways: The role of bridging and bonding social capital experiences. *Journal of Social and Personal Relationships, 32,* 516–534.

Engstrom, C., & Tinto, V. (2008). Access without support is not opportunity. *Change, 40*(1), 46–50.

Epstein, J. (2011). *School, family, and community partnerships: Preparing educators and improving schools* (2nd ed.). Boulder, CO: Westview Press.

Ferrara, M. M. (2015). *Parental involvement facilitators: Unlocking social capital wealth.* Retrieved from http://files.eric.ed.gov/fulltext/EJ1066216.pdf

Ford, D.Y. (2013). *Recruiting and retaining culturally different students in gifted education.* Waco, TX: Prufrock Press.

Fullan,M. & Quinn, J. (2016). *Coherence: The right drivers in action for schools, districts, and systems.* Thousand Oaks, CA: Corwin.

Grantham, T. C., Ford, D. Y. Henfield, M., Trotman, S. M., Harmon, D., Porchér, S., & Price, C. (2011). *Gifted and advanced Black students in school: An anthology of critical works.* Waco, TX: Prufrock Press.

Greene, T. G., Marti, C., & McClenney, K. (2008). The effort-outcome gap: Differences for African American and Hispanic community college students in student engagement and academic achievement. *Journal of Higher Education, 79*(5), 513–539.

Jensen, E. (2009). *Teaching with poverty in mind: What being poor does to kids' brains and what schools can do about it.* Washington, DC: ASCD.

Kaplan, L. S., & Owning, W. A. (2013). *Culture re-boot: Reinvigorating school culture to improve student outcomes.* Thousand Oakes, CA: Corwin.

Khalifa, M. A., Gooden, M. A., & Davis, J. E. (2016). Culturally responsive school leadership: A synthesis of the literature. *Review of Educational Research, 86,* 1272–1311.

Leana, C. R., & Pill, F. K. (2014). *A new focus on social capital in school reform efforts.* Retrieved on February 7, 2017 from http://www.shankerinstitute.org/blog/new-focus-social-capital-school-reform-efforts

Lederman, D. (2013). *Building students' cultural capital.* Retrieved from https://www.insidehighered.com/news/2013/11/05/can-colleges-build-students-cultural-capital-and-should-they

Long, C. (2016). *Community schools bridging the gap between schools and home.* Retrieved on February 6, 2017 from http://neatoday.org/2016/08/09/community-school-bridging-the-gap/

Lucero, E., Maes, J. B., & Klinsmith, L. (2014). African American and Latina(o) community college students' social capital and student success. *College Student Journal, 48,* 522–534.

Madhlangobe, L., & Gordon, S. P. (2012). Culturally responsive leadership in a diverse school: A case study of a high school leader. *NASSP Bulletin, 96*(3), 177–202.

McCray, C., & Beachum, F. (2011). Culturally relevant leadership for the enhancement of teaching and learning in urban schools. In T. Townsend & J. MacBeath (Eds.), *The international handbook of leadership for learning* (pp. 487–502). Dordrecht, The Netherlands: Springer.

Morimoto, S., & Friedland, L. A. (2013). Cultivating success: Youth achievement, capital, and civic engagement in the contemporary United States. *Sociological Perspectives, 56,* 523–546.

Putnam, R. (2000). *Bowling alone.* New York, NY: Simon & Schuster.

Schultz, A. (2006). Home is a prison in the global city: The tragic failure of school-based community engagement strategies. *Review of Educational Research, 76,* 691–743.

Smith, D., Frey, N., Pumpian, I., & Fisher, D. (2017). *Building equity: Policies and practices to empower all learners.* Washington, DC: ASCD.

Straus, V. (2015). *How students with top test scores actually hurt a teacher's evaluation.* Retrieved from https://www.washingtonpost.com/news/answer-sheet/wp/2015/04/01/teacher-how-my-highest-scoring-students-actually-hurt-my-evaluation/?utm_term=.01649adc84bb

University of Chicago. (2012). *Teaching adolescents to become learners: The role of non-cognitive factors in shaping school performance: A critical literature review.* Retrieved from https://consortium.uchicago.edu/sites/default/files/publications/Non-cognitive%20Report.pdf

US Department of Education. (2013). *Partners in education: A dual capacity-building framework for family-school partnerships*. Retrieved on February 6, 2017 from https://www2.ed.gov/documents/family-community/partners-education.pdf

Winter, N. (2003). *Social capital, civic engagement, and positive youth development.* Retrieved on February 7, 2017 from http://www.policystudies.com/studies/?id=57.

Yosso, T. J. (2005). Whose culture has capital? A critical race theory discussion of community cultural wealth. *Race, Ethnicity and Education, 8*(1), 69–91.

PART 1

ACCOUNTABILITY STRUCTURES

PART 1A

LEADERSHIP CAPACITY

CHAPTER 1

THE ROLE OF SCHOOL LEADERS MANAGING SOCIAL CAPITAL WITHIN URBAN AND RURAL SCHOOL SETTINGS

John Crutchfield, Sarah Bailey, and Jandel Crutchfield

How best to educate students within urban and rural settings is of international concern. Students attending schools in both rural and urban settings can suffer from the effects of poverty, underfunded school systems, and limited access to resources (McFarland et al., 2017). Forty-eight percent of rural students and 59% of urban students in the United States lived at the poverty level based on data from the 2014–15 school term (National Center for Educational Statistics, 2017). International perspectives report unequal access to opportunities based on student residence within urban and rural settings (Qian & Smyth, 2008; Sayed, 2010; Stelmach, 2011; Ye, 2010; Young, 1998). For example, the disparities evidenced by the widening achievement gap in urban and rural schools throughout East Asia supports the existence of a universal challenge faced by school leaders in urban and rural settings (Liu, 2009; Othman & Muijs, 2013; Zhang & Pang, 2016; Zhao et al., 2012). This universal challenge regarding how to secure and steward resources to eliminate or minimize barriers to success for disadvantaged students

Contemporary Perspectives on Social Capital in Educational Contexts,
pages 5–21.

5

faces all school leaders. School leaders must assume responsibility for leveraging internal and external resources and human and fiscal resources to ensure equity in education and access to academic and social supports for every child. Of particular interest are the social and institutional resources, or "social capital" needed by school administrators to educate students served by urban and rural school systems.

It is the purpose of this chapter to define social capital under the management of the educational leader, review available research on the management of social capital in a variety of school contexts, and to make recommendations of considerations leaders should make in light of the understanding thereof. School leaders must be aware of the commonalities and disparities in the available capital between urban and rural school settings, and what their role is in managing such resources.

DEFINING SOCIAL CAPITAL FOR SCHOOL LEADERS

Social Capital is "so much a part of the fabric of people's working lives that it tends to be invisible…" (Cohen & Prusak, 2001). Because of this entrenchment in daily life, Bartee & Brown (2011) highlight the difficulty in finding a standard definition. Vorhaus (2014) offers an interpretation which emphasizes social capital as a vehicle to acquire institutional resources and build trust and relationships through social networks. Lee (2010) defines social capital by explaining the connection between group membership, interpersonal ties, and access. Also, the definition considers the use of resources available as a result of those relationships. Putnam (1995) describes social capital as the relationships and connectedness of a community as essential for the success or failure of that community. He further defines social capital as networks of shared norms, trust, and values that facilitate this connectedness and collaboration.

Defining social capital for schools varies when applied to each stakeholder, as students, teachers, leaders, and parents benefit from the resources available through the relationships, trust, and networks forged within each educational context. The recently revised standards for educational leadership, Council of Chief State School Officers (CCSSO), Professional Standards for Educational Leadership 2015 (PSEL, Standard Five), National Policy Board for Education Administration (NPBEA), and National Educational Leadership Preparation Standards (NELP, Standard Five), re-emphasize the expectations for school leaders set forth by the CCSSO, Interstate School Leaders Licensure Consortium Standards 2008 (ISLLC, Standard Four) NPBEA, and the Educational Leadership Constituent Council Standards 2011 (ELCC, Standard Four) regarding building and nurturing relationships with community partners to secure academic and social resources for the school. Thus, school administrators must consider and understand how, though wide-ranging, resources and benefits are interconnected as accessibility for each stakeholder ultimately aids in the advancement and improvement of the school community (Chen, Anderson, & Watkins, 2016). Securing and mobilizing resources to address the comprehensive needs of the school is an important consideration as school leaders seek to create and manage school-wide social capital. Fostering a school environment where social capital provides access to an integrated network of resources for students, teachers, leaders, and parents is the standard for effective school leadership (ISLLC 2008, CCSSO, 2008, NPBEA, 2011, CCSSO, 2015, NPBEA, 2018, ELCC, 2011, PSEL, 2015, NELP, 2018).

Social capital, as it relates to students, can be viewed as a "portfolio of instrumental and expressive resources spanning multiple microsystems" (Rose, Whoolley, & Bowen, 2013). It further encompasses family, school, neighborhood, and peer groups which can be organized (Brunie, 2009; Dika & Singh. 2002; Woolley, Kol, & Bowen, 2009). When organized, social capital forms a supportive network for students (Fraser & Galinsky, 2010). Chattopodhay (2014) suggests the existence of a 3R framework for student social capital, including relationships, resources, and readiness. These serve as the medium through which social capital is activated for students by school leaders. Relationships serve as the basis of networks students can access as the result of "school-facilitated contexts, processes, and protocols" (Rose et al., 2013). The "resources of others" are accessible to students in "material, informational, and psychosocial" forms when student social capital is accessible (Rose et al., 2013). Readiness is referred to as "sociability" by Bourdieu (1987) and represents the knowledge, skills, and capacity students possess which guide how social capital resources are drawn upon when necessary(Rose et al., 2013).

Putnam's (2000) *Bowling Alone: The Collapse and Revival of American Community* positions the conversation of social capital as shifting over time and across location. He discusses how, over time, networks have withered as suburbs have formed and created communities that are less connected and less social. This chapter adds to the variety of perspectives captured in these definitions and places the focus on the responsibility of school leadership to manage social capital in the context of urban and rural school settings. The school leader must consider how changing community relationships might impact available networking and in turn student achievement.

SOCIAL CAPITAL IN LEADERSHIP DEVELOPMENT PROGRAMMING

The efforts of professional organizations such as the Council of Chief State School Officers and the National Policy Board for Educational Administration with the creation and adoption of the Educational Leadership Policy Standards: Interstate School Leaders Licensure Standards (ISLLC, 2008) address the need to prepare school leaders for the communication, culture and leadership building, and community relations necessary to mature social capital within the educational context. For example, Standard 4 of the ISLLC Standards 2008 articulates that the "educational leader promotes the success of every student by collaborating with faculty and community members, responding to diverse community interests and needs, and mobilizing community resources."

Such efforts are complemented by the National Council for Accreditation of Teacher Education (NCATE) and its support of the NPBEA ELCC Standards (2011), which includes standards suggesting how to appropriately train school leaders to prepare to build the necessary networks for successful school operations. Some programs include internships and practice-based experiences, which provide prospective school leaders with entrenched opportunities to begin to establish relationships with faculty, staff, and community members.

Less evidence, however, is available to demonstrate how principals are being trained to address schools where these social networks are not as established as others, which can be broken in places where schools have high attrition rates for school leaders or experienced consequences of malpractice or malfeasance.

The Leadership Education and Development (LEAD) program is one program which, when evaluated, considered social capital in its framework. The goal of the program designers was to develop leaders capable of increasing efficiency within organizations, through methods that included building leadership capacity to communicate, coach, and manage social networks. Participants in the program were divided into small groups and discussed issues related to intergroup cooperation. Outcomes of the program suggested better communication and the creation of connections between resources and participants was necessary for organizational improvement (Roberts, 2013).

One study examined the efforts of the University of Ottawa's Management Leadership Program (MLP). Findings suggest that the programs support for the interaction of colleagues and the relationships that continued long after the program ended were of substantial benefit to participants (Terrion, 2006). The program strengths resulted in recommendations around diverse representation, relationship building, informal conversation, and other linking activities.

How are school leader preparation programs, whether they be university level, alternate route, the private sector, or school district based, adequately providing aspiring leaders opportunities to gain the experiences required to manage social capital? The variety of components that make up social capital as understood by a school leader might be as comprehensive as the variety of job duties inherent to the position. Not only must school leaders create effective networks with parents, but also with business, community, authorizing bodies, and policy boards. Preparation programs should ensure leaders have the experiences necessary to begin practicing the work of managing social capital. They might also aid leaders in building and sustaining capital even after graduation.

SOCIAL CAPITAL AS APPLIED BY LEADERS IN K–12 EDUCATION SETTINGS

Collins and Hansen (2011) discuss how excellent leadership is aided by a higher capacity for collective decision making and their ability to build a strong culture within successful companies. This collaborative approach to decision making is extended by and serves to expand social capital within these companies, and allows them to outperform competition over the long term repeatedly. Similarly, principals who have taken the time to nurture the social networks in their schools are often seen as highly effective. Harris (2013) suggests that the ability of the principal to build collaborative teams that are efficient adds to that effectiveness. School leaders have the important charge of managing social capital in a way that leads to not just high student achievement in one school year, but high student achievement across multiple years. This charge includes supporting parental involvement networks, community and business relationships, professional development within a school, student-staff relationships, and the maintenance of operational relationships (Gleeson et al., 2009). The administration charged with supporting these efforts instantly realizes a dependency upon social capital as foundational. In other words, what relationships have been fostered to allow for effective collaboration?

One method for principals to utilize in fostering social capital are professional learning communities (PLCs), which are evidenced to increase shared values around student learning and classroom practices (Jones & Harris, 2014). These frequent and normed group meetings between teachers allow for discussions of academic and behavioral data, along with suggested strategies to intervene for struggling students. Basileo (2016) discusses the strength of relationships between teachers through PLCs as central to effective public education. ."..A high functioning PLC will act, in essence, as a knowledge-generation system for teachers." (Basileo, 2016, p. 3).

Principals also foster social capital through the use of distributive leadership, where teacher leaders work together with school principals (Nappi, 2014). In these environments, social capital is fostered through increased teacher retention rates when teachers feel empowered to grow school achievement using their creativity. The school leader builds relationships with teacher leaders by supporting an expansion of their roles and in turn distributing some of their responsibilities. When teachers stay in the classroom, this serves as additional social capital for the school community. The longevity of relationships, established school culture, and increased content knowledge are a few examples. The role of the principal in establishing student and staff relationships that build community and a sense of trust, while managing diverse populations and expectations from stakeholders, proves to be a delicate balancing act (Riley, 2013).

PARENTAL INVOLVEMENT AS SOCIAL CAPITAL FOR SCHOOL LEADERSHIP

The level of support from a child's parent has been observed as a protruding factor in explaining behavioral outcomes in school, particularly around a parent's involvement in parent-teacher organizations and parent-child discussion (McNeal & Ralph, 1999). Access to social capital improves behavioral outcomes for more affluent and advantaged students. Parents from majority groups exhibit higher levels of parental involvement, and this involvement has strong correlations with higher academic achievement (Lee & Bowen, 2006). Some research suggests that families may be "more powerful than schools in promoting child and adolescent well-being" (Parcel, Dufur, & Zito, 2010). Schools and parents should work together to determine what appropriate performance is for students, as a mechanism of social control (Hill & Taylor, 2004). African-American parents are less likely to be involved in at-school activities (Eccles & Harold, 1996), even though increased parental involvement at school can result in improved performance at school. White parents are more likely to be involved in at school activities (Hill & Craft, 2003).

The managerial styles of principals can influence the level of parental involvement in schools (Griffith, 2001). When considering the type of managerial roles as reported by principals, the role of master teacher and gamesman was associated with greater feelings of parental empowerment across ethnic groups. School leaders should consider their role as a possible influence on parental motivation when parents consider whether to participate in at-school involvement opportunities.

Considering the literature, school leaders should view parents as an invaluable resource to align themselves with for school improvement. School leaders should recognize parent voice in shaping their positions and policies, and in on-going decisions related to school improvement initiatives. Their decision to include or neglect, whether intentional or unintentional, could have effects on their rates of success regardless of their intent. Of particular concern should be the manner in which parents perceive their role as principals attempt to manage them as a resource. Should parents perceive school leaders as formal administrators or managerial figureheads, they will be less likely to attend meetings or to feel as if they can create change (Gleeson et al., 2009).

Instead, school leaders who frequently engage parents for their ideas, demonstrate investment in their child's interests, and drive a school vision may garner additional parental support. Positive school climates and increased student achievement are the intended outcome of such parental social capital management.

As a response to the work of Griffith (2001), we suggest there is a link between social capital and an involved parent community. This perspective aligns with the idea that social capital has a value that becomes a resource to those to whom is it available or lack thereof to those to whom it is not available. School leaders should consider varying research regarding strategies to engage parents of differing demographics and develop cultural competence. To involve more African-American parents, the school leader may want to consider at-home approaches to communication and empowerment. To address more Anglo-American parents, the school leaders may take more traditional approaches to communication and empowerment at school.

COMMUNITY AND BUSINESS RELATIONSHIPS AS SOCIAL CAPITAL FOR SCHOOL LEADERSHIP

Another type of social networking necessary to create social capital, as identified by Portes (1998), is extra-familial networking which provides connections to individuals outside of the family unit. Additional agencies and opportunities often result in access to the necessary academic, economic, and social supports for the upward mobility of disadvantaged students. Community partnerships formed and accessed to improve student academic outcomes, provided community-based opportunities for mentoring, tutoring, and afterschool enrichment through programming and services specific to the community context (Kremer et al., 2015). School reform models also provide a framework to guide school leaders as they work to address challenges specific to the school setting. The full-service community school model prioritizes creating social capital by integrating academic, social, and health services to meet the diverse needs of disadvantaged students and their families more comprehensively (US Department of Education, 2014).

From the onset, school leaders should consider pre-established networks between their schools and local and external community partners. School leaders should ask about the history of these relationships, determine the contributions made by the partnerships, and seek to strengthen existing and establish additional relationships. The benefit of such relationships includes additional resources for student mentoring, tutoring, and afterschool programming. But the benefits may not stop there, as philanthropic support, facility improvement, student and family health support, and other systemic quality of life enhancement may be a well yet fully tapped.

In urban settings, businesses and community organizations often partner with leaders to offer services such as mentoring, after-school tutoring, enrichment, and counseling. How principals engage these groups and coordinate these services can be of significant value to school operations and academic enhancement. The decisions school leaders should nurture these relationships, as long-term implications of school leader decisions often impact these links for future leaders serving urban schools.

In rural settings, the school system may be the most significant employer and primary source of synergy within the community. Also, strong ties are inherent which makes rural communities fertile ground for cultivating social capital for students, teachers, leaders, and parents. However, due to the geographical locale of rural schools and districts and, in some instances, limited fiscal resources, opportunities to collaborate with local organizations and businesses to benefit the school community are sometimes minimal. Moreover, access to the full spectrum of benefits may be limited to school principals and students in communities where schools are divided along racial and cultural lines. Therefore, school leaders in rural settings should devise and utilize a strategic approach when identifying and building relationships with community gatekeepers, agencies, and organizations to build a network of support for the school.

A FOCUS ON URBAN AND RURAL CONTEXTS

Because of the large number of students, families, and communities within metropolitan and urban areas, it would seem that there is greater access to social capital in these areas. However, much of the literature suggests that it is rural communities that demonstrate extensive amounts of access to social capital (Beaudoin & Thorson, 2004; Jiang, Sun, & Marsiglia, 2016; Symeou, 2008). Both geographic and non-geographic social capital exists to a higher degree in rural communities. Given that rural communities include neighborhoods that are often diverse regarding income and education levels, social networks can exist with individuals that can provide access to each other within these different realms (Debertin,1996). However, in some geographical regions, access to social capital in rural communities may be limited to individuals who are members of micro-social networks, small and exclusive networks, which afford resources to only certain members of the community. School leaders serving in rural areas should be prepared to address the issue of equity of access to social capital in communities where barriers or disparities in access are evident.

In contrast, urban neighborhoods tend to lack diversity in income and educational levels as evidenced by how housing segregation purposely tries to maintain a homogenous group of individuals within neighborhoods. Poor, middle class and wealthy individuals often do not all live in the same neighborhoods in urban areas. Instead, they are segregated by income levels. Within neighborhoods based on income, it is often the case that there may be rigid rules from neighborhood associations that are enforced. This is as opposed to unspoken neighborhood rules that are commonly seen in rural areas, where neighbors all tend to know each other and may even work as one social network to get things accomplished without the oversight of an association (Beaudoin & Thorson, 2004).

When considering parental involvement as social capital, a pattern of increased social capital within rural communities has also been demonstrated in the literature (Ishimaru, 2013; Symeou, 2008). When interviewed regarding their perspectives about local education, rural parents showed more appreciation and satisfaction for teachers and believed that school officials should receive respect as a result. Urban parents were more critical of teaching practices, in cases such as their skepticism of teacher attitudes towards students. The demonstration of increased social capital is also apparent in the higher level of trust between rural parents and school officials. Higher parental engagement from rural areas is documented as well (Debertin, 1996). In rural settings where high teacher and leader attrition is evident, parental distrust of the school is a factor school leaders should address when considering parents as social capital.

Social capital demonstrates itself as ties between community members are also stronger and more active in rural areas (Symeou, 2008). Schools needing connections within smaller rural communities likely know precisely who to ask, not only from past benevolence but possibly because school officials grew up in the rural communities themselves. When a business tie is desired, for example, a principal may be able to call her dad's good friend who owns a business. While urban school leaders can make these calls as well, the building of those relationships has probably occurred long before any particular leader takes the position in a rural school.

According to Sorenson (2016), urban areas may have an advantage in social capital when the different forms of it are introduced, namely bridging and bonding.

Sorenson (2016) defines bonding social capital as the trust and networking within communities while bridging social capital includes the social networks among individuals both within and outside of a local community. Rural areas may indeed have an advantage in bonding social capital, but urban areas have an advantage in creating bridging social capital. For example, smaller rural communities can compensate community members for limited goods and services by using community ties. In contrast, urban areas have numerous goods and services and thus don't need to connect within communities as often. Given that many people move-in and out of urban areas, some of the social networks formed are from other communities. This may explain why urban areas have more bridging social capital.

This is the environment that both urban and rural leaders enter when striving to build social networks with parents and the community. Knowing the potential for rural areas to provide more access to bonding social capital, researchers explore methods for both rural and urban leaders to form these social networks between parents and the community. Leaders in more rural communities should focus on creating trust within the social networks among community members. This includes local businesses, parents, churches, and other social groups. Leaders should tap into these strong networks as a resource to gain resources for their schools. In urban areas, while leaders may use links within an immediate community, they can more successfully build bridges to other communities, networks, and organizations to gain needed resources for their schools.

Portes (1998) outlined three social networking conditions which aid in building social capital: close-knit communities, parental support, and support beyond the family. Close-knit communities foster an environment of high expectations for all students with respect to academics and behavior resulting in community pressures associated with success and failure. Parental support and high aspirations for children results in strong social capital as the resources available to the parents expands the network of the child. Portes further asserted social capital is strongest in two-parent families with one parent primarily responsible for rearing the children resulting adequate attention to the needs of children and a posture of achievement. Support beyond the family, or membership in networks, results in increased individual mobility socially and professionally.

An ethnographic study conducted by Bagley and Hillyard (2014), in two rural schools located in separate English villages, found social capital flourished when the principal held a clear philosophy with respect to school-community relations integrating the school into the community. The importance of a school leader serving as the steward and manager of social capital is evident by the standards set forth for school and district leaders. Without consideration of the diverse barriers to success inherent in urban and rural settings and a framework for navigating these social and economic contexts, school improvement and promoting the success of students and staff may prove to be an arduous task for novice and experienced educational leaders. It is necessary that school leader preparation programs understand both the ranges of resources available between urban and rural school settings, and make specific efforts to build school leader capacity to manage this social capital. In doing so, leader preparation programs can support the application of school leaders to not just one particular school context, but across many regardless of the resources available to that school.

CASE VIGNETTE AND LEADERSHIP APPROACHES

The choice of leadership style is often based on the level of social capital available to the school. In light of the literature regarding rural and urban social capital, consider the following case vignette of a school leader faced with the task of managing social capital.

Jennifer S. is a 38-year-old assistant principal at an urban middle school in a large city in the southeastern United States. She has submitted applications for a principalship in her current city and other large cities within a 30-mile radius for the past two years but has not secured a position. As she considers applying for a principalship for the third year, she is introduced to the superintendent from a smaller, rural school district 40 miles from her current city. She goes through the interview process but does not believe she will receive the job and believes it would not be her first choice for a position. When the superintendent calls her to offer her the principal position, Jennifer S. is faced with a decision about moving into a very different school environment than justified by her previous experience. While the rural school is not Jennifer's first choice, she accepts the position, hoping to catalyze her career as a principal.

Upon visiting the school for an initial walkthrough, she notices a distinctly different culture marked by deep familiarity between staff, parents, and local community members. While this is somewhat different than her experience in the urban school, she begins to see the potential benefits of such a culture and hopes to learn more to build on these relationships. The staff in this school regularly collaborate with peers and share expertise, although this collaboration is limited to within school networks. This is likely a result of limited external links between the school and other neighboring towns. Teachers ensure that their students' individual learning needs are met by adapting instruction. School leaders appear to model self-reflection, but need to offer more opportunities for professional development. While the school has dedicated parents, the school could make it more welcoming for new parents to participate. Also, the school has an effective role for parents on advisory teams. Parents on the advisory teams express interest in having more decision-making authority. Due to the smaller community, the school staff and leaders are very friendly with community members. This relationship is not systematic, however. This sometimes makes it difficult for newcomers to the community to navigate building connections with the school.

For new administrators who are also encountering different contexts such as moving from urban to rural or rural to urban schools, the task of maximizing social capital may be a challenge. One useful tool to assess levels of social capital and develop concrete needs and steps to meet the challenges is the Social Capital

Gap Analysis for Schools, which integrates School Turnaround Principles and related research on social capital in schools. Using the information from the case vignette, Jennifer completes a gap analysis (Table 1.1) based on her new rural school environment.

The Social Capital Gap Analysis for Schools template above offers a critical analysis of the needs of the school described in the case as they relate to social capital. The gap analysis provides possible solutions to the challenges a new principal may encounter in rural school communities where social capital is limited. Strategic planning, parental and community engagement strategies advocacy for disadvantaged students, budgeting, and building teacher capacity were the leadership behaviors employed to formulate the plan of action, each of which are aligned to the ELCC Standards. In addition to specific action steps, the tool requires the school leader to anticipate potential barriers to success which ensures the leader thinks strategically about potential challenges and devises a plan to overcome barriers.

Recommendations/Action Steps for Leader Preparation Programs

Recommendations	Question for Leaders to Consider
Provide opportunities for collaboration with diverse groups of stakeholders through the course of leadership studies	• In what ways do aspiring leaders have opportunities to talk, work, plan, and troubleshoot with others of a different socio-economic status, race, gender, and educational background during the program?
Provide educational programming surrounding school contexts that are diverse, differing in access to parental involvement, business relationships, and partner support throughout leadership studies	• In what ways does coursework prepare aspiring leaders to work with schools that have more or fewer degrees of parental engagement, business involvement, or partner support than is familiar to his/her prior experience?
Further delineate professional leadership standards to include specific experiences that increase available resources available to school leaders after program completion.	• What specifically will be done within each content standard to ensure aspiring leaders are communicating and investing in the relationships necessary to improve success outcomes?
Differentiate and Discuss Urban and Rural Contexts and Applications when approaching issues of access to various capital	• In what ways does coursework differentiate between educational settings with discourse around urban and rural considerations?
Consider K–12 parental participation in the preparation and delivery of educational leadership programming	• How do parents participate in the process of shaping the training of educational leaders? How could parents be engaged in the process of shaping future training?
Provide on-going opportunities for networking between prepared school leaders and diverse groups of stakeholders even after the completion of the program?	What methods are used to foster communication and cooperation between leaders after program or employment end dates?

TABLE 1.1.

Effective Teachers

Status of Social Capital	Needed Improvements	Steps Needed to Improve Status	Barriers to Best Practice Implementation
• Staff regularly collaborates with peers, shares expertise, and holds themselves accountable for professional learning and improved practice. • Teachers regularly adapt resources and instruction to address learning differences in their students.	• Collaboration with networks outside of the community may be able to increase social capital.	• Identify school leaders and schools with a track record of improving student outcomes for intra-school collaboration • Develop partnerships with regional education consortiums • Principal to use linkages from a current urban environment to foster out of network collaboration.	• Accountability sometimes limited to rural connections; not external links.
• School administrators build staff capacity by encouraging and modeling a self-reflective culture.	• Leaders need to provide more leadership development opportunities for staff.	• Develop a budget line for professional learning. • Facilitate conversations with staff focused on improving professional practice and developing leadership capacity. • Seek external resources to support the professional growth of staff. • Provide staff the opportunity to model best practices for each other.	• Budget in a rural area may be limited for professional development. Staffing limitations may limit the ability of teachers to travel for extended professional development days.
Parental Involvement			
• School has dedicated parents that participate in school activities.	• School should attend to factors that make it more inviting and welcoming to students, parents, and community.	• Poll current parents and families for ideas about inclusivity. • Develop and implement a strategy to increase positive school/community interactions • Develop and implement a strategy to integrate and invest new staff into the school community • Provide multiple times and locations for parent and community participation	• Parents in smaller communities who have negative histories with schools may be influential in blocking others from becoming involved.

• The school includes families on advisory teams and parent-teacher organizations.	• Families want to provide more input into school improvement through surveys and committee decisions and recommendations.	• Conduct focus groups to identify garner parental perspective on student, parent, and community needs • Schedule meetings at various times and in various locations to accommodate parent schedules • Create annual beginning and end of the school year surveys for parents. • Identify lists of decisions for which parental input is requested and publicize list.	

Community Engagement

• Leaders, teachers, and staff are friendly and willing to include communities regarding children's learning. • School and community partners collaborate to meet students' social and emotional needs.	• The school needs a more systematic process in place to get input from the community that is communicated clearly. • School-wide strategies should be increased to know students and their needs well.	• Identify community engagement strategies to address the needs of the specific school/district context • Identify community gatekeepers who are greatly respected in the community and establish lines of communication • Strategically utilize staff who are respected in the community to establish and nurture community relationships • Plan community nights at the school and invite stakeholders to attend. • Identify and establish partnerships with regional agencies to support the social, emotional needs of students • Invite community members to leadership team meetings; offer mentorship opportunities to further knowledge of students and needs.	• Parental and community distrust of the school/district • Competing community events/businesses. • Geographic alliances of stakeholders may bar new community members from participating. • Limited resources due to geographical locale • Students in smaller towns may be more readily defined by family history rather than their performance/attributes.

ONCLUDING THOUGHTS

Current literature regarding differences in urban and rural school access to social capital is invaluable for school leaders. Whether leaders are in small rural towns or large urban centers, a portion of their success as school leaders is maximizing school capital to benefit all stakeholders in their school and community. In the areas of parental involvement, community and business stakeholders, and leadership development programming, research documents methods used by school leaders to access social capital for the improvement of each. Many leaders switching between urban and rural environments give scant attention to potential challenges and benefits inherent to each type of environment. Using the recommendations and gap analysis in this chapter will provide school leaders a resource for understanding how to succeed in their quests for increased social capital across urban and rural settings. Future scholarship must examine the role of leader preparation and continuing education programs in equipping school leaders to access social capital across these two types of settings.

REFERENCES

Bagley, C., & Hillyard, S. (2014). Rural schools, social capital and the Big Society: A theoretical and empirical exposition. *British Educational Research Journal, 40*(1), 63–78.

Basileo, L. (2016). Did you know? Your school's PLCs have a major impact. *Learning Sciences International,* 1–5.

Beaudoin, C., & Thorson, E. (2004). Social capital in rural and urban communities: Testing references in media effects and models. *Journalism and Mass Communication Quarterly, 81*(2), 378–399.

Bourdieu, P. (1987). What makes a social class? On the theoretical and practical existence of groups. *Berkeley Journal of Sociology, 32*(1987), 1–17.

Brunie, A. (2009). Meaningful distinctions within a concept: Relational, collective, and generalized social capital. *Social Science Research, 38*(2), 251–265.

Chattopadhay, T. (2014). School as a site of student social capital: An exploratory study from Brazil. *International Journal of Educational Development, 34*(2014), 67–76.

Chen, M. E., Anderson, J. A., & Watkins, L. (2016). Parent perceptions of connectedness in a full-service community school project. *Journal of Child and Family Studies, 25*(7), 2268–2278.

Collins, J. C., & Hansen, M. T. (2011). *Great by choice: Uncertainty, chaos, and luck. Why some thrive despite them all*. New York, NY: HarperCollins Publishers.

Council of Chief State School Officers. (2008). *Educational leadership policy standards: ISLLC 2008*. Retrieved from http://www.ccsso.org/Resources/Publications/Educational_Leadership_Policy_Standards_ISLLC_2008_as_Adopted_by_the_National_Policy_Board_for_Educational_Administration.html

Council of Chief State School Officers. (2015). *Professional standards for educational leaders: PSEL 2015.* Retrieved fromhttp://ccsso.org/resource_library/professional-standards-educational-leaders

Debertin, D. L. (1996). *A Comparison of Social Capital in Rural and Urban Settings.* Paper No. 159375, University of Kentucky, Department of Agricultural Economics.

Dika, S. L., & Singh, K. (2002). Applications of social capital in educational literature: A critical synthesis. *Review of Educational Research, 72*(1), 31–60.

Eccles, J., Harold, R. (1996). Family involvement in children's and adolescents's schooling. In A. Booth & J. F. Dunn (Eds.), *Family-school links: How do they affect educational outcomes?* (pp. 3–34). Hillsdale, NJ: Lawrence Erlbaum Associates, Inc.

Fraser, M. W., & Galinsky, M. J. (2010). Steps in intervention research: Designing and developing social programs. *Research on Social Work Practice, 20,* 459–466.

Gleeson, J. P., Wesley, J. M., Ellis, R., Seryak, C., Talley, G. W., & Robinson, J. (2009). Becoming involved in raising a relative's child: reasons, caregiver motivations and pathways to informal kinship care. *Child & Family Social Work, 14*(3), 300–310.

Griffith, J. (2001). Principal leadership of parent involvement. *Journal of Educational Administration, 39*(2), 162–186. doi.org/10.1108/09578230110386287

Harris, A. (2013). *Distributed Leadership Matters.* Thousand Oaks, CA: Corwin Press.

Hill, N. & Craft, S. (2003). Parent-school involvement and school performance: Mediated pathways among socioeconomically comparable African American and Euro-American families. *Journal of Educational Psychology, 95*(1), 74–83. doi. org/10.1037/0022-0663.95.1.74

Hill, N. E., & Taylor, L. C. (2004). Parental School Involvement and Children's Academic Achievement. *Current Directions in Psychological Science, 13*(4), 161–164. doi. org/10.1111/j.0963-7214.2004.00298.x

Jones, M., & Harris, A. (2014). Principals leading successful organizational change: Building social capital through disciplined professional collaboration. *Journal of Organizational Change Management, 27*(3), 473–485. doi.org/10.1108/JOCM-07-2013-0116

Ishimaru, A. (2013). From heroes to organizers: Principals and education organizing in urban school reform. *Educational Administration Quarterly, 49(1)* 3–51.

Jiang, G., Sun, F., & Marsiglia, F. (2016). Rural-urban disparities in adolescent risky behaviors: a family social capital perspective. *Journal of community psychology, 44*(8), 1027–1039.

Kremer, K. P., Maynard, B. R., Polanin, J. R., Vaughn, M. G., & Sarteschi, C. M. (2015). Effects of After-School Programs with At-Risk Youth on Attendance and Externalizing Behaviors: A Systematic Review and Meta-Analysis. *Journal of Youth and Adolescence, 44*(3), 616–636. doi.org/10.1007/s10964-014-0226-4

Lee, J.-S., & Bowen, N. K. (2006). Parent Involvement, Cultural Capital, and the Achievement Gap Among Elementary School Children. *American Educational Research Journal, 43*(2), 193–218. doi.org/10.3102/00028312043002193

Lee, M. (2010). Researching social capital in education. *British Journal of Sociology of Education, 31*(6), 779–792.

Liu, M. (2009). Education management and performance after rural education finance reform: Evidence from Western China. *International Journal for Educational Development, 29*(5), 463–473.

McFarland, J., Hussar, B., de Brey, C., Snyder, T., Wang, X., Wilkinson-Flicker, S., Gebrekristos, S., Zhang, J., Rathbun, A., Barmer, A., Bullock Mann, F., & Hinz, S. (2017). *The condition of education 2017 (NCES 2017-144).* U.S. Department of

Education. Washington, DC: National Center for Education Statistics. Retrieved from https://nces.ed.gov/pubsearch/pubsinfo.asp?pubid=2017144

McNeal, J., & Ralph, B. (1999). Parental Involvement as Social Capital: Differential Effectiveness on Science Achievement, Truancy, and Dropping Out*. *Social Forces*, *78*(1), 117–144. doi.org/10.1093/sf/78.1.117

Nappi, J. S. (2014). The teacher leader: Improving schools by building social capital through shared leadership. *Delta Kappa Gamma Bulletin, 80*(4), 29–34.

National Policy Board for Education Administration. (2011). *Educational leadership program standards: 2011 ELCC building level.* Retrieved from http://www.ncate.org/LinkClick.aspx?fileticket=zRZl73R0nOQ=

National Policy Board for Education Administration. (2015). *Professional standards for educational leaders 2015.* Retrieved from http://www.ccsso.org/Documents/2015/ProfessionalStandardsforEducationalLeaders2015forNPBEAFINAL.pdf

National Policy Board for Education Administration. (2018). *National educational leadership preparation standards.* Retrieved from http://www.ucea.org/initiatives/the-draft-nelp-standards-are-available-for-public-comment/

Othman, M., & Muijs, D. (2013). Educational quality differences in a middle-income country: The urban-rural gap in Malaysian primary schools. *School Effectiveness and School Improvement, 24*(1), 1–18.

Parcel, T., Dufur, M., & Zito, R. (2010). Capital at home and at school: A review and synthesis. *Journal of Marriage and Family, 72*(4), 828–846. Retrieved from http://www.jstor.org.umiss.idm.oclc.org/stable/40864948

Portes, A. (1998). Social capital: Its origins and applications in modern sociology. *Annual Review of Sociology, 24*, 1–24.

Putnam, R.D. (1995). Tuning in, tuning out: The strange disappearance of social capital in America. *Political Science and Politics, 28*(4), 664–683.

Putnam, R. D. (2000). *Bowling alone: The collapse and revival of American community.* New York, NY: Simon & Schuster.

Qian, X., & Smyth, R. (2008). Measuring regional inequality of education in China: Widening coast–inland gap or widening rural–urban gap. *Journal of International Development, 20*(2), 132–144.

Riley, K. (2013). Walking the leadership tightrope: Building community cohesiveness and social capital in schools in highly disadvantaged urban communities. *British Educational Research Journal, 39*(2), 266–286.

Roberts, C. (2013). Building social capital through leadership development. *Journal of Leadership Education, 12*(1), 54.

Rose, R. A., Woolley, M. E., & Bowen, G. L. (2013). Social capital as a portfolio of resources across multiple microsystems: Implications for middle-school students. *Family Relations, 62*(4), 545–558.

Sayed, Y. (2010). Globalisation, educational governance and decentralisation: Promoting equity, increasing participation, and enhancing quality? *Compare: A Journal of Comparative and International Education, 40*(1), 59–62.

Sorenson, J. (2016). Rural-urban differences in bonding and bridging social capital. *Regional Studies, 50*(3), 391–410.

Stelmach, B. L. (2011). A synthesis of international rural education issues and responses. *The Rural Educator, 32*(2), 32–42.

Symeou, L. (2008). From school-family links to social capital: Urban and rural distinctions in teacher and parent networks in Cyprus. *Urban education, 43*(6), 696–722.

Terrion, J. L. (2006). The development of social capital through a leadership training program. *MountainRise: The international Journal for the Scholarship of Teaching and Learning, 3*(2). Retrieved from http://mountainrise.wcu.edu/index.php/MtnRise/article/view/69/47

U.S. Department of Education. (2014). *Full-service community schools program.* Retrieved from http://www2.ed.gov/programs/communityschools/index.html

Vorhaus, J. (2014). Education, social capital and the accordion effect. *Journal of Philosophy of Education, 48*(1), 28–47.

Woolley, M., Kol, K., & Bowen, G. (2009). The social context of school success for Latino middle school students direct and indirect influences of teachers, family, and friends. *29*(1), 43–70.

Ye, X. (2010). China's urban-rural integration policies. *Journal of Current Chinese Affairs, 38*(4), 117–143.

Young, D.J. (1998). Rural and urban differences in student achievement in science and mathematics: A multilevel analysis. *School Effectiveness and School Improvement, 9*(4), 386–418.

Zhang, J., Pang, N.S.-K. (2016). Investigating the development of professional learning communities: Compare schools in Shanghai and Southwest China. *Asia Pacific Journal of Education, 36*(2), 217–230.

Zhao, N., Valcke, M., Desoete, A., & Verhaeghe, J. (2012). The quadratic relationship between socioeconomic status and learning performance in China by multilevel analysis: Implications for policies to foster education equity. *International Journal for Educational Development, 32*(3), 12–422.

CHAPTER 2

SOCIAL CAPITAL AND SCHOOL REFORM

The Role of School Leaders in Fostering Relationships Amongst Stakeholders

Denver J. Fowler

INTRODUCTION

In the PreK–12 educational setting, much of the focus on school reform initiatives have been embedded in the analysis and utilization of assessment data derived from standardized tests, efforts to improve the curriculum, and a focus on the pedagogical skills of teachers (Blink, 2007; Leana, 2011; Leana & Pil, 2014; Midgley, Stringfield, & Wayman, 2006). However, in more recent years, research suggests that fostering social capital[1] in the school context leads to school-wide change and improved student performance (Leana & Pil, 2009, 2014). Subsequently, we have begun to see a shift in focus towards an emphasis on school leaders promoting a positive school climate and culture as the foundation of any school improvement

---

[1] Social capital in the school context refers to the relationships and interrelationships amongst all stakeholders, including students, staff, parents, community members, and business owners.

Contemporary Perspectives on Social Capital in Educational Contexts,
pages 23–33.

initiative (Gordon, 2015; Gruenert & Whitaker, 2015; Jones, Yonezawa, Mehan, & MCClure, 2017; Loukas, 2016). Keeping with this theme, there is no doubt that social capital plays a vital role in the makeup of the climate and culture of a given school building and/or district. Furthermore, it may be argued that social capital could (and should) be recognized and promoted in all schools (Catts & Ozga, 2005). Building on the extant literature, this chapter aims to clearly outline social capital as it relates to the PreK–12 educational setting, and its role in school reform. Additionally, an emphasis will be placed on the requisite for school leaders to promote and foster social capital in the school ecosystem in an effort to improve student achievement. Finally, this chapter intends to clearly delineate a school leaders' role in fostering the relationships amongst all stakeholders, including students, staff, parents, community members, and business owners.

SOCIAL CAPITAL

In many respects, in reviewing the extant literature on social capitol, one may unearth multiple and varying definitions of social capitol. In fact, researchers and scholars alike have previously reported this phenomenon (Fukuyama, 1999). Of such publications, Acar (2011) most animatedly expounds this portent writing "there seems to be no unanimous definition of social capital…social capital has been given a number of definitions, many of which refer to its manifestations rather than to social capitol itself" (p. 456). Of such definitions, the simplest, and perhaps most accurate, is that social capitol is an instantiated informal norm that promotes cooperation between two or more individuals (Fukuyama, 1999). This definition is useful as it applies to the PreK–12 educational setting in that it encompasses items such as trust and networks, both concomitant with social capitol (Fukuyama, 1999). Moreover, one might argue that both trust and networks arise due to the result of school leaders fostering social capitol. Nonetheless, Fukuyama (1999) wrote "not just any set of instantiated norms constitutes social capital; they must lead to cooperation in groups and therefore related to traditional virtues like honesty, the keeping of commitments, reliable performance of duties, reciprocity, and the like." Thus, we might contend that social capitol really is defined by its purposes, versus its indications.

SOCIAL CAPITAL AND THE PreK–12 EDUCATIONAL SETTING

Social capital in the PreK–12 educational setting can refer to items such as parental expectations (for students, staff, and the school, in general), perceived obligations, and the many social networks that exists within a given school community (Ho, 2017). More unambiguously, academic success can be directly ascribed to a school leaders' ability to foster social capitol in schools. Thus, there is no doubt that academic achievement can either be reinforced or inhibited based on the social capitol characteristics that exist in a school ecosystem. Such characteristics include the expectations parents have with regards to both the school educating their children, and their obligations as a parent in educating their child. In addition, societal networks that exist in the school community such as the connections between a school and the stakeholders in which the school serves, including students, staff, parents, community members, and business owners, contributes to the school's success or failure in educating its students. Additionally, elements such as the school climate and culture, and cultural norms play a vital role in the education of students in the PreK–12 educational setting. This certainly is not a new concept. Dating back to the 1980s, Coleman (1988) made the connection between social capital and other constructs in the school setting. In fact, Coleman (1988) argued that "social capital is part of a general theoretical strategy" in combating issues that arise in the school environment. Nonetheless, social capital specifically, is a term that has largely been ignored in the PreK–12 educational setting by practitioners. Furthermore, school leaders still struggle with how to effectively bridge the gap between the school and the community in which it serves. Nonetheless, in more recent years, there has been a significant shift towards, and focus on, the importance of school leaders fostering a positive school climate and culture in schools. Therefore, social capital, either directly or indirectly, has been regarded as an important aspect of a school's success (or failure), as the physiognomies of social capital often are part of, and contribute to, the overall climate and culture of a given school.

Historically, student achievement scores have indicated a school's success (or failure) in educating its students. Research has shown when social capital in schools is evident, student achievement scores are higher (Leana, 2011). The focus on social capital, again, either indirectly, directly, or by chance in the PreK–12 educational setting has certainly become more prevalent in more recent years, namely as it applies to certain aspects of a given school's climate and culture. In fact, one might argue that in order to be an effective school leader in the 21st Century, school leaders in the PreK–12 education setting must copiously understand the importance of investing much needed time and resources in an effort to build social capital. More specifically, school leaders must be able to lead for, and articulate, the role social capital plays with regards to school-community engagement. In a nation where a child's zip code often determines the quality of education they receive, and in some cases (if not all) their future, the need for collaboration between schools and the community are vital to a school's success in educating its students, perhaps especially in schools that are located in areas of high poverty. There is no doubt that one strategy to combat these quandaries is utilizing community input as it relates to school improvement initiatives. "We must confront the segregation and concentrated poverty that make sustained school improvement virtually impossible, and ground school improvement efforts in community input so that the key voices are heard, valuable assets are leveraged, and critical needs are met" (Noguera, 2016). Nevertheless, school leaders continue to struggle in many respects with regards to school-community engagement as an opportunity for school reform initiatives. However, proven and effective models on how school leaders can best foster collaboration between schools and community-based organizations are prevalent.

BUILDING SOCIAL CAPITAL IN SCHOOLS

Perhaps one of the most highly regarded models focused on the importance of school leaders investing time and resources in building social capital was generated by Warren (2005). In this model, Warren (2005), identifies three main approaches; (1) the service approach; (2) the development approach; and (3) the organizing approach. "All three models seek to build new, stronger, and more collaborative relationships between and among parents, educators, and community members. In conceptual terms, they work to build social capital and relational power. But each model does so in different ways, which gives them distinctive strengths and weaknesses" (Warren, 2005, p. 163). Although the model and approaches are notably focused on urban school reform, one might conceive its effectiveness in all school district locales including urban, suburban, and rural. All three models are succinctly and eloquently described below as shared by Theoharis and Scanlan in *Leadership for Increasingly Diverse Schools* (2015, p. 168):

The service model-epitomized in community schools-uses schools as hubs that house a range of support services for families. For instance, community schools frequently include health clinics and provide adult education classes. Second, the development model involves the community sponsoring a new school, investing resources in creating the school as a vital organization in the neighborhood. Third, the organizing model uses schools as one partner amongst many local organizations working in a concerted manner to reform the quality of life in a neighborhood. One lesson across all the models is the importance of investing resources in building social capital.

Warren (2005) further contends successful school reform starts with linking the school to the community. This includes the educational leadership practice of boundary spanning[2] where school leaders function as "organizational navigators" and "knowledgeable information brokers" (Miller, 2009, p. 619). Essentially, one may argue that schools are social frontiers[3] in their own right. "The metaphor of social frontiers is a useful one for school leaders to apply to the complexities inherent to building productive relationships with families and with communities" (Theoharis & Scanlan, 2015, p. 163). A school leader who is a boundary spanner, acts as a link between stakeholders and the school, bringing people together who might otherwise be isolated from one another (Theoharis & Scanlan, 2015). This intersection of social networks and the schoolhouse, and the inclinations that arise

---

[2] Educational leaders who are "institutional infiltrators organizing for community advancement," who are "in" and "of" communities (Miller, 2008, p. 372).

[3] Social frontiers as described by Theoharis and Scanlan, (2015) as "places where different social worlds collide, forcing interaction of people who would otherwise tend to be isolated from one another" (p. 163).

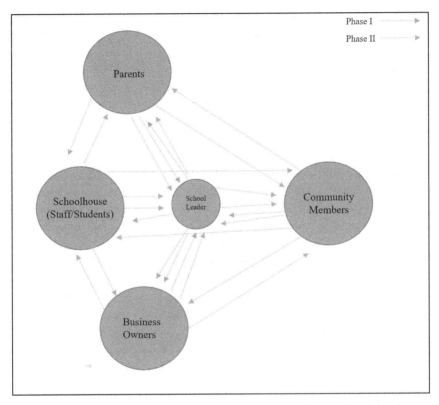

FIGURE 2.1. The Role of a School Leader in Fostering Social Capital in Schools

from these fostered networks, most undoubtedly lead to networks of people do-ing things for each other (Becker, Coleman, & Bourdieu, 2017). Catts and Ozga (2005) contend that "social capital bonds people together and helps them make links beyond their immediate friends and neighbors" (p. 1). In many ways, the school leader acts as the liaison between the schoolhouse (staff and students) and the stakeholders; parents, community members, and business owners (See Figure 2.1). Although the school leader may help foster the initial connections between the schoolhouse and the stakeholders (Phase I), the long-term goal is for these dif-ferent groups to sustain strong relationships with each other and the schoolhouse, dependent of the school leader (Phase II). However, one might argue that the school leader should continue to play a significant role in fostering these relation-ships, even in Phase II (See Figure 2.1).

Social Capital and School Climate and School Culture

Although school climate and school culture are often used interchangeably, some scholars argue they are in fact two separate entities. For example, Whitaker (2015) utilizes a weather analogy to explain the difference between climate and culture. Essentially, he argues that the *school climate* is the weather today, whereas the *school culture* is the weather over a given academic school year. That is, keeping with the weather analogy, it may be warmer in Alaska than in California on a given day (daily forecast-*climate*), but over a year's time, one might conceive it is colder in Alaska (yearly forecast-*culture*). "Changing a school's culture has to start with changing the school's climate" (Whitaker, 2015). Essentially, to change the culture of a school, a school leader must change what happens in the school on a daily basis (school climate). School leaders must be able to understand the role that social capital plays in fostering a positive school climate and culture at the schoolhouse. "School climate refers to the general tone of social relations in and around schools: how people in the school relate to each other, the culture that emerges among these people, the norms that they construct" (Crosnoe, 2007, p. 1). Thus, by this definition, one could easily argue that social capital certainly plays a vital role in relation to school climate. In using Crosnoe's (2007) definition of school climate, one can easily see how social capital and school climate/culture intersect. Moreover, a research brief (Wellbeing at School, 2012) contended that "school climate is the quality and character of school life. School climate is based on patterns of students,' parents' and school personnel's experience of school life; it also reflects norms, goals, values, interpersonal relationships, teaching and learning practices, and organizational structures" and that a positive school climate includes characteristics such as "students, families, and educators work(ing) together to develop and contribute to a shared school vision." Thus, one might contend that, when a school leader effectively builds social capital throughout the school ecosystem, naturally, either directly or indirectly, the school climate/culture improves. There is a vast amount of literature connecting a positive school climate/culture to improved academic achievement (Gordon, 2015; Gruenert & Whitaker, 2015; Jones, Yonezawa, Mehan, & McClure, 2017; Loukas, 2016). Nonetheless, as previously reported, much of the focus on school reform initiatives have been embedded in the analysis and utilization of assessment data derived from standardized tests, efforts to improve the curriculum, and a focus on the pedagogical skills of teachers (Blink, 2007; Leana, 2011; Leana & Pil, 2014; Midgley, Stringfield, & Wayman, 2006). In an era of school reform that requires school leaders (and teachers) to collect vast amounts of data (on a daily basis), and use it to drive instructional practices (i.e., classroom instruction, intervention, enrichment, etc.), school leaders must not discount the importance of relationships in the school community. After all, we know that positive school relationships lead to increased student motivation, student engagement and academic outcomes (Vink, 2015). In essence, one might argue that social capital should be at the forefront of any school reform initiative.

SOCIAL CAPITAL AND SCHOOL REFORM

Fostering social capital in the education setting no doubt leads to school-wide change and improved student performance (Leana & Pil, 2009, 2014). In fact, "recent research has found social capital to be a better predictor of student achievement" (Kagle & Galosy, 2017). However, some researchers and scholars have made a case that social capital in schools is on the decline. Putnam (1995) argued that social capital in general, not only as it applies to the school setting, has been on the decline in the United States for the past forty years. Years later, Longo (2007) reported that the school community is suffering from a decline of social capital. Years earlier, Coleman (1966) documented the connotation of community support as it applies to schooling detailing how students with greater social capital are more successful in school. Interestingly enough, Putnam's work on social capital led him back to the schoolhouse, where he was able to make connections between social capital and educational achievement (Putnam, 1995). Putnam's (1995) findings indicated that social capital had a major influence on the educational process as a whole. Perhaps Longo's (2007) analysis of Putnam's work is described best (p. 8):

> In examining comparative statewide educational performance in the United States, Putnam finds a strong correlation between social capitol and educational performance-a connection that is even stronger than that between socioeconomic or racial characteristics and educational performance.

Years earlier, Coleman (1966) documented the connotation of community support as it applies to schooling detailing how students with greater social capital are more successful in school. Conceivably, at no other time throughout history, does there need to be a gallant and averred effort on the part of our nation's school leaders to utilize social capital as it applies to school reform initiatives and implementation. At the very least, social capitol should be an aspect of any initiative in the school ecosystem. When school leaders work as a liaison between the school (including staff and students) and parents, community members, and business owners (See Figure 2.1), a climate and culture is fostered in such a way that all stakeholders are contributing to the objective of the school; to provide a high-quality education to each and every student, and prepare them to be college, career, and life ready. By working to connect all stakeholders to the schoolhouse, a school leader can tap into the expertise and resources that exist throughout the school community. In doing so, not only are school leaders "boundary spanning" and cultivating relationships across "social frontiers," in essence, they are creating an environment where there is shared responsibility for the quality of education students receive in the school community. This schoolhouse-community network becomes the driving force behind all initiatives at the school, and as previously mentioned, contributes to the school climate and culture in a positive manner. By involving and connecting different stakeholders, that might not otherwise interact, one might envisage how this may "increase the relevance of a quality education… by improving ownership, building consensus, reaching remote and disadvantaged groups, and strengthening institutional capacity" (Acar, 2011, p. 458). When it comes to school reform, school leaders must include social capitol in the blueprint. In fact, some may argue it is the cornerstone of any school initiative. In a study by Acar (2011), it was revealed that "social capital's concrete benefits for education can be seen as: (1) higher achievement on tests; (2) higher graduation rates; (3) lower dropout rates; (4) higher college enrollment; and (5) greater participation in school and community organizations" (p. 460).

SUMMARY

The role of school leaders in fostering relationships amongst stakeholders has implications that, in many facets, are unending and all of the benefits aside from the obvious ones are hard to truly measure. That is, although researchers have found correlations between social capitol and academic achievement (Acar, 2011; Coleman, 1966; Leana & Pil, 2009, 2014; Putnam, 1995), the by-product of building social capitol in schools may be more impactful than previously thought. If social capital truly is the cornerstone of any school reform initiative, then school climate/culture and academic achievement are the masonry stones arranged directly to the left and right. In essence, the three are somewhat interconnected, and in many ways, cultivate one another. Thus, one may argue that a school cannot truly have a positive school climate and culture without the existence of social capital. Likewise, one might argue that you cannot have strong academic achievement without the existence of a positive school climate and culture (See Figure 2.2).

After all, we might very well conceive that any effective school leader would not want one without the other. To do so, might be deemed as unethical, namely as it applies to the ethics of care or relational ethics. As Noddings (1992) wrote, "the first job of the schools is to care" (p. 16). Acar (2011) further reinforced the need for the ethics of care in schools writing "ethics of care; indeed, like the concept of social capitol, the ethics of care deal with relationships involving care, responsibility, trust, trust worthiness and compassion among individuals and organizations" (p. 459). Perhaps no one more eloquently articulates this concept of care better than Acar's (2011) interpretation of Starratt's (1994) work focused on addressing the "characteristics of schools and school communities that are committed to ethics of care" by writing (p. 460):

> The integrity of human relationships should be held sacrosanct, both in school and out of school. Educators should also develop sensitivity to the dignity and uniqueness of each person in the school. To do so, educators can attend to the culture tone of schools…school activities and procedures should also reflect caring, as should the school song and other symbols. This ethic should concern itself with the larger purpose of productivity…when successfully applied, the ethics of care as Starratt imagines them are comparable to high social capital in schools and school communities. His suggestion to promote care in and out of school may also be applicable to the

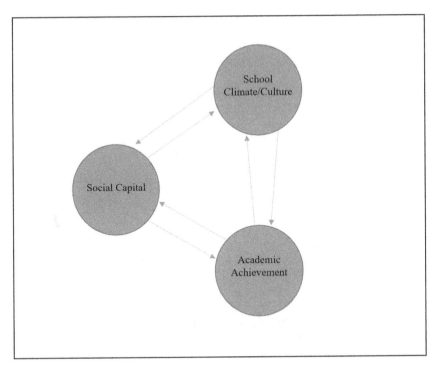

FIGURE 2.2.   Social Capital, School Climate/Culture, and Academic Achievement

promotion of high social capital in other words, when there are people committed to the ethics of care in schools and communities, there is higher social capital. On the other hand, all parties involved in the process of education, including but not limited to, administrators and teachers should not sacrifice the uniqueness and individuality of students for the sake of promoting social capital. Rather, they should try to maintain a balance between these two assets (that is social capital and individuals' unique interests, capabilities, and routes to realization of their potential). In other words, educators should still cherish diversity in the school and in the classroom, while trying to reap the benefits of social capital. This requires respect for decisions made by individuals and elimination of any overt and covert pressure on individuals to mold them into a uniform identity and/or purpose.

REFERENCES

Acar, E. (2011). Effects of social capitol on academic success: A narrative synthesis. *Educational Research and Reviews, 6*(6), 456–461.

Becker, G., Coleman, J., & Bourdieu, P. (2017). *Species of capital.* SlidePlayer. Retrieved from http://slideplayer.com/slide/8936123/

Blink, R. (2007). *Data-driven instructional leadership.* New York, NY: Routledge.

Catts, R., & Ozga, J. (2005). *What is social capital and how might it be used in Scotland's schools?* CES Briefing 36. Centre for Educational Sociology, University of Edinburgh, Edinburgh, Scotland.

Coleman, J. (1966). *Equality of educational opportunity.* Washington, DC: U.S. Office of Education.

Coleman, J. (1988). Social capital in the creation of human capital. *American Journal of Sociology, 94,* 95–120.

Crosnoe, R. (2007). *School climate.* The Blackwell Encyclopedia of Sociology. Retrieved from http://onlinelibrary.wiley.com/doi/10.1002/9781405165518.wbeoss021/abstract;jsessionid=E01A36337D71F179DEA74EFE94A7FD79.f04t03?userIsAuthenticated=false&deniedAccessCustomisedMessage=

Fukuyama, F. (1999). *Social capitol and civil society.* International Monetary Fund. Retrieved from: https://www.imf.org/external/pubs/ft/seminar/1999/reforms/fukuyama.htm

Gordon, J. (2015). *You win in the locker room first: The 7 C's to build a winning team in sports, business and life.* Hoboken, NJ: John Wiley & Sons.

Gruenert, S., & Whitaker, T. (2015). *School culture rewired: How to define, assess, and transform it.* Alexandria, VA: ASCD.

Ho, S. C. (2017). *Social capital and education.* Education encyclopedia. Retrieved from http://education.stateuniversity.com/pages/2427/Social-Capital-Education.html

Jones, M., Yonezawa, S., Mehan, H., & McClure, L. (2017). *School climate and student achievement.* CREATE. Retrieved from https://education.ucdavis.edu/sites/main/files/Yonezawa_Paper_WEB.pdf

Kagle, M., & Galosy, J. (2017). *Teacher social capital and educational improvement.* Knowles Teacher Initiative. Retrieved from: http://kstf.org/2017/03/23/teacher-social-capital-and-educational-improvement/

Leana, C. (2011). The missing link in school reform. *Stanford Social Innovation Review: Informing and Inspiring Leaders of Social Change.* Retrieved from https://ssir.org/articles/entry/the_missing_link_in_school_reform

Leana, C., & Pil, F. (2009). Applying organizational research to public school reform: The effects of teacher human and social capital on student performance. *Academy of Management Journal, 52*(6), 1101–1124.

Leana, C., & Pil, F. (2014). *A new focus on social capital in school reform efforts.* Albert Shanker Institute. Retrieved from: http://www.shankerinstitute.org/blog/new-focus-social-capital-school-reform-efforts

Longo, N. (2007). *Why community matters: Connecting education with civic life.* Albany, NY: State University of New York Press.

Loukas, A. (2016). *What is school climate?* Paper presented at the 2nd Panhellenic Conference, Larissa, Greece. Abstract received from https://www.researchgate.net/publication/265306026_What_Is_School_Climate

Midgley, S., Stringfield, S., & Wayman, J. (2006). *Leadership for data-based decision-making collaborative educator teams.* Paper presented at American Educational Research Association, San Francisco, CA.

Miller, P. M. (2009) Boundary spanning in homeless children's education: Notes from an emergent faculty role in Pittsburgh. *Educational Administration Quarterly, 45*(4), 616–630.

Miller, P. M. (2008). Examining the work of boundary spanning leaders in community contexts. *International Journal of Leadership in Education, 11*(4), 353–377.

Noddings, N. (1992). *The challenge to care in schools: An alternative approach to education.* New York, NY: Teachers College Press.

Noguera, P. (2016). *Poverty is an obstacle to learning: Op-ed in Education Week delineates hunger, health, issues, and trauma as educational barriers.* University of California at Los Angeles's Center for the Study of School Transformation. Retrieved from https://ampersand.gseis.ucla.edu/pedro-noguera-poverty-is-an-obstacle-to-learning/

Putnam, R. (1995). Bowling alone: America's declining social capitol. *Journal of Democracy, 6,* 165–178.

Starratt, R. J. (1994). *Building an ethical school: A practical response to the moral crisis in schools.* London, UK: Falmer Press.

Theoharis, G., & Scanlan, M. (2015). *Leadership for increasingly diverse schools.* New York, NY: Routledge.

Vink, R. (2015). *Relationships matter.* Relational Schools. Retrieved from http://relationalschools.org/2015/01/30/relationships-matter-2/

Warren, M. R. (2005). Communities and schools: A new view of urban education reform. *Harvard Educational Review, 75*(2), 133–173.

Wellbeing at School. (2012). *The importance of building a safe and caring school climate.* Wellbeing at School. Retrieved from https://www.wellbeingatschool.org.nz/sites/default/files/W@S-Building-a-safe-and-caring-climate-research-brief.pdf

Whitaker, T. (2015). *Changing a culture starts with the climate.* ASCD. Retrieved from http://onlinelibrary.wiley.com/doi/10.1002/9781405165518.wbeoss021/abstract;jsessionid=E01A36337D71F179DEA74EFE94A7FD79.f04t03?userIsAuthenticated=false&deniedAccessCustomisedMessage=

CHAPTER 3

BUILDING SOCIAL CAPITAL FOR PARENTS AND FAMILIES THROUGH SCHOOL LEADERSHIP

Roberto Trigosso, Phyllis F. Reggio, and Carlos R. McCray

INTRODUCTION

Research has found that parent, family, and community involvement is instrumental in addressing school dropout rates and promoting student motivation as well as higher educational aspirations (Barton, 2003). For students at both the elementary and secondary level, regardless of the parent's education, family income, or background, parent involvement affects academic achievement across all races (Jeynes, 2003). Students come to school with diverse needs, abilities and backgrounds. These diverse characteristics can influence students' varying levels of social capital, which can be essential in fostering academic success and closing achievement gaps. Parents too, possess diverse characteristics and bring varying levels of social capital as they attempt to navigate their child's education. For some parents, the pathway to their child's academic trajectory is clear—they visit, question, research, and make informed decisions. Others, may lack a basic

Contemporary Perspectives on Social Capital in Educational Contexts,
pages 35–44.

awareness of how to approach such critical choices in the development of their child's academic life.

The aforementioned awareness and ability to make informed decisions is of-tentimes grounded in social capital. Such social capital is found in relationships parents have cultivated with other organizations within the community as well as the school itself. Effective schools provide networks, contacts and resources to parents and families. And effective school leaders also provide the learning op-portunities needed to foster social capital for parents and families.

In order for parents to help their child succeed in their academic life, they need to have learning resources and social capital. While all parents may have social capital to some degree, it may not have the same value or have the greatest im-pact on the students or the school environment (Lareau & Horvat, 1999). Parents' demographics may influence their social capital, which can then influence their behaviors in the interest of their child's achievement. While McNeal (1999) ac-knowledges that all parents can use their social capital, Lareau and Horvat, (1999) emphasize that parents may not activate their social capital due to a variety of reasons, such as a lack of understanding or a belief that their capital is not relevant or beneficial in their environment.

The environment consists of the school organization and the communities that store the social capital that parents can access. For some families, especially those foreign born, the school can be an intimidating place. Others, for example, many highly involved parents, possess a high degree of social capital through infor-mation channels. According to Coleman (1988), these channels produce a high degree of information that is essential for the specific needs of the individual. While the highly involved parents will obtain a high level of information for their children, the parents who are less involved will not have the same level of infor-mation channels or harness their resources for the academic achievement of their children.

Parents may use informational channels for the purpose of academic achieve-ment in their children (Cooper & Crosnoe, 2007). For example, parents may use social capital to ensure a child's admission into a university. These parents use information channels to understand what is needed for entry into certain universi-ties. An additional example can be illustrated when students receive school sched-ules prior to the start of the school year. Parents with social capital who are not satisfied with the student schedule or teacher will view this as a detriment to their child's future. These parents use their capital to advocate changes in their child's school program. While these parents activate their social capital in this regard, other parents may not have the same access to social networks, or they lack an understanding of how teachers or particular courses will benefit their child. In-deed, Fleming, (2012) found parents' education levels and social capital aware-ness could influence how they interpret student grades to monitor progress.

Social capital theory implies purposeful investment on the part of the partici-pants, as it pertains to the academic development of youngsters, Coleman (1988) argued that the mere presence of parental stores of knowledge is insufficient to ensure transmission of that knowledge to children. Instead, parents must make choices to invest in their children's growth and engage in interactions with the child to form the connections which will allow information to pass. While parents may be committed to forming these bonds, many factors can impede their ability to invest and engage in their child's development—languages barriers, cultural boundaries, lack of time and access, for example.

As school leaders, we are responsible to all parents. Gone are the days of parent involvement that focuses on bake sales and fundraisers. All parents are invited to participate in school activities. We believe that effective school leaders create pathways for parental involvement which serves to inform parents, develop their ability to bolster their child's academic progress, and raises their level of social capital through concrete and meaningful strategies.

SOCIAL CAPITAL AND PARENT INVOLVEMENT

In our work as school leaders, we have identified several scenarios in which parents can be actively engaged in opportunities in which their social capital can be deepened. In this chapter, we explore several cases from practice in urban schools through the lens of Joyce Epstein's *Framework for Parent Involvement* (2011) Framework. Our cases capture school leaders who provided a direct link to parents and families of children in high-need, urban schools. We present our cases from the field in three distinct ways as follows:

First, using cases from the field, we link theory to practice. We ask school leaders to articulate how these practices have resulted in academic outcomes for high need students. We demonstrate how these practices reflect Epstein's (2011) model coupled with the National PTA Standards. For example, several school leaders and communities have used technology to teach parents the benefits of social networking within their communities for the benefit of their children (Fleming, 2012). Schools have added Internet based parent portals that give parents instant access to grades and teacher comments. Other school districts have created community technology hubs where parents can access these resources while they are not working. In addition, these centers have been used as training schools to show parents how to use technology for parent networking. These workgroups have focused on teaching parents the value of using their social capital for the academic achievement of their children (Fleming, 2012).

Our cases from the field demonstrate how school leaders have supported parents in leveraging resources, and building social capital resulting in positive consequences for student academic progress. Although schools cannot change parents' educational backgrounds, schools can design specific parental engagement programs to help parents access and gain social capital. While schools embody a range of diversity among parents, schools can design parental involvement programs that engage all parents and support them in participating in activities that are beneficial to all students.

We conclude our leadership cases and parental accounts with specific strategies for school leaders in their work with families. Using cases from the field, we demonstrate our work as school leaders employing parental involvement approaches following the work of Epstein (2011). Specifically, we recommend strategies and implications for school leaders that foster a climate for parents' involvement; a result-oriented approach to building social capital.

LINKING THEORY TO PRACTICE

We propose a model of parental involvement that fosters social capital for families through the lens of school leadership. We apply Epstein (2011) framework for parental involvement due to its comprehensiveness in addressing the major components to parental involvement which are influenced by social capital (Bhering, 2002). In addition, this framework allows us to address concerns from both school leaders and parents by emphasizing six (6) essential categories. The six categories are as follows: (a) parenting, (b) communicating, (c) volunteering, (d) learning at home, (e) decision making, and (f) collaborating with the community (Epstein, 2011). Each of these components to the framework provide opportunities for leaders to put theory into practice with students and parents. In parenting, for leaders to find strategic ways to help parents understand the development of children and creating supportive home environments. For communicating, it is key for leaders to develop programs and structures that increase communication for the improvement of the student's progress. When considering volunteering, leaders must find creative ways to include parents in school related activities that go beyond the traditional bake sales and fundraisers. When considering learning at home, leaders must help parents provide ways to help their children with home related activities. In addition, parents should be incorporated in curriculum related decisions. Leaders should include parents in critical decisions that involve students and the greater school community. Finally, when collaborating with the community, leaders must utilize all community resources that include all stakeholders. This should include individuals that may not have students in the school as well (Epstein, 2011).

The following cases demonstrate how practices from parents and school leaders foster social capital through the components of the Epstein framework. These questions guide our discussion of cases from the field:

- Using Epstein's (2011) Framework, what immediate strategies can school leaders implement to support the academic achievement and outcomes of students?
- What effective strategies and resources can the school employ to build social capital for families?
- What future research can inform school leaders in efforts to build the social capital for parents and families?

The overall purpose of this chapter is to provide preliminary evidence on the effectiveness of our leadership practices that build parent's ability to help their children excel. We utilize a case method to capture the integration of social capital into the work of school leadership. We present three cases from the field and demonstrate how school leaders have implemented practices of parental involvement, as mentioned earlier, by applying Epstein's framework for parent involvement, (2011).

PROMOTING ACADEMIC ACHIEVEMENT THROUGH LEADERSHIP: CASES FROM THE FIELD

Case #1

Rodrigo, has been a Director of ENL (English New Language) and World Languages for over ten years in various urban and suburban school communities. In his role as director he has recognized the importance of parents as partners for the success of his students. His focus was especially for his high need students, the English as a New Language population. He stated how he used Title I funds to develop social events in the evening to encourage parents to visit and learn about the school. These parent events were in addition, to the cultural celebrations that were already in place in many schools. Rodrigo said he found success in parents being advocates in their child's education by also investing in Saturday field trips for students, parents and teachers. He found creative ways in each teacher contract to pay teachers for their time on Saturdays. He acknowledged the impact the events made on parents to help them connect with the school.

Rodrigo believes the outreach events linked a direct outcome to those students' grades. Furthermore, the opportunity for parents to meet each other and network within their community is an essential way to increase social capital. In his final example, he stated how he hires community liaisons that speak the languages of the ENL students in need. For example, he hired one who spoke Mandarin and was able to translate for the growing population of parents who only speak Mandarin. The liaison held a workshop for parents on how to access and utilize the parent portal internet system to review their child's academic progress. The parents who attended this workshop had a clear understanding of how to access and review their child's grades and assignments. He stated how the students whose parents learned how to access the student grades via the internet demonstrated academic improvement. Rodrigo's work with his school is an example of Epstein's framework, Communicating, can be developed with ENL students (Epstein, 2011). Social networking is an effective way to utilize social capital and to increase capital for parents (Fleming, 2012).

Case #2: Epstein Framework: Type of Parent Involvement: Learning at Home

The National Parent Teacher Association (National PTA, n.d.) clearly outlines its mission to engage parents and help students succeed: "The overall purpose of PTA is to make every child's potential a reality by engaging and empowering families and communities to advocate for all children" (para. 1). While the mission for helping children is clear, each school community has to engage parents and community in various ways to foster student achievement. Students with different family backgrounds have varying needs that can be addressed with the help of parents. Parents offer insight in the essential needs of their children and families' success. It is high time for schools to make the best use of this under-utilized social resource. In our next case, one school leader describes his efforts to utilize internet resources.

Enrique is an Assistant Principal of a diverse Middle School in a suburb outside of New York City. He acknowledged that parents are the key to the success of students in his school during middle school and beyond. To engage parents in his community he is working with students to create videos that stream over the internet for parents on current topics that are concerns in his community. These videos help parents understand what students are dealing with in school and out in their community. Reaching out to parents via the internet is a way to engage working parents who may not have the opportunity to visit the school for a parent evening. The administrators in his school are also working on educating parents on mindfulness. This is a strategy they have worked with students to lower their anxiety. They realized that students would benefit more from the learning activities if they asked parents to participate in their own mindfulness. Having parents participate in the learning of the students is a critical way to make learning meaningful to students. Teaching parents coping skills will also help students develop coping skills which they found is a concern in many of their students. Enrique's strategies emphasize, Learning at Home in Epstein's Framework for Parent Involvement (Epstein, 2011). Enrique designed a way to provide parents important information that students were struggling with. In addition, it engaged parents to become involved in their child's learning at home. Parents were essential in this example because all students could not be successful in the goals of Enrique's strategy without the parents help.

Case #3

Building the social capital of parents while their children are transitioning from the middle grades to the high school level is critical. Ferrara (2015) discusses the dichotomy between this most at-risk time for youngsters and the drop in parental involvement at school as children enter teen years. Choosing the high school, a child will attend is a key decision that takes place at this transition time. For parents who lack social capital, this decision can have long-term consequences in their child's future.

New York City, the nation's largest school system, ensures a seat for every eighth-grade student. In 2014 only 7 black students were admitted to the elite Stuyvesant High School, which has over 3000 enrollees (Rosenbaum & Pearson, 2014). During the same year 45% of eighth graders gained entry into their top choices selected in an application process. Those who do not receive their first choice, may have gained admission to one of their other choices or else must wait for a round-two admission process. For many parents, especially those with who speak little or no English, one former New York City middle school principal describes challenges and strategies:

> When the admission letters arrive and the school counselors have to be on hand to support students who may be disappointed especially when they haven't been placed. In my first year as principal, I saw students cheering while some were crying—it was heartbreaking, and the parents had no understanding of how this happens. We learned that we have to get on top of the process early and engage all parents. While the city provides most materials for high school admission in translated formats, we include translators at all our parent events so that all parents have access to information. In my school, most parents are Spanish speakers, but we recently noticed that Polish translators are needed. We have a meeting for all parents beginning in the middle of seventh grade so parents are prepared for the selection year ahead. Next, at the start of eighth grade, we hold a high school night. We help our students visit high schools throughout the fall to support parents in making informed decisions. With all these efforts, still, parents send back the final applications without an understanding of the choices indicated and in many their children have filled in the information on their own. On more than one occasion, student applications had choices where the schools were two hours from their homes—that can influence a child's attendance. We also noticed unrealistic choices were made considering the child's academic record and the small seat counts in many schools. Students were selecting schools where they lacked admission requirements. This is a high concern because once a student is placed in a bottom choice, there is no recourse. If they are in the second round of choices, the playing field is even more limited because seats are already taken. This is the point where the school stops the process from moving forward and individually assists each family prior to sending out the student applications.

One parent commented on how the principal was able to properly guide her child:

> I got a call from the school saying my son picked schools all over the city. Two of his choices were in neighborhoods over two hours from our house. The school asked me to come in and meet with the guidance counselor. She spoke Spanish, and we looked at the book together. We worked with my son and picked choices that made me feel he would be safe—he comes from a small school and he isn't ready to travel far and go to a very large high school. When my daughter went through this, I had no help and we couldn't get her reassigned to a better place.

This New York City principal's experiences illustrate two important components of the Danielson Framework, Communicating and Collaborating with the community. This principal identified a lack of social capital in parents when their children applied to elite New York City High Schools. While this principal found new opportunities to increase parent communication, the principal also used community resources for the advancement of those students. Communication and collaboration with the community were key factors in the school leaders' efforts to support parents who lack social capital needed to ensure good placements for their children. The Epstein Framework, (2011) emphasizes that school leaders need to design creative ways to communicate with parents and follow through with them. This example, is an effective way to communicate but also demonstrates how the leadership created continual events and calls to homes were effectuated. Language barriers were also addressed. In addition, Community collaboration involved forming connections to high school representatives who visited the schools and allowed students and their parents access to open houses.

KEY STRATEGIES FOR SCHOOL LEADERS

Utilize a variety of communication tools: Many school districts have internet programs that can email, text, and phone parents keeping them informed of key dates, events, and online student progress reports. Supplement these systems with take home flyers and translated versions for parents without computer access. Lareau and Horvat (1999) emphasize that parents with lower levels of social capital will need further assistance in communicating. Therefore, it is essential to find multiple ways to communicate (Lareau & Horvat, 1999).

Encourage Parents to Come Into the School by Providing Learning Opportunities. While parents may enjoy cake sales or fundraising events, many working parents value their time. School leaders can plan events that educate parents about the academic program or help them navigate their child through the Pre-K–16 continuum. Connect these learning opportunities to celebrations of student achievement events such as awards evenings, or student presentations where parents can see the progress of their child. When parents can be part of the learning and track the progress of their child, it fosters academic achievement in those students. In addition, when students and parents come together, it promotes an environment of social networking for the advancement of capital and achievement in all students (Fleming, 2012).

Survey Stakeholders. All leaders can learn from self-reflection and current data. It is critical that school leaders take the time to survey parents about how well the school is making connections and collaborating with parents as partners. Some of the best changes and opportunities for school improvement can come directly from parents. Also, when parents feel they have an ownership in the school-based decisions, they are more likely to become partners with regard to academics. Surveys give leaders clear data to work from as they plan parental involvement actions and next step.

Identify and Hire Staff Who Understand The Community's Cultural Backgrounds, Languages, and Interests. Hiring staff is one of the most important jobs as a school leader. When working with students from diverse backgrounds, it essential to hire staff that not only represents the community they serve but also, staff who can help foster social capital in parents by developing close partnerships.

CONCLUSION AND RECOMMENDATIONS

Social capital theorists (Bourdieu, 1986; Coleman, 1988; Lareau & Horvat, 1999; McNeal, 1999; Woolcock, 1998) agree that social capital has a relationship with parents' income, ethnicity, and education. Although schools cannot change how much social capital a parent has or has access to, schools can design specific parent engagement programs to help parents develop parental partnerships and foster social capital. When parents are further engaged in their child's education, they have more information. Parents may use informational channels for the purpose of academic achievement in their children (Cooper & Crosnoe, 2007).

As we have discussed, past research has clearly linked how parents can have an impact on academic achievement (Sui-Chu & Willms, 1996). Our cases provide a glimpse into school leadership efforts that are immediate and aim to close achievement gaps. However, all success needs to build on data, and parents' perceptions must be captured in a formalized way. Thus, we recommend the following steps:

- School leaders should track and monitor parents' perceptions of the supports, interventions, and strategies employed by the school.
- School leaders should track their student success rates after graduation. Many school systems are implementing data systems capable of following students' high school and college completion rates. Schools need to understand the long-range impact of their programs and policies. The urgent question is: Do our efforts serve to keep students in school until graduation? Further, are our students completing college?
- Locally developed practices can benefit from collaborations with institutions of higher education in identifying appropriate staff, translation services, and educational opportunities for parents.

School leaders can develop program and supports that build the social capital of parents and families. These types of programs would be particularly useful to parents who did not receive higher education due to various life circumstances. While schools have parents of various demographics, schools can design parental involvement programs that engage all parents in how to participate in school-related activities that are beneficial all students.

REFERENCES

Barton, P. E. (2003). *Parsing the achievement gap: Baselines for tracking progress.* Princeton, NJ: Policy Information Report, Educational Testing Service.

Bhering, E. (2002). Teachers' and parents' perceptions of parent involvement in Brazilian early years and primary education. *International Journal of Early Years Education, 10*, 227–241. doi:10.1080/0966976022000044762

Bourdieu, P. (1986). Forms of capital. In J. C. Richards (Ed.), *Handbook of theory and research for the sociology of education* (pp. 241–258). New York, NY: Greenwood.

Coleman, J. (1988). Social capital in the creation of human capital. *American Journal of Sociology, 94*, 195–210. doi:10.1086/228943

Cooper, C. E., & Crosnoe, R. (2007). The engagement in schooling of economically disadvantaged parents and children. *Youth & Society, 38*, 372–391. doi:10.1177/0044118X06289999

Danielson, C. (2007). *Enhancing professional practice: A framework for teaching* (2nd ed.). Alexandria, VA: Association for Supervision and Curriculum Development.

Ferrara, M. (2015) Parent involvement facilitators: Unlocking social capital wealth. *School Community Journal, 25(1)*, 29–51.

Fleming, N. (2012, November 6). Schools are using social networking to involve parents. *Education Week*. Retrieved from http://www.edweek.org/ew/index.html

Jeynes, W. H. (2003). A meta-analysis: The effects of parental involvement on minority children's academic achievement. *Education & Urban Society, 35*(2), 202–218.

Lareau, A., & Horvat, E. M. (1999). Moments of social inclusion and exclusion race, class, and cultural capital in family–school relationships. *Sociology of Education, 72*, 37–53. Retrieved from http://www.asanet.org/journals/soe/soe.cfm

McNeal, R. B. (1999). Parental involvement as social capital: Differential effectiveness on science achievement, truancy, and dropping out. *Social Forces, 78*, 117–144. doi:10.1093/sf/78.1.117

National PTA. (n.d.). *About PTA*. Retrieved from http://www.pta.org/

Rosenbaum, S., & Pearson, E. (2014, March 11). 45% of New York City 8th graders got into top high school choice: Education Dept. *Daily News.*

Sui-Chu, H. E., & Willms, J. D. (1996). Effects of parental involvement on eighth grade achievement. *Sociology of Education, 69*, 126–141. doi:10.2307/2112802

Woolcock, M. (1998). Social capital and economic development: A theoretical synthesis and policy framework. *Theory & Society, 27*, 151–208. doi:10.1023/A:1006884930135

PART 1B

RESOURCES, MEASUREMENT, AND MISSION
STATEMENTS

CHAPTER 4

NYEISHA'S MOTHER

An Ethnographic Examination of Urban Schooling and Adopting a Resource Orientation Toward Social Capital

Nicole Mittenfelner Carl

Nyeisha's mother, Ms. Crawford, is a mother of six, soon to be seven children. Three of her children, including Nyeisha, attend Baker School[1]. Ms. Crawford is at Baker School several days a week. Despite this, Ms. Crawford is described by Nyeisha's teacher, Ms. Smith, as a "waste." In this chapter, I consider why Ms. Crawford's interactions with school personnel do not function as social capital that can be leveraged for her and her children. I argue that this is because of a deficit orientation that schools and the individuals within them have toward students and parents in the community. I suggest that taking a resource orientation toward families is a more effective way to engage them and develop bilateral relationships. The paper begins by discussing key theoretical concepts and then overviews the research methods. I then present a case study of Ms. Crawford and discuss her interactions with school personnel. The chapter demonstrates that for Ms. Crawford's interactions to result in positive benefits (i.e., function as social capital), a shift in the way parents' efforts are interpreted in schools needs to occur.

Contemporary Perspectives on Social Capital in Educational Contexts,
pages 47–60.
Copyright © 2019 by Information Age Publishing
All rights of reproduction in any form reserved.

THEORETICAL FRAMEWORK

Capital refers to resources that allow individuals to profit (Bourdieu, 1986; Wacquant, 2008). Capital can be economic (financial and material), cultural (qualifications and goods), social (connections and networks), and symbolic (misrecognized as "natural" competence) (Bourdieu, 1986, 2000). Furthermore, the cultural capital of the dominant group[2] is manifest in schools in ways that reinforce hegemony and reinscribe deficit orientations and that ultimately further sediment inequity (Bourdieu, 1998; Lareau, 2011; Mills & Gale, 2007). In addition, scholars (e.g., Lareau, 2011) have shown how middle-class parents' social capital facilitates their children's success in schools. By privileging certain forms of capital over others, whether consciously or unconsciously, schools contribute to reproducing social inequality.

Whether this process of legitimization is conscious or not, some students benefit while others do not (Henry et al., 1988; Lareau, 2011; Mills, 2008). The ways in which schools legitimate certain capital and habitus (embodied cultural capital) over others is a form of symbolic violence. This violence does not involve physical or bodily harm, and in the same way that symbolic capital is invisibly transmitted, symbolic violence is largely invisible; it is a form of cultural domination in which the symbols and practices of the dominant group are imposed on all of society (Bourdieu, 2001). For example, because schools tend to reproduce the values, tastes, and ideals of the dominant culture (Bourdieu, 1984), symbolic violence, "a gentle violence, imperceptible and invisible even to its victims, exerted for the most part through the purely symbolic channels of communication and cognition (more precisely, misrecognition), recognition, or even feeling" (Bourdieu, 2001, pp. 1–2), is acted upon students because their own habitus and capital are degraded (Bourdieu, 2000, 2001). Symbolic violence tends to be unconscious, occurring in daily interactions (Bourdieu, 2001), and causes individuals "to 'misrecognize' inequality as the natural order of things and to blame themselves for their location in their society's hierarchies" (Bourgois & Schonberg, 2009, p. 14). One example is the way in which schools often assume that all students should exhibit middle-class cultural capital (Henry et al., 1988; Lareau, 2011). Students who do not have these expected forms of cultural capital can experience symbolic violence (Bourdieu, 1984; Henry et al., 1988). As a result of this symbolic violence, some students are "distanced and Othered" because the school legitimizes certain cultures and marginalizes others (Horvat & Antonio, 1999, p. 320). Students with a different "background, however rich in experiences, often turns out to be a liability" (Henry et al., 1988, p. 142), and the racial and class othering that students experience causes pain, trauma, and hurt (Horvat & Antonio, 1999). Social capital operates in the same way. Because schools assume that all parents should behave like middle class parents (e.g., Lareau & Horvat, 1999; Lareau & Schumar, 1996), the efforts of parents with different backgrounds do not result in social capital.

One way to stop "othering" students and families is to consider them through a resource orientation. This involves acknowledging and incorporating the different funds of knowledge (González, Moll, & Amanti, 2005; Moll, 2000) that all individuals bring that may not always be immediately seen. Another part of a resource orientation is recoding forms of capital to acknowledge everyone's many attributes (Yosso, 2005). Finally, ethnographic methods can help to humanize individuals and resist deficit orientations (e.g., Bourgois & Schonberg, 2009; Paulle, 2013).

METHODS

As an ethnographic study, the primary data collection methods included observation and fieldnotes and in-depth interviews throughout a two-year period. Secondary data sources include researcher memos and archival data. Consistent with a qualitative approach, the research design was emergent, evolved based on learnings in the field, and placed a primacy on understanding individuals' lived experiences (Ravitch & Carl, 2016).

Observations occurred in classrooms, at school-related activities and events, during admission and dismissal, at lunch, during after-school programs and activities, at fieldtrips, school dances, report card conferences, in the hallways, in homes, and the like. Observing the school in a variety of settings and contexts helped contribute to a more detailed understanding. Jottings were taken in the field and developed into fieldnotes as close to the actual time of the observation as possible (Emerson, Fretz, & Shaw, 2011).

Qualitative data analysis took place formatively to help develop more nuanced and complex interpretations. During formative analysis, I composed analytical memos that reflected potential themes and contradictions in the data, commented on fieldnote vignettes, and documented difficulties and learnings. I paid specific attention to three important aspects of data analysis including, data organization and management, immersive engagement, and writing and representation (Ravitch & Carl, 2016). These processes entailed consistently maintaining my data corpus so that fieldnotes and other data can be grouped, sorted, and engaged with in multiple ways throughout data collection and analysis. In addition, descriptive and analytic memos were composed throughout data collection and analysis to document emerging learnings, reflect on data, and capture sense-making processes.

Data were also analyzed summatively after all data were collected. I conducted multiple readings of my data corpus and employed open and axial coding processes (Ravitch & Carl, 2016). Open coding processes were as inductive as possible to develop emic understandings of the data (Maxwell, 2013), and axial coding combined inductive and deductive processes. I developed a code set that includes both descriptive and theoretical categories (Maxwell, 2013). Once all data were coded, codes were analyzed to determine key themes and develop thematically based findings (Gibson & Brown, 2009). While developing codes, code definitions, and themes, I deliberately looked for disconfirming evidence and alternative examples and explanations. I also systematically engaged with others to elicit feedback, challenge my interpretations, and scrutinize codes, themes, and findings throughout formative and summative data analysis (Ravitch & Carl, 2016). In addition to thematic coding, I employed connecting strategies to holistically look at data in their entirely rather than solely pulling coded excerpts with the goal of seeing relationships to broader contexts and the entire "story" of the data (Maxwell, 2013; Maxwell & Chmiel, 2014; Maxwell & Miller, 2008). Developing holistic stories of the data helped to keep the findings as contextualized as possible. Consistent with many qualitative approaches and with ethnographic methods, I maintained a fidelity to participants' experiences rather than to specific methods (Hammersley & Atkinson, 2007).

ATTEMPTING TO ACTIVATE SOCIAL CAPITAL: A CASE STUDY

In this section, I present a case study of Ms. Crawford and how she tries to activate social capital to help her children have a better experience at school. Ms. Crawford's efforts are deliberately thwarted by school staff and especially by Nyeisha's teacher, Ms. Smith, who considers Ms. Crawford "a waste" and "worthless." Throughout this section, I analyze ethnographic fieldnote data by discussing the ways that Ms. Crawford attempts to develop and activate social capital and the barriers that she encounters.

The Crawford Family

I learn from Ms. Crawford that she and her children have been in and out of homeless shelters and agencies. After a presentation to the fourth-grade students, Ms. Crawford comes up to me in the auditorium. She is very frustrated. Ms. Crawford explains, "Ms. Smith saw me raising my hand, and she trying to be smart and not let me ask a question. I wanted to ask him [the speaker] about Sister Janice who I met when I was in [name of shelter]." I see the guest speaker leaving, and I introduce him to Ms. Crawford. They speak for a few minutes, and it turns out they have a few connections in common. After their conversation, Ms. Crawford turns to me and states, "You know. My children and me, we are kind of growing up together. And when we are in a program for [homeless] mothers and children, we do good. Then as soon as we are out on our own again, things start to fall apart. It is so hard for me to get my bipolar medicine, and I really be about to lose my shit on these kids." (Fieldnotes, 1/27/16)

Nyeisha, Nadira, and Niles Crawford all attend Baker School. Baker School is a public school in a high poverty neighborhood in Philadelphia. Students attending public school in Philadelphia contend with schooling options that are largely perceived to be inadequate. The School District of Philadelphia is often described as in "crisis," has laid off thousands of employees, and closed dozens of schools in recent years (Quinn & Carl, 2013, 2015). Baker School enrolls approximately 600 students in kindergarten through eighth grade. Its students are 95% African

American, and 100% are classified by the district as economically disadvantaged. The staff at Baker are also predominately African American.

Nyeisha is in fourth grade, Nadira is in second, and Niles is in Kindergarten. The Crawford children are known by most adults in the school, and their reputation is primarily negative. They are frequently late to school, not in uniform, and in trouble. Their teachers often complain to the counselor and other school leaders that the Crawford children smell of urine. Nyeisha is responsible for walking Nadira and Niles to school. I spent considerable time in Nyeisha's classroom, and as soon as Nyeisha opens the classroom door, she is greeted with remarks and questions from her teacher, Ms. Smith, in front of the rest of the class, including, "Why are you late?" or "Late again?"

As noted in the fieldnote at the beginning of this section, Ms. Crawford is self-described as bipolar and often admits that she is overwhelmed and needs help. Members of the school community are aware of this, yet, instead of trying to help the Crawford family, they primarily disparage Ms. Crawford. The staff members look down on Ms. Crawford because she does not work outside of the home. Many comments are made by staff at Baker about how Ms. Crawford receives "welfare." In addition, Ms. Smith often makes comments about how Ms. Crawford "needs to be a mom" and "needs to parent." For example, she states,

> Nyeisha's mom, she is overwhelmed. She needs the help honestly. She has 6 kids with one on the way. Nyeisha needs a mom. Her mom doesn't know what to do. It is chaos in that house. Different dads. Nyeisha and the older kids, two older kids, I think they have the same dad. Then the younger ones have a different one. And the new baby will have a different one. There are at least three dads. The thing is if your mom slacks, you lose. You know she told her Nyeisha that if she is better, that maybe I would be a mother to her. That is not my job. I am conflicted. You know these are my people, and I am really conflicted...You know I was in this neighborhood once. Yes. My sister went to this school. We lived on [street name]. My parents, my mom and dad, were not educated, but they wanted more for us. We, my sister and brother, are educated. We all have advanced degrees. (Fieldnotes, 1/5/16)

Ms. Smith is a middle-aged Black woman who used to live in the neighborhood; her siblings went to Baker. She acknowledges that Ms. Crawford and her children need help. However, Ms. Smith cannot seem to get past feelings of judgment, dislike, and resentment toward Ms. Crawford. Because Ms. Crawford has not achieved social mobility like she has, Ms. Smith does not consider her worthy of engaging with. Although Ms. Crawford has yet to successfully connect with Ms. Smith, Ms. Crawford continues to make attempts to engage Ms. Smith with the goal of leveraging their relationship (i.e., using social capital) to support her daughter. The following sections detail how Ms. Crawford persistently and consistently tries to establish social capital networks for the benefit of her children.

Attempts to Activate Social Capital and Gain Access to Resources

Ms. Crawford is at Baker School at least once a week, and she is often there multiple times in one day. She tries to establish connections with teachers and other staff members. However, school personnel disregard Ms. Crawford's efforts. For example, Ms. Smith tells me first thing one morning, *"Nyeisha's mom was here yesterday. She is a waste, and it is so sad."* (Fieldnotes, 2/10/16). Ms. Smith frequently makes these kinds of comments about Ms. Crawford. In the following fieldnote, Ms. Smith continues to disparage and discount Ms. Crawford without any mention of how many times Ms. Crawford has come to school to try and resolve issues with her children.

> I walk to Ms. Smith's classroom on the second floor. Ms. Smith seems frustrated and says, "Nyeisha complained of a stomach ache. I took her to the nurse, and the nurse said nothing is wrong with her. Nyeisha, she just lies and lies. Her mother is worthless. And it is so sad. It hurts me. She was awful after lunch. You know I think she is so far gone. She is mentally ill." I ask, "Has she been evaluated by a psychologist?" Ms. Smith responds, "No. But she should be. She is just so far gone, and her mom is really so much of the problem. It makes me so sad when she says she doesn't know what to do, but it is because she doesn't listen."

> After school I see Ms. Smith yelling at Nyeisha again in the hallway. I can't hear what she is saying, but I see Nyeisha walk away from Ms. Smith and into the cafeteria and then Ms. Smith turns around and throws up her hands. Ms. Smith walks up the hallway and sees me and says, "You know I just don't know how much longer I can do this." I ask, "How long have you been teaching?" Ms. Smith says, "14 years. I like this population, and they need it, but it is just so hard. It just hurts me." Ms. Smith continues, "She [Ms. Crawford] is worthless. I just don't know. I am not a mother, but I think it is hard to be a mother, I think you have to sacrifice. I know that my sister did for my nephew. She was really strict, and now he is happy and he thanks her. She was tight," Ms. Smith mimics kicking, "and she had to sacrifice a lot." (Fieldnotes, 2/10/16)

As this fieldnote shows, Ms. Smith is frustrated. She frequently discusses how much she cares about "this population." However, she takes out her frustration directly and harshly on students, even though she primarily blames the parents, whom Ms. Smith considers "worthless" and "so much of the problem." Ms. Smith directly deficitizes individuals and does not recognize the structural and systematic forces that impact parents like Ms. Crawford (Gorski, 2011; Valencia, 2010). Ms. Smith expects parents to act like her sister, who is an upper-middle class woman. When they do not parent along these lines, she considers their parenting efforts as "useless." Despite Ms. Crawford's persistent efforts to connect with Ms. Smith so that Nyeisha has a better experience in school, Ms. Smith does not recognize or reward Ms. Crawford's efforts.

Ms. Crawford is aware that she was not making progress with Ms. Smith, and she resourcefully reaches out to others to try and help leverage resources for her children. Ms. Crawford knows that I am an unofficial mentor to Nyeisha, and Ms. Crawford often asks me about how things are going for Nyeisha. For example, Ms. Crawford asks, "Do you be checking up on her [Nyeisha] when she is in the classroom?" I tell her, "Yes. I check in on her." She states, "Ok. Good. Because her and her teacher don't see eye to eye. I don't know what the problem is, but they don't get along" (Fieldnotes, 1/12/16).

Ms. Crawford asks me to help Nyeisha get into the after-school program because she knows I spend time with students and staff in that program as a part of my fieldwork. I tell her I will do what I can, and I ask Mr. James, the director of the after-school program, if Nyeisha could participate. Initially, he is wary because of Nyeisha's reputation as a "problem student." I encourage Mr. James to give Nyeisha a chance stating Nyeisha frequently pushes limits, but I believe that all children do this. A spot opens up in the after-school program, and Nyeisha is allowed to participate despite Ms. Smith's efforts to lobby Mr. James to not allow Nyeisha to be included because "she can't act right." This is an example of how Ms. Smith has such a deficit view of Nyeisha that she does not think that Nyeisha "deserves" to participate in anything remotely positive. Ms. Crawford knows that Ms. Smith would not help to get Nyeisha into the after-school program and so Ms. Crawford activates social capital through her relationship with me (e.g., Yosso, 2005). Because my understanding of Ms. Crawford and Nyeisha was not rooted in a deficit orientation, I could see the many efforts that Ms. Crawford was making toward helping her family as positive as well as the resourceful way that she tapped into my social network in the school.

Despite being thwarted by most school personnel, Ms. Crawford continues to come to school frequently and attempts to navigate the school terrain. Ms. Smith often laments how few parents show up to the report card conferences. Even though Ms. Crawford attends Nyeisha's conference, Ms. Smith has nothing positive to say during the conference. After their meeting, Ms. Smith asserts that Ms. Crawford is "the problem." The following fieldnote highlights a portion of this interaction:

Ms. Smith begins the conference by saying, "Nyeisha is going to be retained if she doesn't start doing her work." Ms. Crawford turns to me and asks, "What is retained?" I say, "It means Nyeisha would repeat the fourth grade again." Ms. Smith jumps in, "It means left back." Ms. Crawford gets upset, "Well, Ny Ny [Nyeisha's nickname], I told you your teacher likes you or else she wouldn't leave you back. I want more for you, Ny Ny. I didn't graduate eighth grade, but I got farther than you are now." Nyeisha's mother is always trying to convince herself and Nyeisha that Ms. Smith likes Nyeisha. She wants Ms. Smith to care about Nyeisha, and Ms. Smith decidedly states, "That is not my job."

Two of Nyeisha's younger siblings, Nadira and Niles, are in Ms. Smith's room running around during the conference. Ms. Smith gets frustrated with them and sends them to another teacher's room. At the end of the conference, I am curious what our game plan is moving forward, and I ask, "Do we have a plan?" Ms. Smith responds, "Nyeisha is going to get it together. Right?" Nyeisha smiles sheepishly. Ms. Crawford states, "You are checking in on her right, Ms. Nicole? How is she doing in the after-school program?" Before I can respond, Ms. Smith states, "You know I have been talking with Mr. James (the director of the after-school program), and he said she is acting up in the after school and that she might get kicked out. I have been talking with the people in the [behavior support program], and Nyeisha might get sent to an alternative school." Ms. Crawford states, "I am just so tired. I am so tired." Ms. Smith asks, "What about Nyeisha's father? Is he around? Can I get his number?" Ms. Crawford states, "Yes. Call her father. I can't do all this by myself. Ny Ny, give your teacher your dad's number." Ms. Smith states, "I've asked for it. Nyeisha says she doesn't know it." Ms. Crawford responds, "She knows it. Give it to her. Nadira and Niles, let's go get your report cards." (Fieldnotes, 2/24/16)

In addition to coming to the school weekly, Ms. Crawford attends her children's conferences. Ms. Crawford wants her children to be successful. She continues to try and make connections with Ms. Smith, but Ms. Crawford is consistently thwarted. In the previous interaction between Ms. Crawford and Ms. Smith, Ms. Crawford is trying to establish connections with Ms. Smith by stating how she "likes Nyeisha." Ms. Smith sees these comments as evidence that Ms. Crawford wants Ms. Smith to act like a parent toward Nyeisha, which reinforces Ms. Smith's deficit orientation toward Ms. Crawford and other parents to include that they do not parent.

Ms. Smith's understanding of parents as "the problem," prevents parents, like Ms. Crawford, from successfully connecting with her. A frequent comment Ms. Smith makes to and about her students is "they don't get it." She is referring to life in general and specifically what they need to do in order to be successful. Ms. Smith believes that the stakes are higher for the students at Baker because they have so many challenges to overcome. For Ms. Smith, "the parents need to be parents." She states,

They [referring to her students] don't understand how hard it is. They don't understand work because their parents don't work. They think that rent is just based on your income, that utilities are just paid. They don't know that the stakes are so high and they don't know about working for things." I ask, "What can we do?" Ms. Smith responds, "I don't know if there is anything we can do. The parents need to be parents. They are so young and they don't know how to parent. You know, I am not a parent, but I know it is hard. My sister is a doctor, and she was a single mom, and she stayed on my nephew. She rode him so hard, and now he thanks her for it. He is at Harvard getting his MBA. He worked for the NBA in finance. He is probably going to be the chairperson of the NBA. Oh we are so proud of him. My sister did so good, but you know it wasn't easy. She was on him like a hawk. She didn't let him get away with anything. His dad is a doctor too, but he wasn't around and didn't do anything." I ask her again, "So what can we do for students who don't have parents like your sister?" Ms. Smith states, "I don't know. They need to step up. They need to be parents. I don't know. I don't think there is anything we can do. All I know, and I keep telling my students this, is that if Trump gets elected, they better watch out. A lot is going to change. There is not going to be all of this free stuff anymore. I mean I work so hard, and I pay taxes, although I work to not pay that much taxes, but I pay my share. These kids don't understand that all of these handouts are going to stop." (Fieldnotes, 4/1/16)

Ms. Smith perpetuates negative narratives of parents whom she describes as not working and receiving, as she states, "handouts." According to Ms. Smith, Ms. Crawford fits into this category, and that is another one of the aspects Ms. Smith uses to judge Ms. Crawford. Ms. Smith is attempting to educate her students about the culture of power (Delpit, 1995), and this comes with unintended consequences.

To Ms. Smith, the stakes are incredibly high for students at Baker. Ms. Smith attempts to provide students with cultural capital (see e.g., Lareau, 2011) and to help them navigate the culture of power (Delpit, 1995). She says that she wants her students to be successful, which she thinks of primarily in terms of economic social mobility. Ms. Smith frequently makes comments similar to this one: "They [referring to her students] aren't bad. They just drive me crazy. I am trying to keep them from ending up like their parents" (Fieldnotes, 5/17/16). For Ms. Smith, the parents are the problem, and she has zero tolerance for them. Ms. Johnson, the counselor, explains, "Ms. Smith is trying to save the world. She means well, but she can be really hard on the kids sometimes. I tell her that we can't make parents be parents. We can only do so much." (Fieldnotes, 6/14/16).

Ms. Johnson is not as derogatory about parents as Ms. Smith, but she, like many staff members, also has a deficit orientation toward them. Parents are viewed as "lacking" and "not parenting." It is important to contextualize the schooling context at Baker. For example, Ms. Johnson is the only counselor for a school of 600 students. Teachers are exhausted and facing many competing priorities as well as changing administrative guidelines. In the following fieldnote, Mr. James discusses how Nyeisha's issues can be difficult and that staff do not have enough training.

I ask Mr. James how Nyeisha is doing. He states, "She is ok. She has been picking on a second grader, and I mean really picking on her. The second grader came to me again and told me she was really scared. Nyeisha was getting in her face and yelling at her. And making her really scared." I ask, "Why is she doing that?" Mr. James says, "I don't know. Nyeisha has a life of instability, and it has impacted the way she operates in school. You can just look at her and tell that she is less groomed than the other kids. She doesn't look well taken care. There are little trauma signs." I ask, "What are those?" Another after school administrator states, "She doesn't look you in the eyes, for example. She also appears to be in a flight or fight mode all the time." James tell me, "I'm not going to kick her out, but after school can't handle 20 kids with issues. One or two. The staff don't have enough training. Nyeisha needs lots of one on one." (Fieldnotes, 3/21/16)

Teachers and other staff at the school tend to focus on putting out fires and dealing with day to day issues. Baker does not have the financial resources that might be necessary to better engage parents. The school is not functioning, is in disrepair, and does not have basic staff such as a full-time nurse. This situation with parents is emblematic of the larger systemic disinvestment of urban public schools like Baker in which they are not given the resources and investment to be successful (e.g., Anyon, 2005; Ladson-Billings, 2006). However, adopting a resource orientation toward parents and families does not require additional funds, and it has the potential to greatly benefit all stakeholders.

DISCUSSION AND IMPLICATIONS

Ms. Smith is rooted in a deficit understanding of the community (Gorski, 2011; Valencia, 2010) and appears to lack a funds of knowledge (González et al., 2005; Moll, 2000) approach about her students and the community. This means that she does not celebrate their strengths and different forms of capital and is thus not able to be as transformative as she would like. Ms. Smith wants her students to be successful, yet, by rejecting Ms. Crawford's attempts to connect with her (i.e., activate social capital), Ms. Smith ends up not helping Nyeisha and other students. Ms. Smith recognizes the value of the culture of power (Delpit, 1995); however, her deficit orientation toward individuals who do not exhibit middle class cultural capital prevents her from engaging with and developing a bilateral relationship with students and families. Consistent with a Delpit informed approach, it is the role of the teacher to educate students (and parents) about the culture of power and thereafter it is the students' and parents' responsibility to behave in these normalized ways. A resource orientation that stems from a funds of knowledge approach (González et al., 2005; Moll, 2000) encourages the teacher to re-frame his/her understanding of capital (e.g., Yosso, 2005) and to value the multiple resources that all individuals have.

Parents are central stakeholders in education. Yet, urban public school systems tend to not view them as such. Despite trying for decades to increase parental involvement, public school systems continue to try to engage parents, many of whom are living in poverty, in the same ways that they engage middle class parents (Lareau & Horvat, 1999; Lareau & Schumar, 1996). Although these strategies of engagement do not work (and never have), schools and districts continue to engage parents in these ways and are surprised that they get the same results of what is considered low parental engagement. Because the behaviors of these parents do not conform to middle class parenting values, parents in these environments tend to be perceived as "not caring," "uninvolved," and "lazy." This rhetoric is a classic example of a deficit orientation (Valencia, 2010), and describing parents in these terms overlooks the systematic failure of multiple systems that has contributed to lack of economic and educational opportunities (Anyon, 1997, 2005). The education system was not "successful" for many parents whose children attend Baker, and yet educators and policy makers are consistently asking parents to trust and believe in this system. Furthermore, the educators' deficit orientations toward families limits parents' attempts to develop and activate social capital. For example, Ms. Crawford tells Nyeisha, "I want more for you," and Ms. Crawford tries to help Nyeisha by consistently attempting to network within the school for resources. A bilateral relationship between parents and the school could help to better engage parents and the local community as well as improve the school.

The case study of Ms. Crawford shows the ways that she tries to activate social capital on behalf of her children. In the instances she is not successful, it is largely because school personnel discount her efforts. A resource orientation toward families is crucial so that they can build social capital networks at school and with teachers. Neither parents, teachers, nor students are helped when teachers and other school personnel consistently judge, disparage, and discount parents' efforts. Taking a funds of knowledge and a resource approach to families includes recognizing that they care for their children. Their parenting and their attempts to navigate resources for their children may look differently than those of middle-class parents, but it is not because they do not care or are not trying. Opening up ways for parents to have positive experiences in schools and to build relationships with staff members that are not based in negative behavioral problems is important for all school stakeholders.

Despite the systemic lack of resources and disinvestment in inner-city public schools, individuals, primarily students and parents, are blamed and thought about as "unmotivated" and "undeserving" of a better, more equitable education. This research offers important lessons for school leaders as well as policy makers about ways to think about a resource orientation toward students and families as well as ways to foster social capital networks that value, respect, and support students and families. This resource orientation includes thinking about ways to help school staff shift their worldviews to consider other, non-dominant, forms of capital as valuable with the ultimate goal of making schools more humane places for students and families.

In addition, this study suggests that future research is needed about ways that schools and policies can think about engaging parents. Instead of blaming urban parents when they do behave like middle class suburban parents (Lareau & Horvat, 1999; Lareau & Schumar, 1996), schools and districts should re-think what parental involvement could look like and, most importantly, include parents in the reform and design processes. This research study highlights how parents at Baker are struggling with multiple, complex issues. Ms. Crawford, for example, states on multiple occasions that she is struggling and needs help. However, the school environment disparages and blames Ms. Crawford and expressly situates her as "the problem." Thus, a new set of questions regarding ways to consider parents as partners who have important capital and resources that must be acknowledged.

Furthermore, this research suggests a need for increased dialogue between parents and school personnel not just to increase parental engagement in school but primarily to help develop mutual understanding. This could help parents like Ms. Crawford be more successful in establishing relationships with school personnel.

Humanizing parents and recognizing the way that the system has failed them, is an important part of stopping the cycle of the deficit orientations at Baker. It will also help develop a dialogue between the school and the parents that situates parents as a resource and a partner instead of a problem. Having social capital entails that connections result in positive benefits. For this to happen, parents at schools like Baker should be seen as partners instead of "the problem."

NOTES

1. The name of the school and all individuals referenced in this paper are pseudonyms.
2. The dominant group refers to "the group that controls the economic, social and political resources" (Mills & Gale, 2007, p. 435).

REFERENCES

Anyon, J. (1997). *Ghetto schooling: A political economy of urban educational reform.* New York, NY: Teachers College Press.

Anyon, J. (2005). *Radical possibilities: Public policy, urban education, and a new social movement.* New York, NY: Routledge.

Bourdieu, P. (1984). *Distinction: A* social critique of the judgement of taste. (R. Nice, Trans.). Cambridge, MA: Harvard University Press. (Original work published 1979)

Bourdieu, P. (1986). The forms of capital. In J. Richardson (Ed.), *Handbook of theory and research for the sociology of education* (pp. 241–258). New York, NY: Greenwood Press.

Bourdieu, P. (1998). *Acts of resistance: Against the new myths of our time.* (R. Nice, Trans.). Cambridge, UK: Polity Press.

Bourdieu, P. (2000). *Pascalian meditations.* Stanford, CA: Stanford University Press. (Original work published 1997)

Bourdieu, P. (2001). *Masculine domination.* (R. Nice, Trans.). Stanford, CA: Stanford University Press. (Original work published 1998)

Bourgois, P., & Schonberg, J. (2009). *Righteous dopefiend.* Berkeley, CA: University of California Press.

Carl, N. M. (2017). *A hidden curriculum of control: The inequities of urban schooling.* Doctoral dissertation. University of Pennsylvania, Philadelphia, PA. Dissertations available from ProQuest. AAI10278583. Retrieved from http://repository.upenn.edu/dissertations/AAI10278583

Delpit, L. D. (1995). *Other people's children: Cultural conflict in the classroom.* New York, NY: The New Press.

Emerson, R. M., Fretz, R. I., & Shaw, L. L. (2011). *Writing ethnographic fieldnotes* (2nd ed.). Chicago, IL: The University of Chicago Press.

Gibson, W., & Brown, A. (2009). *Working with qualitative data.* London, UK: Sage Publications.

González, N., Moll, L., & Amanti, C. (Eds.). (2005). *Funds of knowledge: Theorizing practices in households, communities, and classrooms.* New York, NY: Routledge.

Gorski, P. (2011). Unlearning deficit ideology and the scornful gaze: Thoughts on authenticating the class discourse in education. In R. Ahlquist, P. Gorski, & T. Montaño

(Eds.), *Assault on kids: How hyper-accountability, corporatization, deficit ideology, and Ruby Payne are destroying our schools* (pp. 152–173). New York, NY: Peter Lang.

Hammersley, M., & Atkinson, P. (2007). *Ethnography: Principles in practice* (3rd ed.). Hoboken, NJ: Taylor & Francis.

Henry, M., Knight, J., Lingard, R., & Taylor, S. (1988). *Understanding schooling: An introductory sociology of Australian education*. Taylor & Francis e-Library, 2001. London, UK: Routledge.

Horvat, E. M., & Antonio, A. L. (1999). "Hey, those shoes are out of uniform": African American girls in an elite high school and the importance of habitus. *Anthropology & Education Quarterly, 30*(3), 317–342.

Ladson-Billings, G. (2006). From the achievement gap to the education debt: Understanding achievement in US schools. *Educational Researcher, 35*(7), 3–12.

Lareau, A. (2011). *Unequal childhoods: Class, race, and family life* (2nd ed.). Berkeley, CA: University of California Press.

Lareau, A., & Horvat, E. M. (1999). Moments of social inclusion and exclusion: Race, class, and cultural capital in family-school relationships. *Sociology of Education, 71*(1), 37–53.

Lareau, A., & Shumar, W. (1996). The problem of individualism in family-school policies. *Sociology of Education, 69*, 24–39.

Maxwell, J. A. (2013). *Qualitative research design: An interactive approach* (3rd ed.). Thousand Oaks, CA: Sage.

Maxwell, J. A., & Chmiel, M. (2014). Notes toward a theory of qualitative data analysis. In U. Flick (Ed.), *The SAGE handbook of qualitative data analysis* (pp. 21–34). London, UK: Sage.

Maxwell, J. A., & Miller, B. A. (2008). Categorizing and connecting strategies in qualitative data analysis. In S. N. Hesse-Biber, S. Nagy, & P. Levy (Eds.), *Handbook of emergent methods* (pp. 461–477). New York, NY: Guilford.

Mills, C. (2008). Reproduction and transformation of inequalities in schooling. *British Journal of Sociology of Education, 29*(1), 79–89.

Mills, C., & Gale, T. (2007). Researching social inequalities in education: Towards a Bourdieuian methodology. *International Journal of Qualitative Studies in Education, 20*(4), 433–447.

Moll, L. C. (2000). Inspired by Vygotsky: Ethnographic experiments in education. In C. D. Lee & P. Smagorinsky (Eds.), *Vygotskian perspectives on literacy research: Constructing meaning through collaborative inquiry* (pp. 256–268). Cambridge, UK: Cambridge University Press.

Paulle, B. (2013). *Toxic schools: High-poverty education in New York and Amsterdam*. Chicago, IL: University of Chicago Press.

Quinn, R., & Carl, N. M. (2013). Occupy our schools: The power and promise of parent organizing in the School District of Philadelphia. *Perspectives on Urban Education, 10*(1).

Quinn, R., & Carl, N. M. (2015). Teacher activist organizations and professional agency. *Teachers and Teaching: Theory and Practice, 21*(6), 745–758.

Ravitch, S. M., & Carl, N. M. (2016). *Qualitative research: Bridging the conceptual, theoretical, and methodological*. Thousand Oaks, CA: Sage.

Valencia, R. R. (2010). *Dismantling contemporary deficit thinking: Educational thought & practice*. New York, NY: Routledge.

Wacquant, L. (2008). Pierre Bourdieu. In R. Stones (Ed.), *Key sociological thinkers* (pp. 261–277). New York, NY: Palgrave Macmillan.

Yosso, T. J. (2005). Whose culture has capital? *Race, Ethnicity and Education, 8*(1), 69–91.

CHAPTER 5

THE PAST, PRESENT, AND FUTURE OF SOCIAL CAPITAL MEASUREMENT AMONG TRANSITION-AGE YOUTH

Sarah Ryan and Lisa Romero

The role of social relationships in child and adolescent development has long captured the attention of researchers from a range of disciplines (Lee, 2014). It was Coleman's (1988) foundational research, however, that launched social capital theory into the educational research mainstream, and the concept of social capital has since become a mainstay in scholarship addressing a host of youth outcomes (Lee, 2014). Social capital theory posits that individuals gain access to valued information, advice, and assistance via personal relationships (Bourdieu, 1986; Coleman, 1988; Lin, 2001; Portes, 1998; Putnam, 1995), making it an especially popular framework through which to explain how youth access (or not) resources critical for successfully navigating postsecondary transitions (for recent summaries see Almeida, 2015; Stephan, 2013).

Grounded in the notion that successfully navigating college preparation and enrollment requires information and assistance from one's social ties, social capital theory has been increasingly applied in research on the transition to life after

Contemporary Perspectives on Social Capital in Educational Contexts,
pages 61–77.

high school (Ryan, 2017). A long line of scholarship suggests that group-level differences in opportunities to develop, access, and use social capital—for example along the lines of racial/ethnic, socioeconomic, and linguistic status—help to explain inequitable patterns of educational and social mobility (see, for example, Bourdieu, 1986; Coleman, 1988; Lin, 2001; Ream, 2005; Stanton-Salazar, 2001). Nonetheless, this body of research has been limited by incomplete, even inaccurate, metrics for quantifying access to social capital (Harpham, 2002; Morrow, 1999; Ryan & Junker, 2019; Smylie, 2015). There is a critical need for the development of more valid and reliable measures of social capital among youth, and this need is especially critical when it comes to understanding the role of social capital within the domain of postsecondary transitions.

In this chapter, we argue that more, and more rigorous, research focused specifically on the measurement of social capital among transition-age youth between the ages of 16 and 24 is needed. We begin by emphasizing that a lack of valid and reliable tools for measuring social capital has resulted in the persistent inability to convincingly document how inequitable access to resources via social networks invariably leads to stratified opportunities and outcomes, especially for students of color. From there, we summarize current challenges and limitations when it comes to social capital measurement among youth, including inadequacy in the conceptualization of social capital (Dika & Singh, 2002; Ream, 2005), the relative absence of empirical research in this area (Billett, 2012; Harpham, 2002; Smylie, 2015), and the tendency to equate structural properties of networks with social capital (Ryan & Junker, 2019).

Next, we turn to new advances in efforts to measure social capital among youth. We summarize several recent studies that aim to measure social capital among youth directly, rather than relying on indirect or proxy measures of this construct. In particular, we highlight recent research (Ryan & Junker, 2019) that uses Lin's (2001) theory of social capital to develop and pilot an instrument to measure youth social capital in the context of postsecondary transitions. The results offer preliminary evidence that dimensions of youth social capital can be reliably measured and that these dimensions are interrelated in a manner consistent with theory.

Finally, we conclude by reviewing some of the primary outstanding issues that future research on measurement of social capital among youth should address. This section is informed by our stance that better measures of youth social capital could help the field better understand and address longstanding group-level inequities in postsecondary transitions and outcomes.

THE DIVERSE CONCEPT OF SOCIAL CAPITAL AND PROBLEMS WITH ITS MEASUREMENT AMONG TRANSITION-AGE YOUTH

In both the higher education and sociological research literature, social capital theory is frequently used to explain differences among social groups in access to information and other resources needed to make well-informed decisions about postsecondary options. The knowledge and resources required to develop and execute postsecondary plans must be learned and acquired (Stephan, 2013), often via relationships with family members, school staff, friends, and others (Almeida, 2015; Ryan & Ream, 2016). For instance, information, assistance with college enrollment, high expectations, and social norms have all been described as resources available via students' networks that influence postsecondary transitions (Perna, 2000; Stephan, 2013).

All children and youth are situated in multiple networks through which they access various resources for diverse purposes. In other words, all youth have social capital. However, the structure and content of these networks, as well as the extent to which young people are able to mobilize network resources, often vary in predictable patterns based on individual characteristics, social group membership, and context (Lin, 2001). Among transition-age youth, including adolescents and young adults between the ages 16 and 24, it has been consistently hypothesized that variation in the characteristics of individual networks leads to subsequent variation in outcomes in postsecondary preparation and enrollment (Perna, 2000; Stephan, 2013). However, efforts to empirically confirm this hypothesis have been hampered by a lack of clarity regarding the concept of social capital and its measurement among adolescents and young adults (Ryan & Junker, 2019). As a result, application of the social capital concept to transition-age youth and their postsecondary endeavors remains limited.

The Debated Concept of Social Capital

Access to resources through one's relationships lies at the core of definitions articulated by most prominent social capital scholars (Bourdieu, 1986; Coleman, 1988; Lin, 2001; Portes, 1998; Putnam, 1995). Yet, debates persist over the constituent dimensions and value of social capital across domains, over whether social capital is a property of individuals or groups, and over whether it is an entity or a process (Fulkerson & Thompson, 2008). Many of the debates derive from the fact that social capital theory draws from more than one sociological tradition (Portes & Sensenbrenner, 1993).[1] This characteristic provides social capital theory with the unique potential to integrate ideas from each of the four major sociological traditions (Collins, 1994), but has also divided the debate into competing camps (Fulkerson & Thompson, 2008).

In one camp are normative social capitalists (Fulkerson & Thompson, 2008) who, drawing on the Durkheimian notion of social integration, view social capital as those features of social structure that give rise to collective action aimed at providing shared benefits for the group. This functional perspective on social capital is perhaps best exemplified in the work of Putnam (1995), Coleman (1988), and Fukuyama (1995). This perspective views social capital as a property of groups (e.g., schools, neighborhoods, nations) and emphasizes how social norms, rules, and trust result in collective assets for group members.[2]

In contrast, resource social capitalists (Fulkerson & Thompson, 2008), who draw upon interactionist and conflict traditions (see Collins, 1994), typically ground their work in Bourdieu's (1986) definition of social capital as comprising both the network of social relationships that allow access to resources and the quantity and quality of those resources. Resource social capitalists, who take a more critical stance than their normatively-oriented peers, view social capital as vital to explaining inequalities in the accumulation of tangible (e.g., educational attainment, wealth) and intangible (e.g., power, prestige) resources. Moreover, they view intangible resources as especially critical to the capacity of social capital to function as a hidden form of capital (Bourdieu, 1986), and thus a mechanism of stratification (Ream, 2003, 2005; Stanton-Salazar, 2001). This camp is also more likely than normative social capital theorists to acknowledge the influence of context on access to and activation of social capital.

Current Challenges in the Measurement of Social Capital among Transition-Age Youth

Ultimately, differences between the normative and resource perspectives have generated not only conceptual confusion but also measurement challenges.[3] One problem is inadequacy in the conceptualization of social capital (Billett, 2012; Dika & Singh, 2002; Ryan & Junker, 2019; Smylie, 2015). A normative perspective on social capital typically locates social capital at the collective level (e.g., community, nation), while a resource perspective most often locates social capital at the level of individuals within a network. Viewing social capital as a property of groups rather than individuals simultaneously positions social capital as a cause and an effect, whereby social capital produces positive group-level outcomes and its presence is assumed based on those same outcomes (Portes, 1998). This concern has generated support for the position that social capital becomes clearest when measured at the individual level (Lin, 2001; Portes, 1998).

A second problem in the measurement of social capital among youth is simply that there has been little empirical research in this area. More often than not, young people have been viewed as passive recipients of social capital rather than as agents capable of activating the resource potential of their own networks (Harpham, 2002). Further, commonly used measures constructed using items from large national secondary datasets (e.g., number of parents in the home, number of siblings, parent-child discussion) are, at best, rough approximations of social capital (Dika & Singh, 2002; Krasny, Kalbacker, Stedman, & Russ, 2015; Morrow, 1999; Ryan & Ream, 2016). More specifically, considering applications of social capital theory in research focused on postsecondary transitions, most studies have relied predominantly on proxy measures from large secondary data sets reflecting the attributes of youth and their parents. This includes, for example, youth attributes such as the number of parents or siblings, the importance of grades to friends, friends' postsecondary plans, whether a parent volunteers at school, whether a parent knows friends' parents, and the frequency of discussions and activities with parents. Such variables have certain advantages over attitudinal measures insofar as they are more amenable to external verification, and many indeed demonstrate positive associations with postsecondary preparation and enrollment (for example, see Carbonaro, 1998; Coleman, 1988; Dika & Singh, 2002; Ream & Palardy, 2008; Ryan, 2017; Ryan & Ream, 2016). However, common statistical measures derived from these and other datasets (e.g., parent-child discussion, Catholic school attendance, educational expectations) are inadequate indicators of social capital, offering limited information about relational characteristics and access to resources via personal networks (Dika & Singh, 2002; Stanton-Salazar, 2001).

Previous studies have called much-needed attention to the role of sociability for educational processes and outcomes. Yet, many proxy measures are limited in their ability to fully reflect the concept of social capital given that they fail to chart "who is related to whom in what context" and thus where, how, and for what purpose social capital is generated (Lee, 2014, p. 455). In addition, the wide array of measures used to represent social capital among youth indicates disagreement, and perhaps confusion, about just which constructs to measure, and arguably reflects the measurement challenges raised by attempts to incorporate both normative (trust, expectations of reciprocity, social norms, and values) and resource (network composition, locations, and resources) perspectives (Harpham, 2002). All of this is further complicated by the fact that different dimensions of social capital may share different relationships with particular outcomes of interest (Furstenberg & Hughes, 1995).

A final concern is a tendency to equate structural properties of networks with social capital. Recent advances in social network analysis have made it possible to study the structural properties of specific, bounded networks constituted by individuals or any set of relationally connected entities. For example, researchers from the fields of sociology and education have studied structural properties of social networks among both youth (e.g., Frank, Muller, & Mueller, 2013) and educators (e.g., Daly & Finnigan, 2010), including patterns of association within a school, network density and centrality, and properties of dyadic relationships. Although social network theory and social capital theory overlap, the structure of one's network in a particular domain (e.g., school, work) is not synonymous with one's social capital. The measurement of social capital must recognize the related but distinct dimensions of network structure and content (Gamoran, Turley, Turner, & Fish, 2012), which in turn reflect the similarly related but distinct normative and resource perspectives on social capital. The structure of social capital refers to the pattern of social relationships, including the location of individuals within a network as well as the collective assets (e.g., norms, trust) that characterize the network (Lin, 2001). The content of social capital refers to the resources deployed through the social network. Analyzing network structure as though devoid of content paints an incomplete picture of an individual's social capital, as does focusing on content without considering the generating structure of relations.

In the United States, some amount of postsecondary learning beyond high school has become a basic requirement for individual economic success and social mobility, and social capital may be an especially salient factor influencing youth transitions to postsecondary education. Yet, given the above limitations, the field continues to lack a clear understanding of how social capital is developed, accessed, and used among youth in this and other domains. College information, assistance, contacts, emotional support, and social norms are often described as social capital resources potentially available in students' networks which arguably influence whether or where students enroll in some type of postsecondary institution (Perna, 2000; Ryan, 2017; Ryan & Ream, 2016; Stephan, 2013). But as researchers have long-argued, group-level differences in access to college- and career-specific social capital likely structure inequitable access to postsecondary pathways most likely to promote social mobility, in part because the utility of students' social capital for the college enrollment process likely varies by factors including race/ethnicity, socioeconomic status, linguistic background, and the context in which its exchange is attempted (Perna, 2000; Ryan, 2016, 2017; Ryan & Ream, 2016). Unfortunately, much of what is social about the process of education and upward mobility is often overlooked in educational policy and practice (Ream & Palardy, 2008), perhaps because technical aspects (e.g., test scores) of education are more readily quantified. Particularly in an era of evidence-based policy making, with its insistent call for more robust measures of inputs and for more rigorous evidence about the impact of those inputs on outcomes of interest, the need for clearer and more careful measurement of social capital among youth is all the more pronounced.

EMERGENT RESEARCH ON THE MEASUREMENT OF SOCIAL CAPITAL AMONG TRANSITION-AGE YOUTH

Few studies have focused on measuring social capital among youth themselves, and such research has been especially rare when considering transition-age youth (Krasny et al., 2015; Ryan & Junker, 2019; Smylie, 2015). Of those studies that have addressed social capital among adolescents and young adults, most have been conducted using qualitative methods (for example, see Stephan, 2013). Such studies provide important insights about, for example, which individuals adolescents typically turn to for social support (Billett, 2012), about how the distribution of social capital may vary systematically according to race/ethnicity, social class, gender and other socially meaningful groups (Ream, 2005), and about how creating social networks within schools around college access may generate social capital useful for successfully navigating college enrollment (Stephan, 2013).

Qualitative research will continue to be essential for developing and refining explanatory models related to the development and mobilization of social capital among youth. However, the ability to make externally valid generalizations about whether and how relational aspects of postsecondary transitions impact educational and social outcomes requires the development of instruments that validly and reliably measure social capital among transition-age youth. It is an encouraging sign, therefore, that a number of recent studies have begun to explore different approaches to more directly measuring social capital within this group.

In one recent example of social capital measurement research from a resource perspective (Hill, Bregman, & Andrade, 2015), researchers examined how the role-composition (parent, teacher/counselor, peer, self) of a student's college information network is related to the selectivity of the college s/he would most like to attend. This research was based on the administration of a researcher-developed name generator instrument to approximately 300 youth in grades 10 and 12. The findings documented by Hill and colleagues suggest that, net of other factors, students whose college information networks were dominated by peers were significantly less likely to identify an institution in the "most selective" category as their first choice college. The researchers acknowledge, however, that their instrument and analyses were limited by a lack of information collected about the nature of students' ties and about the nature and quality of the information and guidance provided by each member of a student's network.

In contrast, Krasny and colleagues (2015) grounded their measurement research in the normative perspective on social capital by developing a survey based on constructs used with adults in the National Social Capital Benchmark Survey, including social trust, informal socializing, diversity of friendship networks, civic leadership, and associational involvement. After administering the instrument to youth (ages 14–18) participants in environmental education programs, the authors reported reliability statistics ranging from 0.64 to 0.74 for three of the five constructs (no reliability statistics were reported for the other two constructs). However, Krasny and colleagues did not present analyses of construct validity, which is an important limitation given questions about the extent to which social capital scales developed for use with adults are applicable among youth (Billett, 2012).

Recent work by Ryan and Junker (2019) offers one of the few examples of measurement research that attempts to integrate normative and resource perspectives. These researchers develop a multidimensional measure of social capital among youth in the domain of postsecondary transitions, grounding their work in Lin's network theory of social capital. Lin (2001) breaks social capital into three dimensions intersecting network structure (location and collective assets), network content (resource access), and action (resource mobilization).

Using confirmatory factor analytic techniques, Ryan and Junker investigated whether dimensions of youth social capital reflecting network structure and content could be reliably measured. The pair examined three components of the network structure dimension in their exploratory research. The first was network location (Lin, 2001), as indicated by closeness, trust, and network density. Networks in which most people know one another (dense networks) and which are characterized by close and trustworthy relationships may be more likely to facilitate access to at least some kinds of resources (Coleman, 1988). The other two components of network structure reflected collective network assets (Lin, 2001), including network norms and belongingness (Harpham, 2002; Morrow, 1999). Networks that are characterized by a sense of belonging and pro-academic norms may support successful college and career transitions. To assess network content, Ryan and Junker considered student access to resources specific to the domain of college preparation and enrollment. Finally, these researchers examined action, or mobilization of network resources, by exploring links between network structure and content, on the one hand, and outcomes associated with successful postsecondary transitions, on the other hand. In addition to exploring dimensional structure, the researchers also considered the extent to which their proposed measure of youth social capital offered evidence of construct validity.

The results of this study offered preliminary evidence that dimensions of youth social capital, including dimensions of network structure and network content, can be reliably measured and that these dimensions of social capital are interrelated in a manner consistent with theory. The results also provided initial support for the validity of the social capital construct as conceptualized by Ryan and Junker (2019) within the domain of postsecondary transitions. The structural regression models the authors used to explore the predictive validity of their social capital measure explained between 18% (attendance) and 45% (four-year plans) of the variability in several related outcomes. Specifically, both network structure and network content were positively and significantly associated with a participant's GPA, with his or her attendance rate, and with his or her plans to enroll in a four-year college or university following high school.

FUTURE DIRECTIONS FOR THE MEASUREMENT OF SOCIAL CAPITAL AMONG TRANSITION-AGE YOUTH

Rapid change and numerous transitions characterize the circumstances of youth between the ages of 16 and 24, as they continually form and reform identities and networks during this life stage (Smylie, 2015). For many young people in the United States, one of the most significant transitions during this period is the transition to life after high school. Continued research is needed to better understand the role of social capital during this important transition which will, most importantly, require more valid and reliable measures of youth social capital (Ryan & Junker, 2019; Smylie, 2015). In the remainder of the chapter, we discuss directions for future research related to the measurement of social capital among transition-age youth. We begin by describing the need for research focused on the validity of the social capital construct among youth. Following this, we discuss the related need for research focused on several other aspects of the social capital construct among this population.

The Need for Closer Examination of Construct Validity

Construct validity refers to how well a construct, such as a concept, idea or behavior, is operationalized or translated into a functioning reality. Social capital has been hypothesized as both represented by and related to an extremely diverse range of concepts, which has not only placed the concept at risk of losing any distinct meaning (Portes, 1998) but has also created challenges for assessing construct validity. Nonetheless, measurement results based on partially developed theories can be used to refine and elaborate theory, in turn providing a stronger foundation for subsequent construct and theory validation research (Strauss & Smith, 2009).

In their research, Ryan and Junker (2019) explored several aspects of construct validity for their measure of youth social capital. Considering discriminant validity, the modest correlation between network structure and network content suggested that these two latent factors discriminated between the two distinct aspects of social capital. However, in this and other recent studies on the measurement of social capital among youth, concurrent validity—or the extent to which the results of a particular measure correspond to those of a previously established measurement for the same construct—has been harder to evaluate given a lack of established measures. Turning to predictive validity, the authors demonstrated that both network structure and network content were positively and significantly associated with participants' GPA, attendance rate, and plans to enroll in a four-year college or university following high school.

Particularly with respect to predictive validity, future research on the measurement of social capital among youth will need to better address the issue of endogeneity (Mouw, 2006), or the possibility that any observed effect of social capital arises in part due to the fact that individuals exercise choice when forming relationships and this nonrandom process could reflect a selection effect rather than a relational effect. One of the most effective ways of overcoming the issue of endogeneity when it comes to the effect of social capital on youth transitions would be to experimentally manipulate youth social capital (for example, by randomly assigning youth to programs hypothesized to build social capital among transition-age youth). Continued progress in the development of instruments that validly and reliably measure social capital among youth would provide the field with outcome measures that could be used in studies of this nature. Further, research focused on the impact of interventions that attempt to shift relational dynamics would be especially valuable to the field given that few studies have addressed whether and how policy or institutions may intentionally foster the creation of social capital (Coburn & Russell, 2008; for a recent exception among parents of school-age children, see Gamoran et al., 2012). Future research must also begin addressing concurrent validity by comparing results from emerging measures of youth social capital across domains, as well as comparing results from these more direct measures to proxy measures used in previous research.

Distinguishing, and Integrating, the Different Aspects of Social Capital

Addressing the issue of construct validity in research will also require determining how to simultaneously capture both the normative and resource aspects of social capital. As previously mentioned, the normative aspect, sometimes referred to as cognitive social capital, is reflected in the pattern of one's social relationships, including the location of individuals within a network (i.e., closeness or intimacy), and in the collective assets (e.g., norms, trust) that characterize that network (Lin, 2001). The resource aspect, also referred to as structural social capital, is reflected by both the resources that are accessible through an individual's network and by the resources that s/he ultimately mobilizes. To date, most research on social capital among transition-age youth has focused primarily on one aspect or the other. Moreover, social capital research among youth, more often than not, treats social capital as a generalized (i.e., "I trust most people here," "I get advice about college from teachers") rather than as an interpersonal construct evidenced within the context of bounded networks. This approach is problematic to the extent that youth, like adults, are simultaneously embedded in multiple relational networks. Advancing the measurement of social capital among transition-age youth will require dedicating greater attention to the question of how to capture both aspects within specific domains.

The combined use of name generator and interpreter items has proven effective for the measurement of normative and resource aspects of social capital with adults (Ryan & Junker, 2019). Name generator instruments can be used to measure the structural properties of domain-specific networks by eliciting a list of names (ties) from the participant. To capture the normative aspect of social capital, researchers can use a series of follow-up name interpreters to collect specific information about the participant's ties. Although the use of name generator and name interpreter items has occurred infrequently with young people (Appel et al., 2014), this approach holds promise as a means to more validly and reliably measure the multidimensional social capital construct among transition-age youth (Ryan & Junker, 2019).

Identifying the Role of Trust

As the field grapples with how to measure different dimensions of social capital among youth, this will also require paying special attention to the role of trust. Almost since Coleman (1988) first posited trust as a form of social capital, scholars have debated the relationship between trust and social capital, asking, for example, whether trust is a precursor to or a dimension of social capital. In terms of youth social capital, student trust (i.e., in teachers, mentors, and schools) has demonstrated an association with academic optimism, belonging, identification with school, behavior, discipline, academic achievement, and college ambition (Ream, Lewis, Echeverria, & Page, 2014; Romero, 2015; Tschannen-Moran, Bankole, Mitchell, & Moore, 2013). Most research on student trust, however, focuses on the K–12 context. There is a relative paucity of research that seeks to understand the role of trust when it comes to youth social capital in other domains, including the domain of post-secondary transitions (but see Ream et al. [2014] for an important exception).

Like the broader literature on social capital, research on trust faces conceptual and measurement challenges stemming from the lack of a common definition of trust. Despite agreement that trust has multiple dimensions, consensus about the nature and number of these qualities remains elusive (Romero & Mitchell, 2018).[4] What scholars can agree on is that trust allows individuals to act in situations where they are vulnerable and must rely on confidence in another's good will and expertise (Bryk & Schneider, 2002).[5]

The role of trust in the generating, accessing, and/or using social capital continues to be the subject of debate. What is clear, however, is that without trust, transition-age youth, and most particularly historically marginalized youth, may find it difficult or impossible to gain access to the kinds of resources necessary to identify and pursue pathways to postsecondary success and upward social mobility. Among young people across social groups in the United States, access to college and career related resources, both tangible and intangible, often occurs via family and friendship networks (Ryan & Ream, 2016; Ryan, 2017). For youth from more advantaged backgrounds, these networks tend to include numerous close ties with personal experience navigating the often-opaque nuances of the U.S. system of higher education. In contrast, while the family and community ties of youth from historically marginalized backgrounds draw upon various forms of cultural wealth to support their academic goals (Yosso, 2005), societal stratification may nonetheless limit these students' access to social networks in which information about how the educational system works are embedded (Perna, 2006; Ryan, 2016). This latter group, therefore, must often rely more heavily on the good will and expertise of institutional agents in the more formal school context, arguably requiring greater personal vulnerability than their peers from more advantaged backgrounds (Stanton-Salazar, 2001).

Future research is needed to better understand the extent to which trust functions as a precursor to as opposed to a dimension of social capital. And we need to better understand not only how, and for whom, trust is productive, but also the circumstances in which *mistrust* arises and with what consequence for postsecondary transitions and social mobility. Moreover, does trust function in the same way for all youth? Or, are there differential returns based on markers of social significant group membership, including, for example, race, ethnicity, and gender? Few studies in the field of education explicitly compare how trust differs by race/ethnicity or gender (exceptions include, for example, Crosnoe, Monica, & Glen, 2004; Ream et al., 2014; Romero, 2018). This stands in marked contrast to other fields where there have been numerous considerations of the interaction between race and trust (Romero, 2018; Smith, 2010).

Characterizing Bridging versus Bonding Social Capital

Trust has been invoked as essential to both bonding (i.e., "interpersonal" trust) and bridging (i.e., "generalized" trust) social capital, and this bonding/bridging distinction is deemed essential for gauging the quality, and not simply the quantity, of network-based resources among adults. For example, Granovetter (1973) suggested that weaker ties (i.e., bridges) provide better access to information, and Lin (2001) suggested that the embeddedness of resources (i.e., the wealth, status, and power of one's ties) contributes to variability in the potential for social capital to generate returns. Characterizing the extent to which students' networks include ties from socially similar (bonding) versus socially dissimilar (bridging) backgrounds among youth, on the other hand, poses unique challenges. The occupation status, wealth, and education of ties are often used to gauge bridging social capital among adults. Yet recent research suggests that only 24% of high school students are able to accurately report the income of their parents within $15,000 (Anderson & Holt, 2017), and it is even less likely that youth are able to make valid assessments about the socioeconomic characteristics of their peers and other adults.

We are especially interested in the potential for future investigation to develop innovative strategies that can be used to characterize the network ties of young people as constituting access to bonding and bridging social capital in various domains. However, such research must also better recognize that these forms of social capital differ in their importance and nature at different points over the lifespan of an individual. While bonding social capital is typically conceived of as important for social support (i.e., getting by) and bridging social capital is viewed as most relevant to achieving mobility-related gains (i.e., getting ahead), some research suggests that the types of ties that are used to achieve these goals differ between youth and adults. Specifically, Billett (2012) notes that adults use their bridging ties to enable mobility while relying on bonding ties, including close family and friends, for emotional support. In contrast, the majority of young people rely on friends and family *both* as sources of belonging and emotional support *and* as a means to mobilize resources beyond their everyday needs. However, as transition-age youth finish secondary school and begin to consider career options and educational pathways, the types of bridging ties that assist adults in creating upward mobility become essential, especially for adolescents from historically marginalized backgrounds. Identifying how youth are or are not able to begin accessing and mobilizing bridging social capital during the period of transition to college and/or careers is, therefore, also essential.

Understanding the Significance of Social Capital in Shared Virtual Spaces

Adding additional nuance to all aspects of social capital measurement among young people is the fact that, in recent years, a great deal of information about almost anything has become available—if not easily navigated—virtually, including an abundance of information about postsecondary pathways. As Smylie (2015) observes, the increasing use of communication technologies and social media begs the question of whether face-to-face interaction is necessary to produce social capital. Leveraging the availability of new data from communication and social media platforms, researchers are addressing this question as they attempt to understand what some have referred to as "online social capital" (Deil-Amen & Rios-Aguilar, 2014).

Some studies posit that communication technologies and social media are critical to the development of social capital in relationships that transcend place, perhaps especially for rural and disadvantaged youth (Wohn, Ellison, Kahn et al., 2013). At the same time, results from recent qualitative research (Smylie, 2015) that included in-depth interviews with youth ages 16–19 suggest that the relationships through which youth access emotional support, material resources, and information are primarily those that involve regular face-to-face interaction. This is not to suggest that so-called online social capital is not real or of value. However, as Smylie (2015) documents, relationships maintained via social media or other technology-based forms of communication do not appear to have the same significance as relationships involving regular face-to-face contact, and instead tend to revolve around "mundane communication, limited to 'catching up' on the state of each other's social lives" (p. 141).

Few studies have investigated the role of access to resources via online relationships in the domain of postsecondary transitions (Wohn et al., 2013). One critical direction for future research is whether and how the educational importance of online interactions and resources varies by race/ethnicity, gender, socioeconomic status, and other indicators of group membership. For instance, while many adolescents often look to institutional agents such as school counselors and teachers for academic guidance and college information, and while their White and Black peers appear to benefit from seeking information online, Hispanic students tend to rely more on face-to-face interactions with parents and other family members as they navigate college preparation and enrollment (Muñoz & Rincón, 2015; Stanton-Salazar, 2001).

There is a need for more careful attention to the advantages and disadvantages associated with the vast quantity of online resources now available to students and families as they navigate postsecondary transitions. Whether and to what extent these resources constitute so-called online social capital remain open questions in need of research. In the meantime, it will be important to remain mindful of the fact that social media and other online resources can supplement but are not a replacement for other needed strategies that can facilitate student success (Deil-Amen & Rios-Aguilar, 2014)—including better access to information and support via in-person social exchange (Ryan & Ream, 2016).

CONCLUSION

An important feature recommending social capital theory as a powerful lens for understanding persistent inequities in postsecondary destinations and longer-term social and economic mobility among U.S. youth is that it calls attention to a dialectical relation between the *determinative* power of social groups and the *undetermined* motivations of free agents, thus preserving insights across numerous disciplines. To date, however, the measurement of social capital among transition-age youth has not yet caught up with its theoretical nuance.

The lack of valid and reliable tools for measuring social capital has resulted in the persistent inability to convincingly document how inequitable access to resources via social networks invariably leads to stratified opportunities and outcomes, especially for society's most vulnerable youth. As a result, arguably critical relational dynamics of educational processes are too often overlooked when making decisions about education policy and practice, including decisions about the equitable allocation of resources (Ream & Palardy, 2008). As we have argued in this chapter, more rigorous measurement research offers the potential to ground theoretical arguments about the role of social capital in understanding and addressing disparate postsecondary opportunities and outcomes among youth from different social groups in robust empirical evidence.

While the measurement of social capital among transition-age youth has been plagued by numerous challenges and limitations, a number of recent studies have begun to move this body of research forward. The different approaches these studies have taken to addressing the operationalization and measurement of youth social capital reflect not only the interdisciplinary roots of social capital theory but also the range of ways in which social capital has been conceptualized in the empirical and theoretical literature. In so doing, these studies provide a stronger foundation for subsequent construct and theory validation research (Strauss & Smith, 2009). Leveraging these insights, future research on the role of social capital among transition-age youth must continue to iteratively test and refine both theory and measurement.

ENDNOTES

1. Adding to this complexity, the notion of social capital has been employed not only in sociology but across numerous academic disciplines including economics, political science, and anthropology.

2. In their almost singular focus on the social benefits of community and civil society, however, normative social capitalists have been criticized for ignoring the important downside of social capital (Portes & Landolt, 1996). The normative perspective implies that communities are homogenous entities that automatically include and benefit all members, yet while membership in a highly integrated community can bring advantages, it can also incur significant costs for some.

3. The distinction between normative and resource perspectives on social capital parallels the distinction some scholars make between cognitive and structural social capital. Cognitive social capital refers to the more subjective or intangible dimensions including trust and norms of reciprocity, while structural social capital refers to social structures including networks and relational associations (Krishna & Shrader, 1999).

4.   Most scholars propose some combination of benevolence, competence or ability, integrity, regard for others, respect, reliability, openness, fairness, and honesty (Bryk & Schneider, 2002; Romero & Mitchell, 2018).

5.   In the case of interpersonal trust, or what Putnam (1995) referred to as thick trust, trust is relational and involves reliance on known others. In contrast, generalized trust, which Putnam referred to as thin trust, involves an essentially indiscriminate belief in the good will and expertise of one's fellow citizens broadly.

REFERENCES

Almeida, D. (2015). College readiness and low-income youth: The role of social capital in acquiring college knowledge. In W. G. Tierney & J. C. Duncheon (Eds.), *The problem of college readiness* (pp. 89–114). Albany, NY: State University of New York Press.

Anderson, D. M., & Holt, J. K. (2017). *Do high school students know their parents' income?* (Research brief No. 2017-3). Edwardsville, IL: Illinois Education Research Council.

Appel, L., Dadlani, P., Dwyer, M., Hampton, K. N., Kitzie, V., Matni, A. A., & Teodoro, R. (2014). Testing the validity of social capital measures in the study of information and communication technologies. *Information, Communication & Society, 17*(4), 398–416.

Billett, P. (2012). Indicators of youth social capital: The case for not using adult indicators in the measurement of youth social capital. *Youth Studies Australia, 31*(2), 9–16.

Bourdieu, P. (1986). The forms of capital. In J. G. Richardson (Ed.), *Handbook of theory and research for the sociology of education* (pp. 241–258). New York, NY: Greenwood Press.

Bryk, A., & Schneider, B. (2002). *Trust in schools: A core resource for improvement.* New York, NY: Russell Sage Foundation.

Carbonaro, W. J. (1998). A little help from my friend's parents: Intergenerational closure and educational outcomes. *Sociology of Education, 71*(4), 295–313.

Coburn, C. E., & Russell, J. L. (2008). District policy and teachers' social networks. *Educational Evaluation and Policy Analysis, 30*(3), 203–235.

Coleman, J. S. (1988). Social capital in the creation of human capital. *American Journal of Sociology, 94*, 95–120.

Collins, R. (1994). *Four sociological traditions.* New York, NY: Oxford University Press.

Crosnoe, R., Monica, K., & Glen, H. (2004). School size and the interpersonal side of education: an examination of race/ethnicity and organizational context. *Social Sciences Quarterly, 85*(5), 1259–1274.

Daly, A. J., & Finnigan, K. S. (2010). A bridge between worlds: Understanding network structure to understand change strategy. *Journal of Educational Change, 11*(2), 111–136.

Deil-Amen, R., & Rios-Aguilar, C. (2014). From FAFSA to Facebook: The role of technology in navigating the financial aid process. In A. P. Kelly & S. Goldrick-Rab (Eds.), *Reinventing financial aid* (pp. 75–100). Cambridge, MA: Harvard Education Press.

Dika, S. L., & Singh, K. (2002). Applications of social capital in educational literature: A critical synthesis. *Review of Educational Research, 72*, 31–60.

Frank, K. A., Muller, C., & Mueller, A. S. (2013). The embeddedness of adolescent friendship nominations: The formation of social capital in emergent network structures. *American Journal of Sociology, 119*(1), 216–253.

Fukuyama, F. (1995). *Trust*. New York, NY: Free Press Paperbacks.

Fulkerson, G. M., & Thompson, G. H. (2008). The evolution of a contested concept: A meta-analysis of social capital definitions and trends. *Sociological Inquiry, 78*(4), 536–557.

Furstenberg, F. F., & Hughes, M. E. (1995). Social capital and successful development among at-risk youth. *Journal of Marriage and the Family, 57*, 580–592.

Gamoran, A., Turley, R. N. L., Turner, A., & Fish, R. (2012). Differences between Hispanic and non-Hispanic families in social capital and child development: First-year findings from an experimental study. *Research in Social Stratification and Mobility, 30*(1), 97–112.

Granovetter, M. (1973). The strength of weak ties. *American Journal of Sociology, 78*(6), 1360–1380.

Harpham, T. (2002). *Measuring the social capital of children*. London, UK: South Bank University.

Hill, L. D., Bregman, A., & Andrade, F. (2015). Social capital for college: Network composition and access to selective institutions among urban high school students. *Urban Education, 50*(3), 316–345.

Krasny, M. E., Kalbacker, L., Stedman, R. C., & Russ, A. (2015). Measuring social capital among youth. *Environmental Education Research, 21*(1), 1–23.

Krishna, A., & Shrader, E. (1999). *Social capital assessment tool*. London, UK: The World Bank.

Lee, M. (2014). Bringing the best of two worlds together for social capital research in education: Social network analysis and symbolic interactionism. *Educational Researcher, 43*(9), 454–464.

Lin, N. (2001). Building a network theory of social capital. In N. Lin, K. Cook, & R. Burt (Eds.), *Social capital: Theory and research* (pp. 3–29). New York, NY: Aldine De Gruyter.

Morrow, V. (1999) Conceptualising social capital in relation to the well-being of children and young people: A critical review. *Sociological Review, 47*(4), 744–765.

Mouw, T. (2006). Estimating the causal effect of social capital: A review of recent research. *Annual Review of Sociology, 32*, 79–102.

Muñoz, J., & Rincón, B. (2015). Unpacking the layers: Financial aid and Latino high school students' postsecondary plans. In P. Pérez & M. Ceja (Eds.), *Higher education access and choice for Latino students* (pp. 38–54). New York, NY: Routledge.

Perna, L. W. (2000). Differences in the decision to enroll in college among African Americans, Hispanics, and Whites. *Journal of Higher Education, 71*, 117–141.

Portes, A. (1998). Social capital: Its origins and applications in modern sociology. *Annual Review of Sociology, 24*, 1–24.

Portes, A., & Landolt, P. (1996). The downside of social capital. *American Prospect, 7*(26), 18–21.

Portes, A., & Sensenbrenner, J. (1993). Embeddedness and immigration: Notes on the social determinants of economic action. *The American Journal of Sociology, 98*(6), 1320–1350.

Putnam, R. D. (1995). *Bowling alone*. New York, NY: Simon & Schuster.

Ream, R. K. (2003). Counterfeit social capital and Mexican American achievement. *Educational Evaluation and Policy Analysis, 25*(3), 237–262.

Ream, R. K. (2005). *Uprooting children: Mobility, social capital, and Mexican American underachievement.* New York, NY: LFB Scholarly Publishing.

Ream, R. K., Lewis, J. L., Echeverria, B., & Page, R. N. (2014). Trust matters: Distinction and diversity in undergraduate science education. *Teachers College Record, 116*(5), 1–50.

Ream, R. K., & Palardy, G. J. (2008). Reexamining social class differences in the availability and the educational utility of parental social capital. *American Educational Research Journal, 45*(2), 238–273.

Romero, L. S. (2015). Trust, behavior, and high school achievement. *Journal of Educational Administration, 53*(2), 215–236.

Romero, L. S. (2018). The discipline gap: What's trust got to do with it? *Teachers College Record, 120*(11).

Romero, L. S., & Mitchell, D. E. (2018) Toward understanding trust: A response to Adams and Miskell. *Education Administration Quarterly, 54*(1), 152–170.

Ryan, S. (2017). The role of parent social capital and college-aligned actions in explaining differences in intergenerational resource transfer among Hispanic and White youth on the path to college. *Teachers College Record, 119*(10).

Ryan, S., & Junker, B. (2019). The development and testing of an instrument to measure youth social capital in the domain of postsecondary transitions. *Youth & Society. 51*(2), 170–192. Retrieved from https://journals.sagepub.com/doi/abs/10.1177/0044118X16685233

Ryan, S., & Ream, R. K. (2016). Investigating college preparation and enrollment across immigrant generation among Hispanic youth. *American Educational Research Journal, 53*(4), 953–986.

Smith, S. S. (2010). Race and trust. *Annual Review of Sociology, 36*, 453–475.

Smylie, L. (2015). The nature and development of young people's social capital. *International Journal of Child, Youth and Family Studies, 6*(1), 134–149.

Stanton-Salazar, R. D. (2001). *Manufacturing hope and despair: The school and kin support networks of US-Mexican youth.* New York, NY: Teachers College Press.

Stephan, J. L. (2013). Social capital and the college enrollment process: How can a school program make a difference? *Teachers College Record, 115*(4), 1–39.

Strauss, M. E., & Smith, G. T. (2009). Construct validity: Advances in theory and methodology. *Annual Review of Clinical Psychology, 5*, 1–25.

Tschannen-Moran, M., Bankole, R. A., Mitchell, R. M., & Moore, D. M. (2013). Student academic optimism: A confirmatory factor analysis. *Journal of Educational Administration, 51*(2), 150–175.

Wohn, D. Y., Ellison, N. B., Khan, M. L., Fewins-Bliss, R., & Gray, R. (2013). The role of social media in shaping first-generation high school students' college aspirations: A social capital lens. *Computers & Education, 63*(2013), 424–436.

Yosso, T. J. (2005). Whose culture has capital? A critical race theory discussion of community cultural wealth. *Race Ethnicity and Education, 8*(1), 69–91.

CHAPTER 6

DIVERSITY MISSION STATEMENT INCLUSION AS SOCIAL CAPITAL

How the Language of Appeasement Fails Egalitarian Goals in Postsecondary Institutions

Zachary W. Taylor, Alden C. Jones, and Catherine E. Hartman

Institutions of higher education (IHEs) in the United States have made numerous, varied, and longitudinal attempts at diversifying student bodies, thereby imbuing the rapidly diversifying U.S. population with valuable social capital and the earning power of a college degree. Following the lead of the *Brown v. Board* decision, race-conscious admissions policies were implemented by three public institutions—the University of California at Davis, the University of Michigan at Ann Arbor, and the University of Texas at Austin—subsequently generating five Supreme Court decisions (*Bakke*, *Gratz*, *Grutter*, *Fisher I*, and *Fisher II*), all of which have informed institutions across the country on who may be included on a college campus through formal admissions processes. In recent years, need-blind (Morris, 2016; Sutton, 2016) and test-blind (Stewart, 2016) or test-optional (Furuta, 2017) admissions policies have been evaluated and implemented by various public and private institutions to better produce a diverse campus population,

Contemporary Perspectives on Social Capital in Educational Contexts,
pages 79–102.

ostensibly allowing for a more equitable distribution of social capital across marginalized populations and underprivileged groups.

Yet, even as the college-going population in the U.S. has increasingly diversified, one way IHEs in the U.S. have sought to achieve the goal of an inclusive campus environment is to create and implement an action plan for diversity (Wilson, Meyer, & McNeal, 2012). These institutional diversity plans or agendas have generated a significant body of research (Iverson, 2008a; Kezar & Eckel, 2008; Williams, 2013); yet, longitudinal studies have demonstrated diversity plans or agendas—across institutional types—have a high rate of failure (Ahmed, 2007a; Hu-DeHart, 2000; Iverson, 2008b; Sidanius et al., 2008; Williams, 2013). The reasons for this failure are twofold: the static nature of institutional culture and/ or inadequate leadership (Williams, Berger, & McClendon, 2005). Furthermore, as an overwhelming majority of executive leadership on U.S. campuses is White, these leaders are often inexperienced when developing long-term diversity plans or agendas, preferring to hire a chief diversity officer and delegate diversity-related responsibilities accordingly (McMurtrie, 2016).

Because of this struggle, executive leaders have scrambled to adopt on-campus diversity interventions, including racially-conscious living-learning communities (Brown, 2016a), funding campus-wide diversity audits (Brown, 2016b), and hiring diversity consultants to assess campus climate and provide IHEs with a "detached third party whose recommendations are likely to be received with less skepticism than those of administrators on the defensive" (Schmidt, 2016). However, no extant research has examined diversity plans, agendas, and institutional commitments to diversity through a linguistic lens, paying special attention to the social capital (Bourdieu, 1986) bestowed upon the constituents named in the diversity mission statement itself.

According to Packer-Williams and Evans (2013), there has "been a movement by institutions and educational organizations to establish diversity mission statements to publicize a commitment to fostering diversity in higher education" (p. 244). Although institutional mission statements have been exhaustively researched (Bender, 2017; Morphew & Hartley, 2006; Wilson et al., 2012), diversity mission statements have not, even though diversity mission statements are an integral part of the institutional diversity plan or agenda and often outline the beliefs of and goals for diversity within the institution (Williams, 2013). Therefore, it is reasonable to analyze diversity mission statements to answer two simple questions:

1.   Where can an institutional diversity mission statement be found?
2.   Who is included in an institutional diversity mission statement?

In this study, we employ content analysis via grounded theory to linguistically analyze institutional diversity mission statements (IDMSs) from fifty public flagship institutions to answer these aforementioned questions. Our findings articulate which forms of diversity hold institutional value—therefore, social capital—via their presence in IDMSs. Through a Bourdieuian lens (1986) and the work of Tara Yosso (2005), we argue colleges and universities delegate value, and therefore power through social capital, upon addressed audiences and educational stakeholders only through culturally-competent diversity programming and diversity post-programming, namely efforts to increase the cultural competency and pedagogical acumen of the faculty and staff tasked with educating and supporting marginalized populations. Inversely, overarching and ambiguous commitments to diversity result in a maintenance of power structures and institutional hegemony. Finally, we argue our results support Ahmed's (2016) notion of diversity "non-performativity" (p. 3), as the IDMSs often describe the status quo and uphold legal precedent without inviting diverse individuals or groups to the institution, subsequently maintaining extant power structures and limiting the institution's ability to equitably facilitate the acceptance and multiplication of social capital and community cultural capital. This, we argue, ultimately leads to a continuation of Stewart's (2017) language of appeasement.

BOURDIEU, INCLUSION, AND THE LIMITATIONS OF SOCIAL CAPITAL

Bourdieu (1986) wrote, "the structure of the distribution of the different types of capital and subtypes of capital at a given moment in time represents the immanent structure of the social world" (p. 81), with social capital comprised of "social obligations (connections)" which are "convertible into economic capital" (p. 82). Here—engaging with the Platonic notion of representation—Bourdieu (1986) unifies the capital-holding institution and the social world in which the institution operates. Intimately and infinitely interwoven, the institution and the social world conduct social capital transactions, as members of the institution arrive and depart to and from the social world, resulting in a sense of social capital reciprocity in which social capital is fluid. However, Bourdieu's (1986) theory asserts the institution is the gatekeeper of power in this relationship—of capital in all its forms. The institution ultimately decides to whom it delegates capital. This power dynamic effectively allows the institution to create a set of rules under which the social world must comply, lest its members become excluded from the valuable conversion of social capital to economic capital, as Bourdieu (1986) suggested.

Under the rules of the institution, individuals and groups can be included or excluded, depending on their satisfactory compliance with the rules of the institution. This act of compliance is where social inequities find strength, as certain members of the social world are unable, unwilling, or unaware of how to comply to the level of their peers. In the realm of higher education, these rules reach every corner of campus. Admissions deadlines, prerequisite coursework, minimum grade point averages, course syllabi, degree requirements, and compulsory final exams are just a few examples. These institutional rules—codified by their articulation through institutional communication channels to students, faculty, and other educational stakeholders—effectively include or exclude individuals and/ or groups.

It is this notion of inclusion—through compliance with institutional rules—that appropriately defines the purpose of IDMSs. Extant research has already outlined the arduous, time-consuming process of drafting institutional mission statements (Bender, 2017; Morphew & Hartley, 2006; Wilson et al., 2012), which is undoubtedly indicative of the institution drafting rules for inclusion. Unlike admission and graduation requirements, IDMSs express who and what an institution believes is diverse and therefore valuable, as over 90 percent of one national survey's respondents said they value diversity in their social contexts (Berrey, 2015, para. 3). In no uncertain terms, an institution asserting who and what is valued represents "the structure of the distribution of the different types of capital and subtypes of capital at a given moment in time" (Bourdieu, 1986, p. 81).

Bourdieu's (1986) discussion of different types of capital and subtypes of capital lends itself to a discussion of value. What types of capital are valued by the institution, and what happens when certain capital is held in higher value than other forms? Tara J. Yosso (2005) argued traditional notions of social capital are particularly problematic for marginalized populations, framing the discussion of social capital as a flawed, deficit model. Of Bourdieu (1986), Yosso (2005) wrote:

> Bourdieu argued that the knowledges of the upper and middle classes are considered capital valuable to a hierarchical society. If one is not born into a family whose knowledge is already deemed valuable, one could then access the knowledges of the middle and upper class and the potential for social mobility through formal schooling. (p. 70)

Here, Yosso's insights are particularly useful to the discussion of social capital as it pertains to IHEs. As IHEs both include and exclude through formal and informal processes, they ultimately decide which forms of capital are valuable and therefore warrant inclusion, forever perpetuating the Bourdieuian (1986) notion of the multiplier effect. This multiplier effect involves those with capital deliberately organizing and concentrating their capital to strengthen the collective, thus multiplying or intensifying the capital and excluding those without. However, for Yosso and other critical race scholars, IHEs have traditionally valued forms of social capital that maintain a White hierarchical society without valuing and including other forms of capital. Yosso (2005) continued:

> Bourdieu's theoretical insight about how a hierarchical society reproduces itself has often been interpreted as a way to explain why the academic and social outcomes of People of Color are significantly lower than the outcomes of Whites. The assumption follows that People of Color 'lack' the social and cultural capital required for social mobility. (p. 70)

This perceived "lack" is precisely what renders the discussion of IDMSs so salient (Yosso, 2005, p. 70). IHEs do nothing but maintain the status quo unless other forms of capital are valued, ones that do not conform to Bourdieu's (1986) notion of social capital as it contributes to a White, hierarchical, and capitalistic society. In a response to Bourdieu's (1986) social capital theory, Yosso helped define a model of community cultural wealth, comprised of six forms of capital that better represent one's cultural wealth: aspirational, familial, social, linguistic, resistant, and navigational capital (2005, p. 78). Furthermore, Yosso (2005) re-defined social capital as "networks of people and community resources" (p. 79), noting people of color have used their social capital "…to attain education, legal justice, employment and health care. In turn, these Communities of Color gave the information and resources they gained through these institutions back to their social networks" (p. 80).

Therefore, it is important to note Yosso (2005) argued educational stakehold-ers bring capital—in its many forms—to IHEs, just as IHEs can augment and multiply various forms of capital. Instead of considering the prospective student or faculty member somehow deficient, Yosso (2005) asserted critical race theory and the notion of community cultural wealth "shifts the research lens away from a deficit view of Communities of Color as places full of cultural poverty or dis-advantages, and instead focuses on and learns from these communities' cultural assets and wealth" (p. 82). By reconceptualizing both the individual and the in-stitution as wealthy with capital, the Bourdieuian (1986) deficit model of social capital can be informed and replaced by a model of capital that is inclusive of all, regardless of prior definitions of social capital.

Ultimately, it is crucial to investigate these IDMSs—the articulation of institu-tional rules governing diversity—to learn what forms of capital and what groups are included in and excluded from these statements to better understand the many inequities of the social world of contemporary college campuses. Whether from a deficit model or a wealth lens, we see institutions naming and identifying groups who may have capital to bestow or who may seek access to capital to share with social networks.

SIGNIFICANCE OF INSTITUTIONAL MISSION STATEMENTS

Most higher education institutions have a mission statement in some shape or form, serving to outline the purpose and direction of the organization. Such statements can also greatly define an institution and serve as a planning, marketing, and fun-draising tool. Additionally, the organizational culture and espoused goals of the institution can be found within an IDMS, as well as how the institution highlights itself as being different and unique as compared to other schools. However, chal-lenges exist in creating a mission statement. Some of these issues include crafting a statement that all members of an institution value and support. Additionally, "not all mission statements fulfill the ideals of the institution…they [may also be] 'full of platitudes and generalizations far removed from institutional realities'" (Wilson et al., 2012). Therefore, it is likely the process of creating a diversity statement poses similar challenges to that of a mission statement, given the wealth of educational stakeholders invested in its composition. Emphasis is placed on the word *likely* because of the lack of extant research specifically focused on IDMSs and their processes of inception, adoption, and operationalization.

Morphew and Hartley (2006) asserted the literature surrounding mission statements, broadly speaking, demonstrates there are two "benefits" of mission statement thinking in higher education (p. 457). The first notes the benefits of identifying a shared purpose and delineating the institution's priorities, thereby allowing community members to align their own personal idiosyncrasies with "institutional imperatives" and share institutional values with other external constituents (Morphew & Hartley, 2006, p. 457). This view of the institutional mission statement as "blueprint" or "touchstone" for institutional decision making is reinforced in the most current literature (Bender, 2017, p. 41). The second understanding of mission statements is somewhat more cynical in that it conceptualizes such statements as nothing more than collections of buzz words, key phrases, and hot topics cobbled together which are "excessively vague or unrealistically aspirational or both" (Morphew & Hartley, 2006, p. 457). These researchers report most of the analysis around mission statements in higher education rests in this camp. This assessment, while ultimately in reference to institutional mission statements, is useful to deploy in the discussion of our findings, as no extant research has examined IDMSs and their implications for campus continuity, unity, and understanding when considering people from diverse communities.

However, working to ensure a diversity mission statement—and its subsequent campus initiatives—is inclusive of all people is a cumbersome task. Since 2012, only one study has analyzed IDMSs, and these results suggested IHEs simply do not prioritize diversity and the articulation of a campus community's diversity through official mission statements or diversity statements. In an examination of 80 IHEs, Wilson, Meyer, and McNeal (2012) found only 59 four-year institutions directly referenced diversity in their official institutional mission statements, and only 18 institutions had an official IDMS. Surely, more than 18 of 80 IHEs value diverse individuals contributing to a larger, diverse campus community; however, this valuation of diversity is simply not articulated through official institutional statements, rendering institutional commitments to diversity ambiguous and informal. These commitments, according to Ahmed (2006), are the source of some measure of the non-performativity of diversity. According to the participants in her research, such commitments are only tools with which to act, that in fact, cannot stand alone (Ahmed, 2006, p. 113).

Smith's (2015) *Diversity's Promise for Higher Education: Making it Work* noted the notion of identity or of intersectional identities is of critical importance when considering diversity and its operation in IHEs. She pointed out some researchers suggest individuals self-select personal and social identities, while other researchers (Carter, 2008; Monroe, Hankin, & Van Vechten, 2000; Parekh, 2008) are more concerned with a duality of voluntary and nonvoluntary identities. Smith (2015) also asserted the origin of one's identity(ies) is not the most salient detail.

Instead, their significance—that is, how important one identity is with respect to the others held by an individual—is what makes diversity a functioning ideology. In essence, identity catalyzes action. What is most important from Smith's (2015) work is the assertion diversity must not be something that runs parallel to the institutional mission but that it is "wholly integrated" (p. 271). Yet a cardinal challenge remains—operationalizing diversity successfully and unwaveringly incorporating the ideology throughout the institution. A diversity mission statement and campus action plan is admirable, but these institutional elements require action to be optimal for all educational stakeholders.

Diversity Non-Performativity and the Language of Appeasement

The process of performing diversity highlights an important piece of the conversation. IHEs are increasingly investing their financial and human resources into diversity-related initiatives across the country, with all educational stakeholders expecting some sort of on-campus, diversity-related activity (McMurtrie, 2016; Schmidt, 2016). These recent developments highlight Smith's (2015) and many others' work (Iverson 2008b; Kezar & Eckel, 2008; Sidanius et al., 2008; Williams, 2013) that considered diversity an actionable abstraction rather than a purely aspirational one. However, diversity and the focus on action faces its challenges and paradoxes.

For instance, Ahmed (2007a) considered how "the institutional preference for the *term* 'diversity' is a sign of the lack of commitment to change and might even allow organizations such as universities to conceal the operation of systematic inequalities under the banner of difference" (p. 236). However, Ahmed (2007a) also considered how and why diversity functions, imploring, "Does diversity enable action within institutions, or does it block action, or does it do both simultaneously?" (p. 243). In doing so, she indicated the entwinement of diversity language and action may be beneficial or cumbersome to on-campus equity and inclusion efforts. Ahmed (2016) elaborated upon this paradoxical notion of diversity when she introduced the term non-performativity: "To use a word like 'non-performativity' is to reveal something about institutional mechanics: how things are reproduced by the very appearance of being transformed" (p. 2). After Ahmed (2016) interviewed several institutional diversity workers, she realized "...even non-performative speech acts can be useful: if organizations are saying what they are doing, we can show they are not doing what they are saying. Diversity work often takes place in the gap between words and deeds" (p. 3). This revelation is critical to the discussion of IDMSs. Granted, IDMSs cannot encompass the entirety of an institution's diversity initiatives (Wilson et al., 2012); yet, these initiatives should—as Ahmed (2016) suggests—be read as serving those mentioned in the statement. If organizations are truly "saying what they are doing" (Ahmed, 2016, p. 3), it is critical to examine who is benefitting from these speech acts-turned-performances of diversity. And if institutions are not performing diversity for those whom they purport to serve, higher education equity researchers must address this gap between, as Ahmed (2016) puts it, "words and deeds" (p. 3).

Stewart (2017), expanding Ahmed's (2007a, 2016) work, begins to define this gap between words and deeds as the "language of appeasement" (para. 1). In their work, they argued diversity and inclusion rhetoric can work to avoid truly transformative equity and inclusion efforts and bar recognizable institutional change. These changes have been especially difficult to realize when historically-White institutions (HWIs) and their leaders succumbed to the language and politics of appeasement during the student activist eras of the 1960s through the 1980s. According to Stewart, these leaders "quieted complaints and concerns from opposing sides: on the one hand, students of color and their supporters, and on the other, trustees and nervous donors—liberal and conservative—who wanted their colleges and universities out of unflattering public spotlight" (2017, para. 7). In modern contexts, Stewart (2017) suggests history is merely repeating itself:

> Administrative leaders of HWIs are hiring chief diversity officers, establishing special endowments to support increased financial aid, launching cluster hires for faculty of color and investing in diversity programming, speakers and consultants. Those efforts seek to quiet the protesters, trustees and donors at the same time, all the while creating little systemic or transformative change on the campus. (para. 8)

Instead, Stewart (2017) implores HWIs to catalyze real institutional change through efforts to promote equity and justice before diversity and inclusion. Flatly, Stewart asserts, "Diversity asks, 'Who's in the room?' Equity responds: 'Who is trying to get in the room but can't? Whose presence in the room is under constant threat of erasure?'" (2017, para. 10).

Here, Stewart's (2017) work informs that of Morphew and Hartley (2006) and Wilson et al. (2012) and their combined focus on mission statements and IDMSs. Both studies highlighted the binary purposes of these institutional statements: a realistic description of the institution as it stands or an aspirational vision of the institution as it could or should be. Stewart (2017) responds by implying a third purpose all diversity-focused work should adopt: acknowledging marginalized groups who have been historically excluded from the institution and explicitly enacting diversity in a way that facilitates truly equitable access and justice for these groups. For Stewart (2017), diversity must not only enact, but it must specifically work to avoid Ahmed's (2016) notion of non-performativity by taking an active, constant, and iterative role in identifying racially and socially minoritized groups to facilitate equity and justice for these groups.

Ahmed (2006), in her article on the non-performativity of anti-antiracism, notes institutional speech acts "do not do what they say" and only talk about the action they require (p. 104). Thus, to be named by the university, the diversity named is *always already* not going to be achieved. This is what Ahmed (2006) means by the non-performativity of diversity work, that the "work" has already ostensibly been done in the naming, and the outcome is that the naming reifies the lack of diversity, providing a space for the cycle to begin anew (p. 110). According to her, "the nonperformative does not 'fail to act' because of conditions that are external to the speech act: rather, it 'works' *because* it fails to bring about what it names" (Ahmed, 2006, p. 104). She goes on to note the inherent paradox of speech acts for diversity (e.g., institutional mission statements). Specifically, the symbolic act of saying *we welcome diversity* makes it impossible to make such a "commitment" real (Ahmed, 2006, p. 121). Instead, it will have become impossible to welcome diversity because diversity now has parameters that will either never expand and thus will not make diversity welcome or will always change and expand thus making the act of welcoming diversity unintelligible.

Ultimately, to answer our overarching questions, a series of linguistic analyses were employed to examine the diversity mission statement of every U.S. public flagship institution. If as Smith (2015), Ahmed (2006, 2007a, 2012, 2016), and Stewart (2017) suggest, the term *diversity* is an elusive and laborious term to define and operationalize. Therefore, examining the text of IDMSs can further articulate exactly who public flagship institutions believe to be diverse, reframing past and informing future research focused on how institutional diversity initiatives address or do not address these diverse yet marginalized groups and/or individuals.

CONCEPTUAL FRAMEWORK

The researchers centered this study around Bourdieu's (1986) social capital theory, primarily his articulation regarding the necessary delegation of social capital—and thus, power—by a group or institution. Bourdieu (1986) wrote:

Every group has its more or less institutionalized forms of delegation which enable it to concentrate the totality of the social capital, which is the basis of the existence of the group (a family or a nation, of course, but also an association or a party), in the hands of a single agent or a small group of agents and to mandate this plenipotentiary, charged with *plena potestas agendi et loquendi*, to represent the group, to speak and act in its name and so, with the aid of this collectively owned capital, to exercise a power incommensurate with the agent's personal contribution. (p. 88)

Here, Bourdieu (1986) delineated between the institution and its members. The institution is the source and its members the vessels into which social capital can be deposited and then exercised or reproduced on the institution's behalf. In no uncertain terms, a highly institutionalized process and product, such as the process of drafting a diversity statement and the diversity statement itself, is an institutionalized form of social capital delegation. This notion of delegation is particularly useful to understand internal institutional culture (Morphew & Hartley, 2006) but also the values which shape an institution's outward facing external culture (i.e., the culture examined by prospective members of the institutional community, including students, faculty, and staff).

However, it is important to note how Bourdieu's (1986) notion of social capital is limited by its inherent deficit-approach to possession of capital. For Bourdieu (1986), either individuals have capital, or they do not. For critical race theorists like Yosso (2005), the community cultural wealth model envisions prospective members of the campus community—students, faculty, staff, or others—as vessels of wealth that have not been traditionally valued, yet are perpetually valuable. For instance, Yosso's definition of "linguistic capital" (2005, p. 78) is particularly valuable to the discussion of language diversity mentioned in multiple IDMSs included in this study.

In short, inclusion in IDMSs can be viewed as an invitation or offer of social capital to those outside the institution and a delegation of social capital to those inside the institution. This study examines Bourdieu's (1986) notion of social capital delegation as it relates to IDMSs to learn who delegates social capital, who is included, and who is excluded from access to social capital embedded within a group of elite IHEs.

METHODOLOGY

Akin to the foundational work of Wilson et al. (2012), this research depended on content analysis, employing a grounded process of variable identification (Neuendorf, 2017). With an extensive history of usage across disciplines, content analysis has become an increasingly popular method for analyzing communication patterns and characteristics of text to examine the goals, beliefs, and biases therein, especially considering the "proliferation of multimedia content generation tools and applications" that could present traditional text in a nontraditional format, such as an infographic, interactive table, or video (Neuendorf, 2017, p. 230). In this study's sample, no IDMSs were presented in non-text formats on institutional websites, but entering the study, we valued the analytic flexibility of content analysis, given that work specifically focused on IDMSs is limited.

Sample

We selected IDMSs from the public flagship institution in each state across the U.S. (n=50), although not all public flagships published formal IDMSs, which will be discussed later in this study. Public flagships are some of if not the most selective institutions in their respective state and across the country. Chancellor Robert M. Berdahl provided a comprehensive yet clear description of a public flagship in his 1998 address during the Texas A&M University convocation ceremony. Berdahl (1998) asserted, in part, the term *flagship* applies:

> ...to the fully mature public universities serving most of states. In most cases, these institutions were the first public universities to be established in their states. Many [...] were established in the extraordinary period of university building that took place [...] from the mid–1850s to the mid–1880s. Many came into being after the Morrill Act of 1863. (para. 5)

Despite being created to serve the needs of states, public flagships are often sources of inequality (Gerald & Haycock, 2013). Admission to these institutions is competitive, and often the most seemingly meritocratic students are those that possess the necessary cultural and social capital to gain acceptance into these institutions (Guinier, 2015; Warikoo, 2016). However, a meritocratic admissions system does not necessarily result in students of all backgrounds attending or being represented on campus. Warikoo (2016) asserted "meritocracy serves as a tool to legitimate the reproduction of social class (and, by extension, in the United States, race), in contemporary societies in which the overt reproduction of class is no longer accepted as legitimate" (p. 58). Covert, exclusionary practices masked as meritocracy continue to a yield a homogenous student body on campuses. A report by Gerald and Haycock (2013) on behalf of The Education Trust (2013) titled, "Engines of Inequality" noted low-income students and students of color are often underrepresented on flagship campuses. Overall, students of color and students from low socioeconomic backgrounds are disproportionately outnumbered on flagship campuses by White and affluent students (Gerald & Haycock, 2013). Access to (and academic preparedness for) these institutions is a factor in this finding, as students of color and/or students from low socioeconomic backgrounds may not possess the required social and cultural capital necessary to gain admission to elite institutions, as deemed by Bourdieu (1986). If admitted, they may find the capital they possess does not match the forms of capital recognized and rewarded by the institution and its agents, potentially limiting students' ability to gain much needed and different forms of capital or to reproduce that capital once they leave the institution (Bourdieu, 1986).

We have already determined Yosso (2005) would strongly disagree and would raise two very important and pressing questions regarding the elite and exclusive nature of public flagships. How does institutional diversity yield social reproduction? How can social reproduction be facilitated through institutional diversity initiatives such as an IDMS? As previously noted, extant research has attempted to answer these questions. Because the institutions in our sample are public, we assess whether the mounting evidence against these schools as being elitist and exclusive is true or if these schools are, indeed, public, democratic, and egalitarian in nature and in character. If the latter statement is true, this would mean these institutions are inclusive of and support a variety of student populations within their state. Such diversity should, then, be reflected in the IDMSs. A caveat to this is public flagships are highly politicized spaces, and university personnel may not have the same agency to voice their opinions as private institutions do in university communications, such as IDMSs. Public schools are limited in their actions because they are, in fact, public and are held accountable by various political bodies within their states. This characteristic may or may not influence the IDMSs of flagship universities. In order to determine the role of public flagships in social reproduction, each flagship's IDMS is analyzed to determine which student populations are included or excluded.

Data Collection

The ubiquity of the Internet renders the content analysis of institutional websites—namely IDMSs—a particularly important area of research, especially since institutional mission statements of any kind may not appear elsewhere during the recruitment and college choice experience (Gallup, 2013; Rozelle & Landis, 2002) and because the Internet is the leading source of postsecondary information for prospective students (Burdett, 2013).

Given this undergirding research, we extracted IDMSs from official institutional websites in November 2016. Data was re-collected and re-analyzed in August 2017 to add rigor, accuracy, and a longitudinal perspective to the study. Following the mission statement search protocol articulated by Wilson et al. (2012), we employed each institution's domain-embedded search tool to find the term *diversity mission statement*. If this search did not yield a clearly demarcated IDMS, we searched each institution's website to see if the institution featured a dedicated office, department, or division of diversity by searching for the term *diversity* in the institution's domain-embedded search tool. Once we located diversity-focused offices, departments, or divisions, we searched each institution's diversity plan or framework to locate specific IDMSs. These statements were located on different webpages on each institution's .edu domain, including the webpage for offices, departments, or divisions dedicated to diversity-related initiatives as well as the institution's equal employment opportunity (EEO) webpage, the president's institutional webpage, and webpages for other chief institutional officers. In these cases, we used the official IDMS of the diversity office/department/division for our analysis. Out of the 50 public flagships, 49 published formal IDMSs on their websites. As such, the data collection procedure identified the published IDMS of 49 public flagships in November 2016. This procedure was repeated in August 2017 to ensure the accuracy of the IDMSs and to inform the study of any changes to the IDMSs over this period. Interestingly enough, a number of statements drastically changed between the initial data collection period—November 2016—and our final data collection and verification period in August 2017.

While gathering our data, we observed two phenomena. First, IDMSs were not composed or formatted similarly across institutions nor were they included on similar types of institutional websites or underneath the umbrella of similar institutional offices, such as offices of diversity, equity, and inclusion. This differentiation justified our decision to employ a flexible, qualitative methodology and a grounded approach to coding textual variables. Because Bourdieu's (1986) notion of social capital requires consideration of the institutional delegate as well as the intended recipient of the social capital, we made a note of which institutional stakeholder housed the IDMS—whether it be an institutional president's website, an EEO office, or a diversity-focused division. Second, we found many institutions featured IDMSs that were markedly different from their academic and/or discipline specific colleges and schools. For instance, one institution featured a diversity mission statement on its Office of Diversity and Inclusion webpage, yet the same institution's College of Nursing had its own unique diversity mission statement, as did the College of Business. Ultimately, this duplicity reinforced our decision to analyze where institutions housed their IDMSs to help articulate how institutions may view different on-campus structures and units as being more effective or less effective at delegating social capital.

Furthermore, given the time- and resource-intensive process of crafting and publishing institutional mission statements of varying kinds (Bender, 2017; Morphew & Hartley, 2006; Wilson et al., 2012), the research team decided to analyze and code the IDMSs as they were written. We drew no inferred meaning from the exact words as they were included in IDMSs. However, a collection of outliers emerged from the data—those that did not neatly fit into overarching categories that were so common across many statements. These outliers are addressed in our findings, implications, and conclusion sections.

Data Analysis

Once each IDMS was identified, its text was extracted and uploaded into a database for collaborative analysis. Along with the text of the IDMS, we also included the institution title, the URL of the IDMS, and the location of the IDMS (i.e., office, department, division title, etc.). Employing Neuendorf's (2017) process of grounded variable identification, we analyzed the text of each IDMS to identify who is included in IDMSs. This analysis produced sixteen unique variables and one unique category of groups or individuals that were markedly different from other IDMSs and only appeared in one or two IDMSs. These nineteen variables included race, ethnicity, color, culture, gender, gender identity, gender orientation, sexual orientation, socioeconomic status, ability, disability, national origin, geographic location, religion, political affiliation, age, thought, language, and veteran status. For a variable to be coded, it needed to appear in at least three unique IDMSs. All other variables were coded as unique and entered verbatim into the database.[1]

FINDINGS

Institutional Location of Diversity Mission Statements

An analysis of the institutional location of IDMSs of public flagships can be found in Table 6.1. Data in this study suggest an overwhelming percentage of public flagship universities have IDMSs and house them in institutional diversity offices, departments, units, or divisions. It is worth noting 78% of the IDMSs were housed with formal divisions of diversity, equity, and inclusion. As such, it seems diversity-focused structures or institutional units are primary in communicating

---

[1] The database of institutions, the URLs of the IDMSs, the text of each IDMS, and all coded variables are available upon request from the authors.

TABLE 6.1. Percentage Analysis of Institutional Locations of Diversity Mission Statements (n=49)

Diversity-focused office, department, unit, or division	78%
Office of institutional leadership (president, provost, dean)	4%
Board of regents of institutional system	4%
Human resources/equal employment office	2%
Other:	10%
Online institutional policy library	2%
Division of Academic Affairs	2%
Institutional strategic plan	2%
Office of University Community	2%
Publication of the University Senate	2%
No discernible statement	2%

the invitation of social capital to prospective members of the campus community. This positioning of IDMSs is paradoxical per Bourdieu's (1986) notion of the multiplier effect. Bourdieu (1986) consistently asserted the full benefit of social capital is realized when groups are "deliberately organized in order to concentrate social capital" (p. 51), thus maximizing the group's "useful relationships, and symbolic profits, such as those derived from association with a rare, prestigious group" (p. 52). It is unclear whether the entirety of an institution—not merely its diversity-focused office, department, unit, or division—fully embraces and supports an IDMS. Bourdieu argued the "existence of a network of connections is not a natural given" (1986, p. 52). In essence, public flagships may be delimiting the multiplier effect of social capital by isolating IDMSs in diversity-focused structures.

Inversely, public flagships rarely house IDMSs in offices of executive or system-level leadership. Out of 49 statements, we found only eight percent on websites for institutional leadership or a flagship system's governing board. Considering Bourdieu's (1986) multiplier effect, educational stakeholders both within and outside of IHEs must ponder certain questions when considering IDMSs. Which institutional structure (e.g., office, department, unit, or division) has the most power to delegate social capital? What structure (e.g., office, department, unit, or division) is best positioned to achieve a campus community's egalitarian goals? Does agent-to-agent proximity influence Bourdieu's multiplier effect? Bourdieu's (1986) theory asserts that agents—individuals or organizations with or wanting to gain capital—can exchange and grow their capital through closeness of and interactions with the agent's physical or metaphysical position in society. Surely, a governing board does not interact with prospective members of a campus community on the same intimate, personal scale as a diversity-focused office at the institutional level, but the governing board or President likely has more power to achieve an egalitarian goal through admissions criteria reform, the funding and support of diversity-related initiatives, and the tearing down of campus walls for external and marginalized communities. Here, the institution as a capital agent may be positioning its IDMS and too far from the intended recipients of capital depending on where the diversity work occurs (or does not) on campus.

Beyond the aforementioned, the data suggests some institutions choose to house IDMSs in additional institutional structures—apart from diversity-focused structures or units. These institutions are taking an idiosyncratic approach to Bourdieu's (1986) notion of the multiplier effect. One institution included their IDMS on the human resources and EEO website, communicating the message that egalitarian goals of diversity can be achieved through the administrative processes of hiring diverse individuals to lead institutional initiatives. Another institution felt it best to place the IDMS in a university senate publication, thus communicating the message of diversity goals through faculty-supported channels. Similarly, one institution included its IDMS in the online policy library, expressing the opinion that IDMSs are best defined as institutional policies requiring formal positioning alongside other policies to maximize Bourdieu's (1986) multiplier effect. Another institution did not feature its IDMS at all on its website. Here, egalitarian goals either will or will not be accomplished. The message communicated via the absence of a published IDMS is egalitarian goals are not prioritized and will, therefore, potentially not be realized within this institution. As demonstrated by each of these structural examples, the location of IDMSs speaks volumes about an institution's attitudes toward accomplishing diversity-related, egalitarian goals and its perception of the multiplier effect of social capital. This paradox—one of the multiplier effect and agent proximity to IDMSs—has special implications for IHEs truly aspiring to achieve egalitarian goals through efforts focused on inclusion, equity, and access for marginalized and underrepresented populations.

Groups Included within Institutional Diversity Mission Statements

A descriptive analysis of IDMSs of public flagships can be found in Table 6.2. First, it is notable 29% of public flagships choose not to name any groups in their IDMSs, touching upon Stewart's (2017) notion of the politics of appeasement, namely that diversity and inclusion rhetoric works to appease constituencies instead of promoting recognizable, institutional change (para. 11). Here, institutions choosing not to name are defining *diversity* and guiding diversity-focused initiatives in broad terms. Often, these statements embraced students, faculty, and staff without emphasizing marginalized or underrepresented group(s). Hearkening back to Bourdieu's (1986) notion of the multiplier effect, these institutions effectively delegate and amplify social capital by including all, rather than including those most in need. Affixing this philosophy to institutional egalitarian goals, it can be reasoned these institutions—those who do not name—are working to

TABLE 6.2.   Percentage Analysis of Diversity Mission Statements with Named Groups and Demographics

% of IDMSs including:	
Sexual Orientation	55%
Ethnicity	53%
Race	53%
Religion	51%
Age	43%
Disability	43%
Socioeconomic Status	43%
Gender	41%
National Origin	39%
Gender Identity	37%
Veteran Status	27%
Gender Expression	21%
Ability	19%
Geographic Location	19%
Thought Diversity (ideas, opinions, thoughts)	19%
Culture(s)	15%
Political Affiliation	13%
Color	9%
Language Diversity	7%

Note. 74% of the institutional IDMSs explicitly named groups or core demographics (n=49).

achieve these goals by simultaneously including and excluding. The paradox of the multiplier effect and agent proximity emerges once again.

Those institutions specifically naming groups did so in peculiar but familiar ways. First, of the most frequent groups and demographics named in IDMSs—namely sexual orientation, ethnicity, race, religion, age, and disability—derivatives of each and every one of these groups can be found in the U.S. Equal Employment Opportunity Commission's (EEOC) list of "Discrimination by Type" as evidenced on their official website (U.S. Equal Employment Opportunity Commission, 2017). Here, it is fascinating to learn roughly half of IDMSs closely mirror—if not echo verbatim—the rhetoric of anti-discrimination laws. In essence, over half of IDMSs could be read as anti-discriminatory statements, which ultimately twists the language of equity and inclusion to be reactionary and compulsory rather than proactive and authentic. A promise of anti-discrimination informs the marginalized individual of the administrative precedent guiding equal opportunity employment in the U.S.: *We will not restrict you.* Inversely, a proactive invitation to social capital reflects individual institutional values and beliefs rather than simply reiterating federal mandates: *You are invited.* Anti-discrimination is no guarantee of inclusion, leaving marginalized groups to question whether diversity initiatives are catalyzed by truly inclusive beliefs or if these diversity initiatives are merely compulsory.

This study further demonstrates the practice of naming extends far beyond an echoing of EEOC rhetoric. Blanket terminology, such as socioeconomic status, appeared in 43% of IDMSs; however, the entity defining socioeconomic status ultimately decides who is included in a protected group, resulting in an invitation to social capital. Overly broad, nondescript, and blanket terminology pervaded dozens of IDMSs, with terms such as *diversity of ability, culture,* and *thought* appearing in at least 19% of all statements. Once again, *ability, culture,* and *thought* are idiosyncratic, abstract notions easily defined and manipulated by the entity in power and the one delegating social capital. Read by a minoritized individual or group, an invitation to social capital by *ability, culture,* and *thought* is an invitation that is both ubiquitous and ambiguous.

For example, in terms of the inclusion of sexual orientation and gender, the sexual orientations and genders that one may expect to be referenced by the terms *sexual orientation* and *gender* are frequently the non-normative lesbian, gay, bisexual—as though these are the only sexual orientations that need mentioning. Queer, trans*gender, intersex, and genderqueer identities are frequently eclipsed or misconstrued by language that is ostensibly welcoming (because some of these non-dominant identities are named) but neutered in its power to bestow capital by its lack of specificity. Straight people—the dominant holders of capital—are welcomed in this naming too, since the language is *sexual orientation* as opposed to specific sexual orientations, and thus the cycle of diversity non-performativity is reified. This particular example is indicative of what Ahmed (2012) says "diversity obscures" by examining what "recedes from view" when "diversity becomes a view" (p. 14). Here, straightness recedes from view and thus is not named, which leads to misunderstanding or intentionally misinterpreting what is meant by *sexual orientation* in a diversity statement.

In contrast to the aforementioned examples (i.e., including the discussion of sexual orientation and gender), it is important to acknowledge outliers in the data, many appearing in EEOC law language. Diversity mission statement inclusion of terms such as *genetic information, health status, family status, marital status,* or *pregnancy* can be traced to Title II of the Genetic Information Nondiscrimination Act of 2008 (U.S. Equal Employment Opportunity Commission, 2015). Furthermore, subsequent expansions of the original EEOC mandates incorporated in the Civil Rights Act of 1964 included the terms *color, sex,* and *creed* (U.S. National Archives and Records Administration, 2017). All three of these terms were outliers in the data, meaning they were included in two or fewer IDMSs. Once again, data in this study suggest EEOC language is apparent in IDMSs, effectively inviting marginalized groups to access social capital in compulsory, obligatory language mandated externally to the institution and alleged to function there, indicating who is welcome to access capital.

Other outliers in the data were peculiar. One IDMS included fraternities and sororities, athletes, alumni, and other members of the university community. Here, is it important to differentiate between aspirational and realistic mission statements, as articulated by Morphew and Hartley (2006). For this particular institution, descriptions of diversity were reflections of the institution as it existed. Surely, fraternities, sororities, athletes, alumni, and other members of the university community are already reaping the benefits of inclusion, and thus, Bourdieuian (1986) social capital. Augmenting Morphew and Hartley (2006), this study finds IDMSs are both written as aspirational and realistic, describing the potential diversity of a campus and which groups—marginalized or otherwise—contribute to a campus' extant diversity. Considering the equitable delegation of social capital, namely Bourdieu's (1986) multiplier effect, it seems naming groups who are already included and benefitting from the multiplier effect is an operationalization of Stewart's (2017) language of appeasement. Institutions are merely appeasing already-included groups by redundantly including these groups in IDMSs, thus inequitably delegating and multiplying social capital to those groups already possession.

However, the same IDMS that included fraternities, sororities, athletes, alumni, and other members of a university community also included Native American, Asian American, White, Latino, African American, Jewish, Christian, and Muslim individuals. Ultimately an outlier, this IDMS served as an important touchstone in this study. IDMSs that describe those with social capital and those who aspire to gain social capital promote diversity non-performativity at its core. Ahmed (2016) asserted her arguments about diversity non-performativity "were not just calls for action but a recognition of the collective labor that is necessary because of how institutional walls keep standing" (p. 4). If IDMSs describe IHEs as they stand, the statements are effectively exclusive. The statements do not perform diversity. They are, instead, non-performative. Subsequently, the Bourdieuian (1986) social capital of IHEs cannot be delegated to those outside of IHEs, rendering the phenomena of social reproduction and the multiplier effect of social capital wholly obsolete.

Ultimately, this study finds evident Stewart's (2017) language of appeasement and Ahmed's (2016) notion of diversity non-performativity in IDMSs, namely by the echoing of compulsory EEOC rhetoric and redundantly inviting campus community members who already reap and multiply the benefits of social capital. The implications of these IDMSs—the beliefs and values of elite IHEs—are especially salient for marginalized and underrepresented, student populations and those institutions truly attempting to accomplish egalitarian goals related to aspirational diversity.

DISCUSSION AND IMPLICATIONS FOR EGALITARIAN GOALS

The public flagships analyzed within this study must be discussed in conjunction with egalitarian goals, especially those related to IDMSs. If the 2016 Presidential Election was any indication, the U.S. has not entered a post-racial society, nor do current public flagship student enrollments and faculty-makeup support the notion racial and ethnic diversity are institutional priorities. For instance, one public flagship's student population is 20% Latinx, whereas the Latinx population in that flagship's state is nearly 40%. It is then curious to learn race and ethnicity are included in over half of all public flagship IDMSs. For institutions such as the one previously mentioned, racially and ethnically diversifying a student population must be an egalitarian goal, yet is clearly still aspirational. Here, given the current sociopolitical climate across the U.S., it may or may not be possible for a public flagship to compose a truly egalitarian IDMS, when sociopolitical restraints only allow for aspirational rhetoric: a realization of Stewart's (2017) language of appeasement. This implies a public flagship must transgress its own predominantly White norms and the predominantly White norms of its state in order to truly perform diversity in a way that serves the equitable and just aims of racially and socially minoritized groups outside of the institution.

Public flagships also prefer to sequester IDMSs in offices specifically tasked with performing diversity, a slant on Ahmed's (2016) notion of diversity non-performativity. By insisting there is diversity and someone in charge of managing, administering, or supporting it, the university will be able to point to that non-performative naming as the diversity it has *done*. Beyond our tables of findings, it is important to note each public flagship's IDMS is only mentioned once and in one location on their institutional website. Consequently, pressing questions emerge. If IDMSs only appear once and in one place, do institutions in their entirety embrace those statements? Can entire institutions perform diversity, and can entire institutions delegate social capital? Is it possible for members of institutions to recognize and cherish other forms of capital aligned with Yosso's (2005) model of community cultural wealth? Stewart (2017) argues, "Diversity asks, 'Isn't it separatist to provide funding for safe spaces and separate student centers?' Equity answers, 'What are people experiencing on campus that they don't feel safe when isolated and separated from others like themselves?'" (para. 10). Here, sequestering IDMSs in one location may perpetuate Stewart's (2017) equity argument. As Stewart (2017) suggests, campus community members across the country often feel unsafe. If IDMSs avoided the language of appeasement and were embraced by whole campuses (i.e., in their entirety), perhaps diversity would then be enacted in a way that reached beyond the walls of a diversity-focused structures or institutional units.

This strongly implies public flagships—or well-developed institutions as Berdahl (1998) noted—fund diversity offices, departments, units, or divisions to perform diversity on behalf of institutions, otherwise IDMSs would surely appear elsewhere on institutional websites. Here, Ahmed's (2016) diversity non-performativity may not apply to the diversity-focused structure or institutional unit, but it likely applies to the rest of the institution. This implication is particularly important for individuals on the outside of IHEs hoping to gain access. It cannot be assumed aspirant individuals are familiar with an institution's everyday diversity planning and on-campus initiatives because they are outsiders. Surely, diversity programming is important work performed daily by countless institutions across the country, but it is highly unlikely an aspirant student would be familiar with an institution's diversity programming. This unfamiliarity renders the IDMS even more important for aspirant individuals asking, "Am I included?," and who (quite frankly) deserve to be included. As a result, public flagships and other predominantly-White institutions (PWIs) must compose their IDMSs in ways that articulate diversity enactment and embrace Yosso's (2005) model of community cultural wealth, lest their statements remain non-performative and written in the language of appeasement (Stewart, 2017).

Touching upon Yosso's (2005) notion of linguistic capital, it is also salient to note every IDMS was written in English and English alone. Also, few flagships mentioned their institution valued language diversity. Certainly a monolingual, IDMS—by the fact that it is communicated solely in English—connotes a marginal disregard for linguistic capital and the value brought to an IHE by those who speak languages other than English or non-standardized varieties of English. By only situating the IDMS in one location, mentioning it once across the totality of an institution's communicative offerings, and only providing that statement in English, the IHE delivers an ambiguous, sequestered, monolithic notion of diversity to the aspirant individual. Here, diversity cannot perform because it is written in the language of the predominantly-White majority. The diversity statement does not invite racially and socially minoritized groups. As such, Ahmed's (2016) diversity non-performativity is perpetuated by institutions insisting upon Stewart's (2017) language of appeasement.

CONCLUSION

This study began in November 2016 with a broad overview of the IDMSs of a few public flagships. After the initial gathering of data occurred in late 2016, nearly half of all IDMSs were changed or entirely removed by September 2017. In fact, IDMSs included in this study are no longer able to be found on several institutional websites. In many ways, this is unsurprising, as late 2016 and 2017 witnessed some of the most divisive and troubling interpersonal behavior in the U.S. in recent history, beginning with the 2016 Presidential Election and perhaps culminating with the hateful and biased acts of terror committed by alt-right White Nationalists in the city of Charlottesville, Virginia, and on-campus at one of the public flagships included in this study.

These changes to IDMSs cannot be categorized as positive or negative in terms of movement toward egalitarian goals of higher education in the U.S. or elsewhere in the world. Change is precisely what it is: *change*. One institution in this sample removed its IDMS entirely in September 2017 and replaced it with the announcement of a new chief diversity officer and a call for a campus climate survey. Another institution changed its statement between November 2016 and May 2017, removing previously named groups in the statement and replacing these names with a broad definition of what diversity means to the institution. Inversely, another institution changed its statement between November 2016 and May 2017 from a bulleted list of institutional definitions of diversity to an explicit naming of broad constituencies: faculty, staff, supervisors, and students. Over the course of a year (and in some cases less), IDMSs of public flagships were changed to specifically avoid naming groups, were re-written to specifically name groups, and were entirely erased from institutions' outward-facing communication.

Ideally, future IDMSs will enact diversity by moving past merely providing diversity programming for diverse individuals toward a post-programming framework that educates the institution and its members on how to better welcome and embrace those diverse individuals. An institution must first recognize its perpetuation of Stewart's (2017) language of appeasement by reflecting upon its own milieu and identifying "Who is trying to get in the room but can't?" (para. 10). Ahmed (2007b, 2012), too, tells us by acknowledging our (institutional) complicity, we can begin to notice how close we are to the problems that diversity work seeks to address. Ultimately, institutions must recognize themselves as complicit in systems of oppression and work to extricate themselves as individuals and as institutional actors from the perpetuation of such systems, like those previously discussed, in order for any form of capital to be equitably and justly accessed and multiplied by racially and socially minoritized groups.

Ultimately, Bourdieu's (1986) theory of social capital is apparent in this study. Those with power, meaning with social capital, are successfully reproducing it and multiplying it. In order to combat this cycle, powerful institutional actors such as HWIs must change, and public flagships could (and arguably should, depending on their institutional mission statements) lead this change. Those working for these institutions must acknowledge who is being minoritized and value the cultural and social capital these individuals bring to an institution. Antiquated definitions of capital simply do not serve nor perform the tasks required for racially and socially minoritized individuals to be treated equitably and justly by IHEs. In sum, IDMSs, if we must have them, should indicate and reiterate the un-finishedness of *diversity work*. They should demonstrate what is being done, by whom, and to what end. They should be so fully integrated in all of the work in a university setting that its ubiquity serves as the constant catalyst *for more work*. Diversity practitioners like to say they hope to work themselves out of a job, but real *diversity work* can never be finished. If IHEs claim to value diversity, they must at once acknowledge and constantly interrupt their own complicity in inequity.

REFERENCES

Ahmed, S. (2006). The nonperformativity of antiracism. *Meridians: Feminism, Race, Transnationalism, 7*(1), 104–126. Retrieved from http://www.jstor.org/stable/40338719

Ahmed, S. (2007a). The language of diversity. *Ethnic and Racial Studies, 30*(2), 235–256. doi.org/10.1080/01419870601143927

Ahmed, S. (2007b). 'You end up doing the document rather than doing the doing': Diversity, race equality, and the politics of documentation. *Ethnic and Racial Studies, 50*(4), 590–609. doi.org/10.1080/01419870701356015

Ahmed, S. (2012). *On being included: Racism and diversity in institutional life*. Durham, NC: Duke.

Ahmed, S. (2016). How not to do things with words. *Wagadu: A Journal of Transnational Women's and Gender Studies, 16*, 1–10. Retrieved from http://webhost1.cortland.edu/wagadu/wp-content/uploads/sites/3/2017/02/v16-how-not-to-do-ahmed.pdf

Bender, B. E. (2017). College and university missions: Purposes, principles, and perspectives. In B. D. Ruben, R. De Lisi, & R. A. Gigliotti (Eds.), *A guide for leaders in higher education: Core concepts, competencies, and tools* (pp. 40–52). Sterling, VA: Stylus.

Berdahl, R. M. (1998, October 5). *The future of flagship universities*. Retrieved from http://chancellor.berkeley.edu/chancellors/berdahl/speeches/future-of-flagship-universities

Berrey, E. (2015, October 26). *Diversity is for white people: The big lie behind a well-intended word*. Retrieved from https://www.salon.com/2015/10/26/diversity_is_for_white_people_the_big_lie_behind_a_well_intended_word/

Bourdieu, P. (1986). The forms of capital. In J. Richardson (Ed.), *Handbook of theory and research for the sociology of education* (pp. 241–258). New York, NY: Greenwood.

Brown, S. (2016a, May 15). *Are colleges' diversity efforts putting students in 'silos'?* The Chronicle of Higher Education. Retrieved from http://www.chronicle.com.ezproxy.lib.utexas.edu/article/Are-Colleges-Diversity/236441?cid=cp38

Brown, S. (2016b, May 15). *Auditing diversity*. The Chronicle of Higher Education. Retrieved from http://www.chronicle.com.ezproxy.lib.utexas.edu/article/Auditing-Diversity/236428?cid=cp38

Brown v. Board of Education, 347 U.S. 483 (1954).

Burdett, K. R. (2013). *How students choose a college: Understanding the role of internet based resources in the college choice process*. Doctoral dissertation University of Nebraska at Lincoln, Lincoln, NE. Available from ProQuest database. (UMI No. 3590306)

Carter, R. (2008). *Multiplicity: The new science of personality, identity, and the self*. London, UK: Little, Brown.

Fisher I v. Univ. of Texas, 570 U.S. ___ (2013).

Fisher II v. Univ. of Texas, 579 U.S. ___ (2016).

Furuta, J. (2017). Rationalization and student/school personhood in U.S. college admissions: The rise of test-optional policies, 1987 to 2015. *Sociology of Education, 90*(3), 236–254. doi.org/10.1177/0038040717713583

Gallup, M. G. (2013). Academic libraries, institutional missions, and new student recruitment: A case study. *Reference Services Review, 41*(2), 192–200. doi.org/10.1108/00907321311326192

Gerald, D., & Haycock, K. (2013). *Engines of inequality: Diminishing equity in the nation's premier public universities.* Retrieved from https://1k9gl1yevnfp2lpq1dhrqe17-wpengine.netdna-ssl.com/wp-content/uploads/2013/10/EnginesofInequality.pdf

Gratz v. Bollinger, 539 U.S. 244 (2003).

Grutter v. Bollinger, 539 U.S. 306 (2003).

Guinier, L. (2015). *The tyranny of the meritocracy: Democratizing higher education in America.* Boston, MA: Beacon.

Hu-DeHart, E. (2000). The diversity project: Institutionalizing multiculturalism or managing differences? *Academe, 86*(5), 38–42.

Iverson, S. V. (2008a). Capitalizing on change: The discursive framing of diversity in U.S. land-grant universities. *Equity & Excellence in Education, 41*(2), 182–199.

Iverson, S. V. (2008b). Now is the time for change: Reframing diversity planning at land-grant universities. *Journal of Extension, 46*(1). Retrieved from https://www.joe.org/joe/2008february/a3.php

Kezar, A. J., & Eckel, P. D. (2008). Advancing diversity agendas on campus: Examining transactional and transformational presidential leadership styles. *International Journal of Leadership in Education, 11*(4), 379–405.

McMurtrie, B. (2016, May 15). *How do you create a diversity agenda?* The Chronicle of Higher Education. Retrieved from http://www.chronicle.com.ezproxy.lib.utexas.edu/article/How-Do-You-Create-a-Diversity/236427?cid=cp38

Monroe, K. R., Hankin, J., & Van Vechten, R. B. (2000). The psychological foundations of identity politics. *Annual Review of Political Science, 3*(1), 419–447. doi.org/10.1146/annurev.polisci.3.1.419

Morphew, C. C., & Hartley, M. (2006). Mission statements: A thematic analysis of rhetoric across institutional type. *Journal of Higher Education, 77*(3), 456–471. doi/abs/10.1080/00221546.2006.11778934

Morris, C. (2016). Dartmouth and diversity. *Diverse Issues in Higher Education, 33*(9), 14–15.

Neuendorf, K. A. (2017). *The content analysis guidebook* (2nd ed.). Thousand Oaks, CA: Sage.

Packer-Williams, C. L., & Evans, K. (2013). Mentorship in diversity leadership in higher education: Empowering emerging and established leaders. In J. Lewis, A. Green, & D. Surry (Eds.), *Technology as a tool for diversity leadership: Implementation and future implications* (pp. 243–254). Hershey, PA: IGI Global.

Parekh, B. (2008). *A new politics of identity: Political principles for an interdependent world.* New York, NY: Palgrave MacMillan.

Regents of the Univ. of Cal. v. Bakke, 438 U.S. 265 (1978).

Rozelle, A. L., & Landis, R. S. (2002). An examination of the relationship between use of the Internet as a recruitment source and student attitudes. *Computers in Human Behavior, 18*(5), 593–604. doi.org/10.1016/S0747-5632(02)00002-X

Schmidt, P. (2016, May 15). *Demand surges for diversity consultants.* The Chronicle of Higher Education. Retrieved from http://www.chronicle.com.ezproxy.lib.utexas.edu/article/Demand-Surges-for-Diversity/236442?cid=cp38

Sidanius, J., Levin, S., van Laar, C., & Sears, D. O. (2008). *The diversity challenge: Social identity and intergroup relations on the college campus.* New York, NY: Sage.

Smith, D. G. (2015). *Diversity's promise for higher education: Making it work* (2nd ed.). Baltimore, MD: Johns Hopkins.

Stewart, D.-L. (2017, March 30). *Language of appeasement.* Retrieved from https://www.insidehighered.com/views/2017/03/30/colleges-need-language-shift-not-one-you-think-essay

Stewart, P. (2016). Optional, flexible or blind. *Diverse Issues in Higher Education, 33*(18), 14–15. Retrieved from http://search.proquest.com/openview/6801d48a34cff799d9e a64b3506a8301/1?pq-origsite=gscholar&cbl=27805

Sutton, H. (2016). Study advocates for poverty preference admissions at selective institutions. *The Successful Registrar, 16*(3), 9. doi.org/10.1002/tsr.30180/full

U.S. Equal Employment Opportunity Commission. (2015). *Genetic information nondiscrimination act of 2008.* Retrieved from https://www.federalregister.gov/documents/2015/10/30/2015-27734/genetic-information-nondiscrimination-act-of-2008

U.S. Equal Employment Opportunity Commission. (2017). *Discrimination by type.* Retrieved from https://www.eeoc.gov/laws/types/index.cfm

U.S. National Archives and Records Administration. (2017). *The Civil Rights Act of 1964 and the Equal Employment Opportunity Commission.* Retrieved from https://www.archives.gov/education/lessons/civil-rights-act

Warikoo, N. K. (2016). *The diversity bargain and other dilemmas of race, admissions, and meritocracy at elite universities.* Chicago, IL: University of Chicago.

Williams, D. A. (2013). *Strategic diversity leadership: Activating change and transformation in higher education.* Sterling, VA: Stylus.

Williams, D. A., Berger, J. B., & McClendon, S. A. (2005). Toward a model of inclusive excellence and change in postsecondary institutions. *Making Excellence Inclusive,* (1), 1–39. Retrieved from https://aacu.org/sites/default/files/files/mei/williams_et_al.pdf

Wilson, J. L., Meyer, K. A., & McNeal, L. (2012). Mission and diversity statements: What they do and do not say. *Innovative Higher Education, 37*(2), 125–139.

Yosso, T. J. (2005). Whose culture has capital? A critical race theory discussion of community cultural wealth. *Race, Ethnicity, and Education, 8*(1), 69–91. https://doi.

PART II
ACCESS STRATEGIES

PART II.A

INSTITUTIONALIZED ACTIONS AND AGENTS

CHAPTER 7

STILL CHASING THE DREAM

The Possibilities and Limitations of Social Capital in Dismantling Racialized Tracks

Richard Lofton, Jr.

African American students in racially diverse schools often encounter racialized tracking (Tyson, 2011), which has resulted in them not acquiring the necessary academic skills for college and upward mobility. Researchers currently acknowledge the reality of intergenerational tracking, which comprises both parents' and students' academic placement. Building on this research by using qualitative methods to examine the experiences of African American parents, this paper investigates the role social capital plays in a racially diverse middle school and a Black community. Findings suggest that African Americans within their communities developed meaningful relationships to combat inequalities and promote detracking policies. Despite this agency, not all African American parents benefited from the social capital that helped some parents navigate their child's academic placement. In addition, some parents who benefited from the social capital used the politics of respectability to rationalize other African Americans' placement in lower-track classes, without acknowledging the neighborhood inequalities, intergenerational tracking, and the circumstances of poverty that students and families faced.

Contemporary Perspectives on Social Capital in Educational Contexts,
pages 107–123.

Whether consciously or unconsciously, most Americans believe in the American Dream, which posits that through rugged individualism, effort, and determination, individuals can overcome any hurdle they confront to attain success. Even more significantly, many people of color, regardless of socio-economic background, vest interest in this dream (Luhby, 2015). While many African Americans have long bought into this dream and have adopted multiple cultural practices that aim to ensure economic and social benefits, social scientific research paints a different picture. This picture shows huge disparities (Perry, 2011) for African Americans in education (Ladson-Billings, 2006), health (National Center for Health Statistics, 2017), unemployment (Wilson, 2015), incarceration (Alexander, 2010) and wealth (Jones, 2017). In addition, African American neighborhoods are subject to higher rates of exposure to crime (Martin. et al., 2011), violence (Sharkey, 2013), evictions (Desmond, 2016), food deserts (Bower et al., 2014), and liquor stores (Jones-Webb & Karriker-Jaffe, 2013). From this perspective, far too often this dream has become, as Langston Hughes wrote, a dream deferred

One reason this dream is deferred is that powerful social actors within institutions have limited the exchange of social and economic capital in African American homes, schools and communities. As a result, many African Americans have not gained entry into social networks that allow them to fully participate in the exchange and accumulation of these forms of capital. According to the French scholar Pierre Bourdieu (Bourdieu & Wacquant, 1992), social capital allows a person or people to accumulate resources through institutionalized relationships. These relationships demand mutual respect and trust which generate social rewards (Brown & Davis, 2001). While most African Americans have not fully participated in social capital within powerful institutions, they have organically produced social ties and networks in their homes, schools, and communities.

Bourdieu, however, warns of the inequities inherent in social capital and the implication that people benefit in society because of whom they know, not necessarily what they know or how hard they work. In Bourdieu's social reproduction theory, he suggests that social capital can perpetuate social stratification. In this perspective, African Americans may believe in the American Dream, but powerful social networks in their society, city, and school may not value, recognize, and trust their community cultural wealth (Yosso, 2005); as a result, they never fully benefit from mainstream social rewards and access to privileged status.

Schools are one milieu that has struggled to validate the cultural wealth of African Americans students and provide them equal educational opportunities. Some researchers have identified schools as institutions that reinforce inequality and hinder upward mobility for African American and poor students (Anyon, 1997, 2014; Bourdieu & Passeron 1977; Bowles & Gintis, 1976; MacLeod, 1995). One way that schools reinforce inequality for African American students is through academic tracking, sorting students based on perceived talents and abilities (Oakes, 1985). Over the last 40 years, researchers have examined how tracking in schools perpetuates social inequalities (Gamoran, 1992; Oakes & Martin,

1994; Rosenbaum, 1976; Rubin, 2008; Wheelock, 1992). African American students who attend racially diverse schools often experience racialized tracking, in which most African American students are in lower-track classes, while their White peers pursue advanced courses (Tyson, 2011). Current research indicates that racialized tracking leads to intergenerational tracking, further legitimizing an unequal distribution of resources, opportunities, and spheres of knowledge in homes, schools, and communities (Lofton & Davis, 2015). While researchers have gained insight into how tracking reproduces inequalities, ways to dismantle intergenerational tracking are still unclear.

This paper proposes to explore the possibilities and limitations of social capital in dismantling intergenerational tracking, by considering the voices and experiences of twenty-six African American parents whose children attended a racially diverse middle school while living in a poor Black community. Twenty of the parents in this study were enrolled in the same school district as children and were often placed in lower-track classes. Building on detailed insights from African American parents, this research highlights the ways social networks provided an opportunity for a few African American parents to gain information critical to academic success, while also noting how parents without the same social ties did not receive vital information for academic placement. In addition, this chapter illustrates how a framework of respectability politics was used to explain why most African American students were in lower-track placement, without regard for the systemic inequalities they faced in their home, school, and community.

THEORIZING AFRICAN AMERICAN HOMES, SCHOOLS, AND COMMUNITIES

The Struggle for Capital in the Black Habitus

> We have deluded ourselves into believing the myth that capitalism grew and prospered out of the Protestant ethic of hard work and sacrifices. The fact is that capitalism was built on the exploitation and suffering of black slaves and continues to thrive on the exploitation of the poor
>
> —*Martin Luther King, August 1967*

Although Bourdieu has elucidated the role of social capital in generating resources and opportunities within social groups, researchers often do not recognize how capital was developed in the global economy. Martin Luther King suggests that capitalism was built on the exploitation and suffering of African Americans, and some historians agree with him. Historians have determined that slavery was a core contributor to the development of the global economy (Johnson, 2013; Schermerhorn, 2015; Williams, 1944), particularly in the United States, where black bodies were exploited by slave owners who exchanged cotton, tobacco, and sugar produced by their labor to gain economic profit. In fact, some historians have argued that Black bodies were their primary capital (Baptist, 2016; Rosenthal, 2013; Sublette & Sublette, 2015). The profits made were invested in banks, universities and other institutions in the United States. In the 19th and 20th centuries, many Whites accumulated, generated and exchanged benefits derived from this capital, while African Americans were confined at various times by slavery, Jim Crow laws, disenfranchisement, lynching and government-sanctioned housing segregation. The capital that people exchange in today's society is rooted, to a large degree, in the oppression and subjugation of African Americans.

Despite this historical exploitation, African Americans have produced their own cultural knowledge, sense-making, and habits. Racial injustices did not prevent these resilient people from participating in the underground railroad to escape slavery, demanding the right to vote, or calling attention to widespread lynching throughout the United States. Moreover, African Americans were instrumental in developing public education in the United States (Anderson, 1988). Through these initiatives, African Americans navigated the social structures that they had to confront and produced cultural knowledge and agency. Pierre Bourdieu (1990) refers to habitus as:

> Systems of durable, transposable dispositions, structured structures predisposed to function as structuring structures, that is, as principles which generate and organize practices and representations that can be objectively adapted to their outcomes without presupposing a conscious aiming at tends or an express mastery of the operations necessary in order to attain them (p. 53)

In Bourdieu's view, individuals' cognitive sense making is grounded in the social structures they encounter. The "structured structures" produce thoughts, logics and habits. While Bourdieu focused his analysis on social class, African Americans have learned to navigate social structures built not only on social class, but also on racial disparities. The social realities of African Americans are distinct because of their racialized experiences and the sense-making and agency they produce in their homes, schools, and communities, all of which I refer to as the Black Habitus. Building on the work of Bourdieu, this concept captures the African American experience in the United States by acknowledging the structural inequalities African Americans confront because of their race and social class, as well as the cultural knowledge, logic, and practices they produce in their homes, schools, and communities.

Within the Black Habitus, African Americans have developed social ties and networks to gain access to resources and opportunities, but discrimination, poverty, and neighborhood inequalities continue to limit the accumulation of economic capital. Churches, community centers, schools, businesses, and historically black colleges have fostered and created contexts in which social capital is generated and exchanged, but government policies and practices continue to allow an unequal allocation of resources in African American communities (Rothstein, 2017). While social ties and networks are essential to create opportunities, they must be coupled with tangible and meaningful resources to generate economic mobility.

Schools are one site where African Americans can develop their social capital for upward mobility. In fact, in the *Sweatt v. Painter* (1950) and *Brown v. Board of Education* (1954) cases, NAACP lawyers argued that the "intangible" benefits of integrated schools would allow African American students to benefit from the prestige of these schools and to access useful social networks. However, we find today that tracking maintains separate and unequal educational experiences within integrated schools (O'Connor et al, 2011; Tyson, 2011). More than 60 years after the Brown decision, intergenerational tracking in some school districts hinders both parents and their children from acquiring the necessary skills for college and upward mobility.

It is important for researchers who investigate social capital in African American communities to understand that African Americans have a different relationship with capital in the United States because of their historical and current struggles to obtain equality and justice within oppressive and exclusionary markets. Many African Americans confront systemic inequalities and exclusionary practices that hinder the efficacy of the flow of social capital.

METHODS

Illuminating the Role of Social Capital

To uncover the role social capital plays in a racially diverse school and a Black community, the researcher designed a qualitative study using ethnographic methods (Creswell, 2003; Merriam & Tisdale, 2009; Willis & Trondman, 2000) to illuminate the perspectives and practices of 26 African American parents in their homes, schools, and community, a segregated community whose students attended a predominantly White middle school in a school district that mirrors the racial demographics of the United States.

The researcher used interviews, observations, school documents, newspaper articles, and field notes to understand how African American parents made sense of their child's educational experiences, social networks, and systemic inequalities, and the agency these produced in their home, school, and community. Parent interviews (ranging from 1 to 3 hours) were conducted in homes or a community center, following a set interview protocol. Most parents had attended the same school as their children and had encountered similar educational challenges. In the larger study ten teachers, six administrators and five guidance counselors were interviewed. The researcher also conducted community observations at PTA meetings, churches, an African American community center, grocery stores, and restaurants. Community observation covered a span of three years, including six months of intensive interviewing of African American parents.

After each day in the field, the researcher wrote notes on the interviews and observations in the school or community for 50 minutes (Emerson, Fretz, & Shaw, 2011). He also jotted notes during interviews and observations; all interviews were recorded and subsequently transcribed. Notes, memos, and interviews transcripts were included in a coding process using Dedoose, an online software, to help the researcher store data, identify codes, and analyze data. He used field notes and multiple readings of transcripts to develop codes that enabled him to explore specific themes in the data. During this process, he focused on the research question: how is social capital reflected in the data, and what are the benefits and limitations of social capital in the African American community, particularly for African American parents? Through this robust coding, three themes emerged that captured the limitations and possibilities of social capital in the lives of African American parents in a racially diverse school and black community.

FINDINGS

This section addresses three findings regarding the role of social capital in a poor African American community. First, it highlights the benefits a small number of parents gained from social capital in the community to help them navigate their child's academic placement in a racially diverse school. Second, it explores most parents' lack of awareness of pertinent information needed to break free of intergenerational tracking. Third, it highlights the view that parents whose children benefitted academically from their social ties had of other African American parents, the view that these parents lacked the cultural norms and styles required to ensure upper-track placement for their children.

Social Capital in the Black Community

African Americans in this community were dynamic social actors, developing meaningful relationships despite oppression and inequalities. On several occasions, ministers, community leaders, and neighbors came together to address inequality in the city. When African Americans encountered police brutality, community members united in protest. Residents assembled weekly in two small churches to worship and develop trusting and caring relationships. Meaningful social networks and ties helped neighbors navigate their social world.

Many relationships were formed in a community center in the African American neighborhood led by a charismatic director, Ethan, who was known throughout the community and had developed strong relationships with school administrators over the years. He was respected by the middle school principal and the former district superintendent. He also had deep relationships with some African American parents who had children in the middle school. I discovered that many of the African American students in upper-track classes had a parent who had a personal relationship with Ethan. In one family, the father had gone to school with him, and they were lifelong friends. In another, both husband and wife were Ethan's close friends and spent a considerable amount of time at the community center. Another parent worked at the community center. Finally, Ethan's niece was also in upper-track classes. Five of the seven parents whose children were in upper-track classes told me they had had multiple conversations with Ethan regarding the classes their child should attend. As Jessica stated:

Jessica:	Ethan knows, I just go to him, he is the one that told me about the class that she is in. I just listen to Ethan.
Researcher:	She is in an accelerated math class.
Jessica:	That is the one he told me to put her in. I just listen to Ethan.

In the interview with Jessica, I learned that she was unaware of policies and procedures related to academic placement, yet through her relationship with Ethan, she decided to place her child in upper-track classes. Jessica developed a relationship with the community leader and trusted his advice. She did not necessarily have to know all the details; because she trusted and respected the advice that Ethan gave her, she was able to navigate her child's educational experiences.

When I interviewed Ethan, he explained the district's detracking policy. The middle school allowed parents to "self-select" their children's classes, that is, they could override the recommendation of teachers and guidance counselors. A guidance counselor would meet with a student to review the classes he or she should take the following year. Afterward, students would take home a self-select form for parents to sign. At this crucial time, Ethan would make a point to tell parents with whom he interacted to place their children in "accelerated classes." These were the upper-track classes, which offered students environments that would help them develop the necessary skills for college and upward mobility. Ethan's insight, regardless of parents' understanding of the self-select process or impact of these classes, gave people in his social network an advantage compared to other African American parents who did not have a social relationship with him.

Ethan not only informed parents, but also encouraged them to be wary of the social actors in the school that continued to foster intergenerational tracking, and urged parents not to accept a lower-track placement for their children. Tim and Janis, who had two daughters in the middle school, illustrated this point. Janis said:

> He said that they might try to put my two girls in other classes… but I should put them in accelerated math and science classes. They try to put them in other classes, but I told them only honors. I know how they are.

Janis was referring to what Ethan told them about the self-select process. She "knows how they are" because she and her husband were both in lower-track classes when they were students in the district. They wanted to ensure that this did not happen to their daughters. Through their relationship with Ethan, they knew they could and should ignore the recommendation of the guidance counselors. Ethan in this case helped foster agency in his community. He encouraged parents to act against a system that produced intergenerational tracking. Because of his advice, these parents insisted on upper-track placement for their daughters.

Ethan was fully aware of intergenerational tracking in the school district through personal experience. He explained to me:

> All of them, the black males in special education. I was even in special education. I tell parents this, parents can put their children in accelerated classes, they did not have to be in regular classes.

Ethan, through his personal story of being in special education, was aware of the tendency to place African American boys in special education in the district and wanted to stop this over-identification. He made it a point to inform parents in his social network that they could select their children's classes regardless of teachers' and guidance counselors' recommendation. His relationship with members of his social network allowed them to counteract the many decades of tracking in this middle school.

A small number of parents who had a close relationship with Ethan obtained detailed information on academic placement and other practices/policies in the school district. When they did not understand the policies or take-home sheets, they called him for information. If Ethan did not know, he called the school principal. These American parents benefited from their social relationship with this community leader, who had relationships with the middle school principal and former district superintendent. Clearly, the relationships Ethan developed in the school district allowed him to be an institutional agent (Stanton-Salazar, 1997) who negotiated the transmission of valuable information and helped parents navigate academic placement in the middle school. Ethan was known throughout the neighborhood, but only a few parents had a social relationship with him. The other parents did not gain the valuable information needed to navigate their child's academic placement.

When Capital is not (Sufficiently) Social

Many of the 26 African American parents I interviewed did not have this personal relationship with Ethan and therefore did not receive his advice on how to break free of intergenerational tracking in the middle school. African American parents outside of Ethan's network did not have a conversation with anyone about filling out the self-select form that parents/guardian had to sign. These parents were unfamiliar with the term "accelerated" which was used to designate upper-track courses. In some of my interviews with parents, I would show the form to them and ask them to explain the term "accelerated." These are some of their responses:

Researcher: Have you heard of accelerated classes?
Parent: What?
Researcher: Accelerated.
Parent: What's that? No, I didn't. I don't know.

Another parent stated:

Parent: Wait. What are the accelerated courses, because I am confused by this (sheet)?

Another parent:

Researcher: Have you heard of accelerated courses?
Parent: Accelerated courses, no.
Researcher: Did you sign a paper like this?
Parent: Let me look at this some more.... I still do not know what accelerated is.

Another parent:

Researcher: Have you heard of accelerated classes?
Parent: No.
Researcher: Okay. All right. Do you know about the different levels in the school?
Parent: A little bit. I'm not really aware. And that's just through the kids and how they talk.

After interviewing the parents, I realized that most African American parents did not fully understand the terms used to explain the different educational tracks in the school. In addition, the self-select sheet did not give clear and concise information on the different classes and how these classes would affect a child's academic trajectory. Without this information, African American parents were expected to sign the sheet and students were supposed to return it to their guidance counselor. After hearing the voices of most of the African American parents, one wonders if this is indeed a "self-select" policy: these parents did not receive clarification of the terms used to describe the different educational tracks and how these tracks could impact their children's academic trajectory.

Most African American parents did not have an institutional agent to help them decipher the self-select form or other important documents sent home for parents to sign. In interviewing these parents, I discovered that they valued education as much as the other African American parents whose children were in upper-track classes. They also wanted their children to fulfill all their dreams and goals. The only difference was that these parents did not have the social connections that could help them process and navigate academic placement and its impact on their children's academic trajectory. Many of them had also been in lower-track or special education classes while they were in school. School for them was not the great equalizer, but the place where they were told they were unintelligent and not valuable (Lofton & Davis, 2015). The unresolved shame and guilt hindered them from developing meaningful relationships with school staff. However, people like Ethan can help bridge the gap between African American parents and school staff. Community leaders, pastors, and neighbors can develop relationships with school administrators to improve the transmission of information to African American parents. While this will help in the transmission of social capital, the unresolved shame of tracking and other structural inequalities that parents experienced will continue to linger.

Respectability Politics and Social Capital

Four of the seven African American parents who benefited from social ties with Ethan did not perceive that many other African Americans in their community wanted to have their children in upper-track classes or to improve their community. These four parents spoke vividly about the racism they personally encountered and the neighborhood inequalities they faced daily. However, they did not take the racism and neighborhood inequalities into account when discussing the other African American parents. They felt that other African American parents did not value education and or want upward mobility for their children. Instead, these parents focused on certain norms, styles, and behavioral practices they felt African American parents and children should adopt to ensure upward mobility.

Four parents focused on what some critical writers call a "politics of respectability" to gain upward mobility (Cooper, 2017; Smith, 2016). Scholars for decades have identified this politics of respectability in African American communities; at its core, it asserts that to lift the race from oppression, African Americans must adopt certain practices, leading to better treatment and upward mobility (Higginbotham, 1993). In this study, four African American parents distanced themselves from others, suggesting that other parents did not value education and as a result their children were in lower-track classes.

Regardless of the academic placement of their children, in the interviews many parents evoked respectability politics. They indicated that African American boys needed to "pull their pants up," speak "English," and "stop worrying about expensive tennis shoes" and "rap music." African American girls on the other hand needed to "cover their bodies" so they would not get pregnant at an early age and respect older "Black women." In these interviews, many parents spoke about African Americans behaving a certain way to gain economic and social capital in the school and city. They also all spoke about the importance of education and restoring their community. However, a small number of the parents whose children were in upper-track classes felt that some other parents were not aiming to uplift the race.

A few parents felt that some of their peers wanted to maintain a marginalized position because they enjoyed their lifestyle. This lifestyle went against what Ethan wanted for the African American community. Kate made this point:

I truly believe Ethan is trying to change this community for the better, to have everybody on one accord with education, working and to just clean up this community. But then you have many people that don't care. They like their lifestyles. They like to be on Social Services, just sit at home, not do anything, not having any taxes claim, just doing their drugs. There are some people that like that lifestyle.

Kate believed many people in her community did not value education or neighborhood development. She believed many people wanted to do drugs, not play taxes, and rely on social services. Kate contended that the lifestyle of the other African Americans prevented them from aspiring for upper-track classes and the associated long-term economic benefits. For Kate, the root of the problem was the behavior and norms of members in her neighborhood that prevented them from accomplishing their goals. Kate's observation of the high percentage of families on social services and people arrested for possession of drugs was accurate. However, Kate did not relate these higher percentages to the circumstances of poverty, decades of failed educational experiences that resulted in intergenerational tracking, or racial injustices that had collectively affected the material benefits of social and economic capital in the African American community. Instead, she believed that people in her community lacked ambition and were content with their own intergenerational poverty.

Not only did they believe others' lifestyle was responsible for intergenerational poverty, some parents whose children were in upper-track classes felt that it was African American parents' fault they had no information regarding academic placement. Jamie made this point:

Parent-teachers' conference, school board meeting, it's about five parents. Stop crying about the district if you're not going to go up there and see what the district is doing. They'd be surprised what goes on up there but then they start screaming about racism and all this stuff, but you're not up there.

Jamie felt that more African American parents needed to go to the school district and gain information on the policies and practices in the school. For her, parents' failure to attend school-sponsored events caused African American students' absence from upper-track classes. She believed that if African Americans parents would change their behavior and attend these events they would be "surprised" to learn about all of the classes, academic clubs, and educational opportunities available at the school. She also complained that African American parents were "screaming racism" but never attended parent-teacher conferences, PTA meetings, or school-sponsored events. She ignored the impacts of micro aggression (Sue et al., 2007) and racial trauma (Carter & Helms, 2009) on African American parents, and the fact that parents' past educational experiences may have resulted in unresolved shame and guilt. Jamie minimized these toxic experiences, instead focusing only on parents being better parents by participating in school-sponsored events.

Jamie's story is different from that of other African American parents. Her son William is a promising athlete in a sport dominated by Whites. Many students and parents, regardless of race, admire his athletic abilities. William is well liked by many White parents, teachers, and administrators, and his skills are valued in the city, since he received positive recognition by winning a statewide championship at an early age. While William is at practice, Jamie sometimes talks with other parents about school policies. Jamie was the only parent that I interviewed that had a child in upper-track classes but did not rely on the social capital in the African American community to access information on academic tracking. Her son's athletic ability and dedication to his sport gave her access to some of the social capital that White parents benefitted from in her city. Winning a statewide championship on a predominately White team allowed William and his mother to be viewed differently from other African American students and parents. Jamie and William gained access to a social network in the city that allowed them to receive social rewards, since as a star player he was valued by the community.

Although Jamie's status was different from that of other African American parents, she criticized their failure to attend PTA meetings or gain important information. Throughout her interview, Jamie stated that African American parents needed to change and become better parents. Surprisingly, however, later in the interview, I learned that while she strongly recommended African Americans attend school-sponsored events, she only attended sport events in the city. When I asked why she did not attend, she replied:

> Those parents are racists. I am not going up there with those parents. I do not have time to listen to racist parents talk about their kids and how bad our kids are.

Jamie insisted that other parents attend PTA meeting with racist parents, yet she protected herself from the toxic effects of racism by not attending the same meetings. She understood that PTA meetings in this district were a toxic environment for African American parents, because participants at these meetings often blamed African American students for the problems in the middle school. While Jamie was aware of what happened in these meetings, she ignored the effects of this racial tension for other African American parents, and expected them to attend. In other words, Jamie wanted to urge on other African American parents a practice that she herself did not follow.

Parents were not the only ones that needed to change their practices, according to some, who considered African American students' behavior inappropriate for obtaining access to upper-track classes. These students were described pejoratively. One parent described many African American students who were not in upper-track classes as "ghetto." Julie stated:

> No, no. There's a handful of black individuals that's in honor classes in the middle school because most of the kids here are like ghetto kids. I hate to say that but they have no upbringing, they don't care about this. It's like a handful of kids, a handful.

Julie concluded that many African American students in the community were "ghetto," did not have any upbringing, did not care about their education, and as a result were not in honors classes. She, too, placed the blame on the other African American parents for not raising their children correctly.

Another parent whose child was in upper-track classes referred to the children in her neighborhood as her son's buddies. Karen stated

> I want him to be in accelerated because he needs to be challenged and he doesn't need to be in the classroom full of his buddies. That's one thing I don't play. You go to school to learn. Your buddies do not want a scholarship, you do.

Karen placed her child in upper-track classes because she wanted him to be challenged, and to ensure that he was not in a classroom full of his buddies, because she thought the buddies might not want to learn. For Karen, an environment where her son could learn and be challenged meant away from other African American students who were his buddies; she wanted to isolate him from other students who, in her view, might not want a scholarship to go to college.

Most African American parents I interviewed discussed changing the styles and behaviors of African Americans to gain social and economic capital in this city. Changing the styles and behaviors of African Americans is not a new topic, it connects to a larger discussion within the African American community (Patterson, 2006; McWhorter, 2005) Four parents whose children were in upper-track classes felt that the main reason most African American students were in lower-track classes was their own behavior or lack thereof. While these parents benefitted from social networks to help them figure out the academic placement policies, they believed that other African American students and their parents needed to change their lifestyles to ensure academic success and upward mobility. This group of parents felt that most African American parents whose children were not in upper-track classes, were in that situation through their own fault. Some felt that other African American parents neither valued education nor took pride in their community. And, some of these parents considered some of the other African American children as "ghetto" and disinterested in better educational experiences.

Four of the seven African American parents whose children were in upper-track classes did not realize that the social capital they had acquired helped them navigate their children's educational experiences. Researchers have strongly demonstrated that social capital helps students reach their educational goals (Bartee & Brown, 2007; Conchas, 2006; Noguera,2003; Stanton-Salazar,1997). In this study, whether through their relationships with Ethan or with White parents, these select parents benefited from information that helped them navigate their child's academic placement. Instead of acknowledging the social advantage they gained through these contacts, they viewed other parents as not displaying the behaviors and norms required to guarantee upper-track placement. In addition, these critical parents did not recognize that intergenerational tracking had resulted in unresolved guilt and shame that some African American parents carried from prior educational experiences.

CONCLUSION

African American parents in this study encountered neighborhood inequalities, intergenerational tracking, and circumstances of poverty. Despite these many inequalities (Lofton & Davis, 2015; Perry, 2011; Sharkey, 2013) these resilient parents wanted their children to fulfill the American Dream. They attended churches, community events, and block parties that helped foster social ties in their community. African American parents valued education and aimed for their children to obtain academic success. A small number of African American parents were more successful at placing their children on a path that had the potential to lead to academic success. These parents, because of their relationship with a community leader, were able to navigate the academic tracks in the school district and were encouraged to place their children in classes where they could develop skills necessary for college and upward mobility. In addition, their relationship with Ethan allowed these parents to not only gain information, but also act on it. African American parents demonstrated agency to combat intergenerational tracking by rejecting the recommendations of guidance counselors and teachers for their children. Instead, these parents were not afraid to demand upper-track placement for their children.

While Ethan was an insightful community leader with social ties with a select group of African American parents, he was not able to reach all of the parents. The other parents did not have information regarding academic placement and were unaware that certain classes would prepare their children for college and upward mobility. These parents all received a "self-select" form, but many did not have anyone to help them process the information. These parents did not understand the terms used or the potential impact of certain classes on their children's academic trajectory. Therefore, while the community leader provided social benefits for a few African American parents, systemic changes were needed to ensure that all parents would gain pertinent information about academic placement. For example, all parents should receive clear and concise information; key terms like "accelerated course" should be clearly explained and defined. Parents should be advised of the impact of certain classes to their child's academic trajectory. In addition, multiple forms of information should be offered to help parents decipher this information. Take-home slips, social media, and phone calls are a few examples that could be all be used to dismantle intergenerational tracking in some school districts. This information could help all parents process the information and make appropriate decisions for their children. If parents do not have the information, the policy is not necessarily a "self-select" process, because participants lack vital information to make critical decisions.

While information and agency are important to dismantling intergenerational tracking, neighborhood inequities continue to affect students' academic performance. Some African American parents argued that changing the cultural norms, styles, and actions of African American students would ensure them access to upper-track classes. However, the politics of respectability can never address the systemic inequalities that many African Americans confront in their home, school, and community, nor the unresolved guilt and shame associated with African Americans' not reaching the American Dream. Unequal distributions of resources in the city impacted African Americans, who confronted higher rates of crime, violence, police brutality, evictions and unemployment. While some parents whose children were in upper-track classes felt that the root of the problem was the cultural practices of African American students and their parents, they were unable to acknowledge the way unequal distribution of resources had prevented many African Americans from attaining the American Dream.

REFERENCES

Alexander, M. (2010). *The new Jim Crow: Mass incarceration in the age of colorblindness.* New York, NY: New Press.

Anderson, J. D. (1988). *The education of blacks in the south, 1860–1935.* Chapel Hill, NC: The University of North Carolina Press.

Anyon, J. (1997). *Ghetto schooling: A political economy of urban educational reform.* New York, NY: Teachers College Press.

Anyon, J. (2014). *Radical possibilities: Public policy, urban education, and a new social movement.* New York, NY: Routledge.

Baptist, E. (2014). *The half has never been told: Slavery and the making of American capitalism.* New York, NY: Basic Books.

Bartee, R., & Brown, C. (2007). *School matters: Why African American students need multiple forms of capital.* New York, NY: Peter Lang Publishing.

Bourdieu, P. (1990). *The logic of practice.* Cambridge: Polity Press.

Bourdieu, P., & Passeron, J.C. (1977). *Reproduction in education, culture and society.* London, UK: Sage Publications.

Bourdieu, P., & Wacquant, L.D. (1992). *An invitation to reflexive sociology.* Chicago, IL: University of Chicago Press.

Bower, K., Thrope, R., Rhode, & C. Gaskin, D. (2014). The intersection of neighborhood racial segregation, poverty, and urbanicity and its impact on food store availability in the United States. *Preventive Medicine, 58*(1), 33–39.

Bowles, S., & Gintis, H. (1976). *Schooling in capitalist America: Educational reform and the contradictions of economic life.* New York, NY: Basic Books.

Brown vs. Board of Educ. of Topeka, 347 U.S. 483 (1954).

Brown, M. C., & Davis, J. E. (2001). The historically black college as social contract, social capital, and social equalizer. *Peabody Journal of Education, 76*(1), 31–49.

Carter, R. T., & Helms, J. E. (2009). Racism and race-based traumatic stress: toward new legal and clinical standards. *Law Enforcement Executive Forum, 9* (5), 113–129.

Conchas, G. (2006). *The color of success: Race and high-achieving urban youth.* New York, NY: Teachers College Press.

Cooper, B. (2017). *Beyond respectability: The intellectual thought of race women.* Urbana, IL: University of Illinois Press.

Creswell, W. F. (2003). *Research design: Qualitative, quantitative, and mixed methods approaches.* Thousand Oaks, CA: Sage Publications.

Desmond, M. (2016). *Evicted: Poverty and profit in the American city.* New York, NY: Crown.

Emerson, R. M., Fretz, R. I., & Shaw, L. L. (2011). *Writing ethnographic fieldnotes.* Chicago, IL: The University of Chicago Press.

Gamoran, A. (1992). The variable effects of high school tracking. *American Sociological Review, 57*(6), 812–828.

Higginbotham, E. (1993). *Righteous discontent: The women's movement in the Black Baptist Church, 1880–1920.* Cambridge, MA: Harvard University Press.

Johnson, W. (2013). *River of dark dreams: Slavery and empire in the cotton kingdom.* Cambridge, MA: Harvard University Press.

Jones, J. (2017). The racial wealth gap: How African Americans have been shortchanged out of the materials to build wealth. *Economic Policy Institute.*

Jones-Webb, R., & Karriker-Jaffe, K. (2013). Neighborhood disadvantage, high alcohol content beverage consumption, drinking norms, and drinking consequences: a mediation analysis. *Journal of Urban Health.* 90(4), 667-684.

King, M. L. (August, 31, 1967). *The three evils of society.* Address delivered at the National Conference on New Politics. Chicago, IL.

Ladson-Billings, G. (2006). From the achievement gap to the education debt: Understanding achievement in U.S. Schools. *Educational Researcher, 35*(7), 3–12.

Lofton, R., & Davis, J. E. (2015). Toward a black habitus: African Americans navigating systemic inequalities within home, school, and community. *The Journal of Negro Education, 84*(3), 214–230.

Luhby, T. (2015). *Why blacks believe in the American Dream more than whites.* Retrieved from http://money.cnn.com/2015/11/24/news/economy/race-american-dream/index.html

MacLeod, J. (1995). *Ain't no makin' it: Aspirations and attainment in a low-income neighborhood.* Boulder, CO: Westview Press.

Martin, M., McCarthy, B., Conger, R., Gibbons, F., Simons, R., Cutrona, C., & Broady, C., (2011). The enduring significance of racism: Discrimination and delinquency among black. American youth. *Journal of Research on Adolescence. 21*(3), 662–676.

McWhorter, J. (2005). *Winning the race: Beyond the crisis in Black America.* New York, NY: Penguin.

Merriam, S. B., & Tisdell, E. J. (2009). *Qualitative research: A guide to design and implementation.* San Francisco, CA: Jossey-Bass.

National Center for Health Statistics. (2017). *Health, United States, 2016: With chartbook on long-term trends in health.* (DHHS Publication No. 2017-1232). Hyattsville, MD: Author.

Nogura, P. (2003). *City schools and the American dream: Reclaiming the promise of public education.* New York, NY: Teachers College Press.

Oakes, J. (1985). *Keeping track: How schools structure inequality.* New Haven, CT: Yale University Press.

Oakes, J. & Martin, L. (1994). Tracking and ability grouping: A structural barrier to access and achievement. In J Goodlad & P. Keating (Eds.), *Access to knowledge: The continuing agenda for our nation's schools* (pp. 187–204). New York, NY: College Entrance Examination Board.

O'Connor, C., Mueller, J., Lewis, R. L., & Rosenberg, S. (2011). Being Black and strategizing for excellence in a racially stratified academic hierarchy. *American Educational Research Journal, 48*(6), 1232–1257.

Patterson, O. (2006, March 26). A poverty of the mind. *New York Times.*

Perry, I. (2011). *More beautiful and more terrible: The embrace and transcendence of racial inequality in the United States.* New York, NY: New York University Press.

Rosenbaum, J. E. (1976). *Making inequality: The hidden curriculum of high school tracking.* New York, NY: Johns Wiley & Sons.

Rosenthal, C. (2013). Plantations practiced modern management. *Harvard Business Review, 91*(9), 30–31.

Rothstein, R. (2017). *The color of law: A forgotten history of how our government segregated America.* New York, NY: Liveright.

Rubin, R. (2008). Detracking in context: How local constructions of ability complicate equity-geared reform. *Teachers College, 110*(3), 646–699.

Schermerhorn, C. (2015). *The business of slavery and the rise of American capitalism, 1815–1860.* New Haven, CT: Yale University Press.

Sharkey, P. (2013). *Stuck in place: Urban neighborhoods and the end of progress toward racial equality.* Chicago, IL: University of Chicago Press.

Smith, M. D. (2016). *Invisible man, got the whole world watching: A young black man's education.* New York, NY: Nation Books.

Stanton-Salazar, R. D. (1997). A social capital framework for understanding the socialization of racial minority children and youths. *Harvard Educational Review, 67*(1), 1–40.

Sublette, N., & Sublette, C. (2015). *The American slave coast: A history of the slave-breeding industry.* Chicago, IL: Lawrence Hill Books.

Sue, D. W., Capodilupo, C. M., Torino, G.C., Bucceri, J. M., Holder, A. M. B., Nadal, K. L., & Esquilin, M. (2007). Racial microaggressions in everyday life: Implications for clinical practice. *American Psychologist, 62*(4), 271–286.

Sweatt v. Painter, 339 U.S. 629 (1950).

Tyson, K. (2011). *Integration interrupted: Tracking, black students, and acting white after Brown.* New York, NY: Oxford University Press.

Wheelock, A. (1992). *Crossing the tracks: How 'untracking' can save America's schools.* New York, NY: New Press.

Williams, E. (1944). *Slavery and capitalism.* Chapel Hill, NC: University of North Carolina Press.

Willis, P., & Trondman, M. (2000). Manifesto for ethnography. *Ethnography, 1*(1), 5–16.

Wilson, V. (2015). Black unemployment is significantly higher than white unemployment regardless of educational attainment. *Economic Snapshot,* 12.17.2015.

Yosso, T. J. (2005). Whose cultural has capital? *Race, Ethnicity and Education, 8*(1), 69–61.

CHAPTER 8

EMBRACING THE FULLNESS OF POSTSECONDARY PLANNING

Utilizing Social Capital to Serve Students at the Nexus of Navigational Capital and Care

Raquel Farmer-Hinton and Nicole E. Holland

For over a decade, new policies, philanthropy, and practices have solidified the ideal that college is accessible to all students (Allensworth, Nomi, Montgomery, & Lee, 2009; Conley, 2007; Farmer-Hinton & Rifelj, 2018; Harris, 2013; Kelchen & Goldrick-Rab, 2014; Lobosco, 2015, 2017; Lowery & Hoyler, 2009; Miller-Adams, 2009, 2015; Mulhere, 2017; New York City Department of Education, 2016; Perna & Leigh, 2018; Yamamura, Martinez, & Saenz, 2010). Even free and reduced-price college tuition programs are growing exponentially with over 280 programs across 42 states in just a few years (Perna & Leigh, 2018; see also Harris, 2013; Kelchen & Goldrick-Rab, 2014; Miller-Adams, 2009, 2015). Additionally, more school communities and districts are engaging in curricular reforms, enhanced student supports, data systems, and partnerships in order to improve students' postsecondary preparation and transitions (Burris & Wehlner, 2005; Burris, Wiley, Welner & Murphy, 2008; Chicago Public Schools, n.d.; Doughtery & Zavadsky, 2007; Duffy & Darwin, 2013; New York City Department of Educa-

Contemporary Perspectives on Social Capital in Educational Contexts,
pages 125–144.
125

tion, 2016; Stillisano, Brown, Alford & Waxman, 2013). These efforts are well-intentioned with significant shifts toward increasing postsecondary opportunities, but we cannot fail to use this opportunity to re-conceptualize postsecondary planning in order to meet the needs of students underrepresented in higher education.

There is an old adage that guards against putting *new wine in old wineskins*, suggesting that it is problematic to refashion old systems and processes to meet new and emerging trends. Our existing college and career readiness systems and processes are based upon archetypal connotations of college and career readiness that center the experiences of Whites, males, and the middle class (Hossler, Schmidt, & Vesper, 1999; Khan, 2012; Peshkin, 2001; Schneider & Stevenson, 1999). For generations, many individuals from traditionally underrepresented communities faced the stratified nature of our schools and communities such that many low-income families and families of color have not had opportunities to prepare for and transition to college, nor pass along comprehensive postsecondary planning information to their children (Enriquez, 2011; Farrington, 2014; Farmer-Hinton, 2002, 2008; Freeman, 2005; Griffin et al, 2007; Holland, 2014, 2017; Kiyama, 2010; Knight & Marciano, 2013; Perez & McDonough, 2008). These archetypal models also do not take into account the intersections of race, class, and gender, which must be prioritized in order for any genuine efforts to address the consistent disparities in postsecondary preparation and planning (Adelman, 2006; Crenshaw, 1991; Crenshaw, Ocen, & Nanda, 2015; Evans-Winters & Esposito, 2010; Farmer-Hinton, 2008, 2017; Freeman, 2005; M. Holland, 2019; Holland, 2017; Kiyama, 2010; Knight & Marciano, 2013; McDonough, 1997; Savitz-Romer & Bouffard, 2013).

Research has consistently demonstrated the importance of social capital, both school-based and otherwise, in postsecondary preparation and support. For example, the means of postsecondary preparation and planning include a reliance on students' social networks to provide exposure, norms, resources, and support (Farmer-Hinton, 2008; Farmer-Hinton & Holland, 2008; M. Holland, 2019; Holland 2010, 2011; Holland & Farmer-Hinton, 2009; Nagaoka, Farrington, Roderick, Allensworth, Keyes, Johnson & Beechum, 2013). We are also aware that, in general, students' postsecondary preparation and planning is not always culturally-relevant and gender-specific; does not always offer familiar ways of knowing and doing; and is not organized to help students "to safely navigate the potentially oppressive ecological aspects of neighborhood, community, school, and society, while reaping the benefits of those ecological aspects that are developmentally empowering" (Stanton-Salazar, 2011, p. 1078; see also Farmer-Hinton, 2011a, 2017; O'Connor, 2000; Roderick, Nagaoka, & Allensworth, 2006; Savitz-Romer & Bouffard, 2013).

Towards that end, we have taken our professional experiences as university faculty and postsecondary preparation researchers, combined with our lived experiences as college-educated African American women, to create a voluntary, college and career readiness after-school program for African American female students. The objective of this chapter is to share how we created and implemented a college and career readiness program, utilizing the tenets of social capital theory, yet also grounding our practices in cultural affirmations and gender empowerment. Specifically, based on a content analysis of our curriculum and activities from 2014–2017, we explore the ways in which our college and career readiness program informs what college for all can look like in the field.

BACKGROUND

According to social capital theory, schools are social networks where students have access to information, activities, and connections that aid in students' navigation of the educational system, particularly those resources that relate to postsecondary preparation and planning (Coleman, 1988; Lin, 2001; Portes, 1998; Stanton-Salazar, 2011; see also Farmer-Hinton, 2011a; Hill, 2008; Holland, 2010; Roderick et al., 2008). To prepare, students need information about career options, academic preparation, financial aid, and college choices. Due to the inextricable link between school quality and local wealth, these resources are not equally available nor equally accessible (Adelman, 2006; Enriquez, 2011; Farrington, 2014; Freeman, 2005; Griffin et al, 2007; Yun & Moreno, 2006). Yet, students from traditionally underrepresented college-going populations may be particularly reliant on their schools to provide such support if they do not live in communities where adults can provide postsecondary preparation and planning support (Farmer-Hinton, 2008; Gast, 2016; Holland, 2017; M. Holland, 2019; Tierney, Bailey, Constantine, Finkelstein, & Hurd, 2009; Vargas, 2004). Moreover, many students from traditionally disenfranchised populations in general, and African American females in particular, who desire to explore college and career options tend to receive conflicting information about their college bound selves and are not offered the necessary guidance toward an unencumbered pathway after high school (Evans-Winters & Esposito, 2010; Enriquez, 2011; Freeman, 2005; Holland, 2011,2014; M. Holland, 2019; Morris, 2007; O'Connor, 2000; Patton, 2009; Perez & McDonough, 2008).

Navigational Capital

In Yosso's (2005) Community Cultural Wealth Model, she conceptualizes navigational capital as capital that "acknowledges individual agency within institutional constraints, but it also connects to social networks that facilitate community navigation through places and spaces including schools, the job market and the health care and judicial systems" (p. 80). O'Connor (2000), for example, shared how African American girls with school-based support systems or "sponsors" were able to navigate both their school and community contexts (e.g., access to rigorous courses, high expectations for college degree completion, financing college), while the African American girls without such support expressed low expectations for completing college and shared the limited support received around academic skill sets and paying for college (see also Patton, 2009).

As African American female college professors and postsecondary preparation researchers, we are aware of the importance of the postsecondary preparatory content that needs to be shared with African American female students while acknowledging the context that has systematically alienated, marginalized, or ignored traditionally underrepresented college-going populations (Conley, 2005, 2011; Holland, 2017; Yosso, 2005). Crenshaw's (1991) work has helped us further critique the college and career preparation of African American girls and women within the larger structure of racial, class, and gender oppression. She writes:

> many of the experiences that Black women face are not subsumed within the traditional boundaries of race or gender discrimination as these boundaries are currently understood, and that the intersection of racism and sexism factors into Black women's lives in ways that cannot be captured wholly by looking at the race or gender dimensions of those experiences separately. (Crenshaw, 1991, p. 1244)

Our country's higher education system was built upon ideas of white and male supremacy. Preparation for and enrollment in college was shaped by students' race, gender, and social class memberships with elite, white males benefitting from a pipeline from high school to college based upon their and their families' socioeconomic status and networks (Armstrong, 1990; Cookson & Persell, 1985; Khan, 2012; Peshkin, 2001; Powell, 1996). As a result, our contemporary understanding of college and who deserves to go to college is rooted in pathways that were carved to mold elite and white males; these pathways are also embedded with "monocultural educational practices that reproduce social and economic power among the elite" (Farmer-Hinton, 2011a, p. 568; see also Armstrong, 1990; Cookson & Persell, 1985; Khan, 2012; Peshkin, 2001; Powell, 1996). Crenshaw's (1991) work forces us to question the creation and reproduction of such pathways, including the ways in which stereotypical femininity defines how African American girls should interact within their schools (see also Fordham, 1993). Evans-Winters and Esposito (2010) add that monolithic narratives about African American girls (i.e., loud, aggressive and sexual) are dangerous narratives. Morris (2007), for instance, showed how African American female students were disciplined and/or unfairly marginalized based upon their assertiveness and verbal expressions in classrooms such that some teachers preferred middle class and gendered-expressions of femininity (e.g., passivity, quiet mannerisms).

As African American female college professors and postsecondary preparation researchers, we are aware of how navigational capital is extended through our practices. When conceptualizing navigational capital, Yosso heartily cautions appropriate and informed practices so as to not reproduce processes that were "not created with communities of color in mind" (Yosso, 2005, p. 80). In a similar vein, Stanton-Salazar (2011) conceptualized "empowerment agents" to aid in the practice of creating supportive social networks that can help students to navigate pathways toward their intended destinations. He suggests that empowerment agents: a) possess a critical consciousness or ideology about unjust and inequitable structures, b) engage in practices that do not reproduce existing hierarchies within institutions, 3) teach students how to "decode" (p. 1092) and "cope" (p. 1093) within systems/structures; and 4) share "positional" (e.g., work or institution-related) and "personal" (e.g., non-work/institutional related) resources with students (p. 1094).

We understand that discriminatory policies and practices have led to the generational divestment of African American communities over time, leading to entire neighborhoods where adults have not had equal opportunities to pursue higher education (Farmer-Hinton, 2002, 2008). Farmer-Hinton (2008), for instance, shares a map of Chicago where residential segregation exists by college degree attainment with poorer communities of color having as few as 3 percent of adults with college degrees while more affluent communities had 33 percent and higher. While these disparities exist, it is also in these kinds of communities where families of color support higher education and where African American students have credited non-traditional resources and networks in their communities (e.g., places of worship, peers) as being instrumental in their college preparation and enrollment (Holland, 2011, 2014; Kiyama, 2010; Knight, 2003).

Most importantly, we understand how to be un-apologetic in our support of African American female students (see also Collins, 2000; Crenshaw et al., 2015; Dillard, 2016; Evans-Winters & Esposito, 2010; Pratt-Clarke, 2013). We see our role befitting Shirley Chisholm's mantra that "[s]ervice is the rent we pay for the privilege of living on this earth." In addition to shared personal paradigms about "giving back," we call attention to Ladson-Billings' (2006) critique of academics and researchers who have been too fixated on the "documentation of the inequalities and inadequacies" in U.S. schools and not fixated enough on providing schools and practitioners with relevant and culturally-informed research (p. 9). Therefore, with an understanding of cultural wealth, power and privilege, and structural inequalities, we engaged in this work to challenge archetypal practices and to pay restitution to our communities in the form of scholar service (see Farmer-Hinton, 2011b).

Postsecondary Preparation and An Ethic of Care

We, like others (e.g., Delpit, 1988; Ladson-Billings, 1994; Noddings, 1988; Valenzuela, 1999; Wilder, 1999), find it necessary to be mindful of not only *what* we teach, but *who* we teach and *how* we teach. Many traditionally disenfranchised students, (e.g., students of color, students from low socioeconomic backgrounds, students labeled academically "at-risk,"), attend academic institutions that marginalize or disregard their culture and communities; and/or, minimally acknowledge or ignore students' multifaceted identities (Enriquez, 2011; Freeman, 2005; Savitz-Romer & Bouffard, 2013; Valenzuela, 1999; Wilder, 1999). However, when collectively considering what we teach, who we teach, and how we teach there is potential for creating the foundation of culturally relevant teaching and learning contexts wherein students perceive that they are cared for; and, their families, communities, and histories are valued (Dee & Penner, 2017; Valenzuela, 1999; Wilder, 1999; Yosso, 2005). This ethic of care, which can be conceptualized institutionally and/or interpersonally, has been touted as a benefit within educational experiences. For instance, an ethic of care reflects "acts done out of love" wherein educators seek to know their students well; and, for whom practitioners create specific learning objectives while holding high expectations for students (Noddings, 1988).

Research has demonstrated that within teaching and learning an ethic of care can be manifested when organizational arrangements and institutional structures are intentionally put in place to facilitate interpersonal relationships, support academic rigor, and provide guidance for future success (Cassidy & Bates, 2005; Holland & Farmer-Hinton, 2009; Schussler & Collins, 2006; Stipek, 2006). Noddings (1988) indicates that these organizational and institutional goals can reflect an ethic of care through the meaningful allocation of time, physical space, and curricula. Students have been reported to not only be aware of the degree to which these organizational and institutional characteristics reflect an ethic of care, but they often demonstrate notable academic engagement and achievement when appropriate care has been taken to develop culturally relevant curricula and employ culturally relevant pedagogical practices that are aligned with the ways they live, learn, and think (Antrop-González & DeJesús, 2006; Dee & Penner, 2017; Freeman, 2005; Knight & Marciano, 2013; Savitz-Romer & Bouffard, 2013; Wilder, 1999). Further, it has been demonstrated that when schools are organized to provide postsecondary guidance for students from traditionally underrepresented college-going populations; and, this support is offered in a culturally responsive way, students are more inclined to engage with and benefit from school-based postsecondary preparation (Holland & Farmer-Hinton; 2009, Knight-Diop, 2010; Welton & Martinez, 2014).

It is important to note that neither institutional nor interpersonal school-based care matters if students do not perceive the relationship as caring (Valenzuela, 1999; Wilder, 1999). Research has demonstrated that students not only perceive certain environments as caring, but use those contexts to advance their academic careers (Antrop-González & DeJesús, 2006; Cassidy & Bates, 2005; Schussler & Collins, 2006). It is within caring school-based spaces and relationships that policies and practices can be implemented that reflect and support the lives of students; where personnel can get to know students well and appropriately engage and challenge them; and, where students are more likely to receive and accept guidance (Antrop-González & DeJesús, 2006; Cassidy & Bates, 2005; Knight-Diop, 2010; Noddings, 1988; Schussler & Collins, 2006).

Finally, we believe that the enactment of care has rippling effects. Noddings (1998) reminds us that schools are places that have been charged with helping to develop moral and ethical individuals; and, the enactment of care can provide a strong foundation for this endeavor. She indicates that schools should not only teach students to receive care, but to enact it. Others have addressed how this approach can demonstrate the nuances of changing perspectives and empowering youth within oppressive contexts (Cassidy & Bates, 2005; Dillard, 2016; Stanton-Salazar, 2011). Stanton-Salazar (2011) argues that *empowerment agents* should not just provide students with educational richness and options, but they should also encourage students to transform lives and communities. He believes that *empowerment agents* offer students a vision for what youth can do that extends beyond what the youth may be able to envision for themselves. Further, educators, administrators, and policy makers who enact care in their professional work may not only be demonstrating an interest in students, their culture and communities; but, they may also be acknowledging that there needs to be a shift in understanding and appreciating how students arrive to and engage with postsecondary preparation and planning (Enriquez, 2011; Holland, 2017; Kiyama, 2010; Yosso, 2005).

TODAY'S DREAMS, TOMORROW'S REALITIES

We implemented a three-year, college and career readiness program from 2014–2017 called *Today's Dreams, Tomorrow's Realities*. We partnered with a small, public, urban high school and offered free, college preparatory sessions every other week for 1.5 hours on the day the school had early dismissal. Students who participated in the program did so on a voluntary basis and were not required to make any attendance commitments. Because this was a three-year project, we targeted the school's sophomore students. We solicited student participation from 10th grade students by way of school announcements, the distribution of written communications, word of mouth, and invitations mailed to the families of the entire sophomore class. When our program began, there were about 70 students enrolled in the sophomore class at our partner school. Throughout the three years of the program, twenty-nine young women submitted the requisite student and parent/guardian consent, and had some involvement with the program.

Our program emphasized three overarching areas: academic support, college knowledge, and career awareness (see Figure 8.1). Additionally, our approach included multiple forms of exposure to postsecondary preparatory resources and time-on-task with postsecondary preparatory activities. Our program offered intensive and focused dissemination of this type of information, spanning over three years. By offering regular opportunities to use and apply this information, our program was designed to inform students' postsecondary knowledge, preparation, and choice. A major element of the program was to give students a significant amount of time to develop critical thinking skills and habitual behaviors associated with postsecondary preparation and planning. *Today's Dreams, Tomorrow's Realities* is distinctive because through our program's consistent exposure to and association with African American female speakers and volunteers, we also modeled the importance of our students sharing information with other women and girls of color when they become adults.

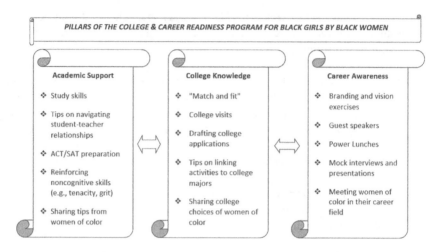

FIGURE 8.1. An illustration of our model for Today's Dreams, Tomorrow's Realities

The objective of this chapter is to share how we created and implemented *Today's Dreams, Tomorrow's Realities* by utilizing the tenets of social capital theory, and also grounding our practices in cultural affirmations and gender empowerment. Specifically, we analyzed our curriculum and activities from 2014–2017 to explore the ways in which our college and career readiness program informs the *college for all* era. In order to conduct our content analysis (see Berg, 2001), we compiled, read, and reviewed the following materials: the biweekly session objectives (including the content covered and skills that were addressed), session scripts that guided how we communicated the content to the students, handouts that the students were asked to complete, descriptions of the class activities and the directors' field notes. As part of our analytical process, we categorized and coded the content then reflected upon the extent to which our analysis revealed patterns. The discussion that follows includes how these patterns illustrated navigational capital (e.g., content and activities related to college match and fit, financial planning, career exposure, branding, cultural and gender representation) and an ethic of care (e.g., content and activities related to culturally relevant pedagogy, communication, relationship building, program management).[1]

Navigating Dreams

On the first day of the program, we established important criteria in preparing students for college and careers: define your passions and dreams. Self-defining passions and dreams was core to our program because African American female students are rarely given the time, space, and resources to do so (Crenshaw, 1991; Crenshaw, Ocen, & Nanda, 2015; Evans-Winters & Esposito, 2010; Pratt-Clarke, 2013). Our students were given the time and space to list, express, and share every dream they ever had from the impractical (e.g., fairy) to the practical (e.g., psychologist). We entertained all possibilities and probed the students for their reasons for wanting a particular career. Over the course of the first year of the program, we used the curriculum, handouts, and activities to help students continue to refine and solidify those dreams. For instance, we talked to students about how they envisioned themselves and asked them to complete activities related to their "brand." The branding exercises were designed for students to analyze their dreams in the context of their current and potential selves. We asked them how they would market themselves on college and/or job applications. What skills did they need? What skills did they have? What skills did they need to develop? We brainstormed with the students about activities in which they could participate and behaviors they could employ to reach their dreams such as volunteerism, leadership, internships, and social action. We helped them think about these experiences in terms of the passions they currently held, the communities with which they were involved, and the activities they were already doing. These branding exercises were aligned with another activity that asked the students to complete a blank college application. There were two major goals for this "college application" activity. The first was to make the students familiar with the multiple aspects of college applications and the types of information that applications generally sought. The second objective was for our participants to be able to self-identify what types of gaps, if any, they would have if they had to submit their applications in the tenth grade. We hoped that this low-stakes, self-evaluative activity would help shape the conversations with our students regarding what types of dispositions, skills, and behaviors they each needed to consider developing as they prepared for college.

We also recognized that, whether students understand it or not, preparing for, enrolling in, and graduating from college is a collaborative process. Towards that end, during the first-year of the program we began having our students think about their college preparatory and enrollment "Dream Team." Most of the students listed their parents and guardians, but after that, the list was less predictable. They began to randomly list people without clear or meaningful reasons. Throughout the remainder of the year, students were asked to interview three adults in their lives: a parent/guardian, a faculty or staff member from their school, and a mentor (or a person in the career that they wanted to pursue). We provided students with an interview protocol that addressed what those adults saw as the student's strengths and what they saw as an area in which the student could develop; where those adults saw the student attending college and why; and, what kind of career the adults thought would suit the student. After the students completed the interviews we provided them opportunities to discuss what they learned. This was another way in which we encouraged the students to be reflective and self-evaluative regarding what they needed to do in order to prepare for college. We revisited the students' Dream Teams throughout the three years of the program and we noted how their criteria for inclusion, as well as the members on the list changed, as the students became more versed in the relevance of their team. We were also surprised and flattered to find out that we were frequently included in various students' lists.

We knew that it may be difficult for 15 year-old students to see themselves as college and career women, so we tried to ease them into thinking about the next phases of their lives.

For example, we shared the biographies of two African American women (Michelle Obama and Oprah Winfrey). Yet, we only shared what these women had accomplished by age 25 in order to reinforce that, even at age 15, the students in our program should be making important choices daily. By the spring of the first year of the program, we asked our students to prepare and present an aspirational autobiography to our invited guest during one designated session. The invited guests were two African American women who had professional experience with college admissions. The aspirational autobiographies were based on a template which allowed students to imagine who they saw themselves as at the age of 25. They were required to consider their anticipated academic achievements, career accomplishments, and community service involvement. We used this activity to help the students see their future selves and begin to use some of the program activities to help them determine what steps they needed to take to achieve their goals. By coaching students through the aspirational autobiography assignment, we were able to have pointed conversations about how to seek support among adults and, we were able to teach writing skills such as how to use evidence to back up claims.

By year two (11th grade), these activities continued, but with more depth. We noticed that our relationships with the students were getting stronger; and, this was noteworthy because our partner school had experienced notable turnover in personnel and many of the students were surprised when we returned to continue working with them. In our field notes, one of us expressed the need for a session on "navigating nonsense." We learned how little the students' visions/ dreams were being supported by the adults around them. During the second year of our program, we had students complete career inventories because they were vacillating among their initial career choices to random and un-related careers due to familial pressures or well-meaning adults. The online inventory tool compiled students' interests and passions then provided three overarching categories of career fields with sample jobs included. We linked this output with weblinks for summer enrichment programs that they could pursue and we offered program time to apply for such programs. We used our program to highlight the students' value and let them know that we believed in them. For example, in one of our field notes, we documented this interaction with a participant: "You see hopeless options for college. I see a great candidate who can contribute to campus." Our students were discouraged that others would believe that their high school was not of the same quality as other schools and that, maybe, they were not be as bright as students from other schools; we helped them to navigate these perceptions to see their unique value and adjust their thinking.

Navigating Actions

In years two and three, we devoted more time explaining and demystifying the essential elements of branding (leadership, extracurricular activities, community involvement, and more); we used these elements as a theme for the sessions occurring in each month. Part of navigational capital is decoding, as Stanton-Salazar (2011) noted. For example, we placed value on and decoded how students who volunteered within their religious communities gained essential skills. We spent time sharing how to link these "branding" elements to participation in local programs like summer jobs and college enrichment programs. We had the students use the school's laptops to search for and apply to internship and summer enrichment opportunities during our sessions.

In addition to lectures and conversations on branding, we helped students navigate the college search and choice process. We found it important to expose students to different types of colleges through college visits, electronic databases, and college comparison exercises. As college professors who research college access issues, we shared our "positional" and "personal" resources with students (Stanton-Salazar, 2011, p. 1094). What appeared to be most useful was clarifying *match and fit* for students (Roderick et al., 2011). Using highly personalized strategies, we helped students decipher colleges' marketing efforts so our students would stay focused on the academic and social support systems that they individually required.

During senior year, our sessions were highly hands-on as students experienced the pressure of taking actions. In addition to general decision-making pressures that college-bound youth have, our students faced additional pressures from a required senior-year course that mandated all students apply to a set number of colleges by a certain date for a passing grade (note that the school was solidifying its reputation in having 100 percent college acceptances). We helped our students navigate this pressure by continuing to humanize the college search and choice process. We continued to provide personalized supports, anchored in their dreams and aspirations from their sophomore and junior years, instead of rudimentary checklists and benchmarks. As students received their acceptances, our work continued into our College 101 sessions about how to navigate college contexts (e.g., time management, self-advocacy, formal and informal campus support systems, study skills, writing skills) and their finances (e.g., money management, cost saving measures).

Creating A College and Career Readiness Program as An Act of Care

When we began this project, we called upon our professional knowledge and skills as university professors and researchers, but it only took one session for us to realize how personal this work was. The personal nature of the work was not because we saw ourselves in these students (although at times we did), but because we SAW our students (Cassidy & Bates, 2005; Freeman, 2005; Wilder, 1999; Yosso, 2005). We saw their ambitions, we saw their strength, we saw their skill sets, and we saw their struggles. From the first time we met the students in the program, they became "our girls," and we knew that we had to approach this endeavor with an ethic of care.

Noddings (1988) has suggested that one indication of the ethic of care is the meaningful allocation of time and space. As visitors to the school we had to negotiate where our program would meet on a semi-regularly basis; and, our time was often adjusted based on the needs of our partner school. While we understood how precious the resources of time and space were, we also recognized that our participants needed a space that was designated for our program. We needed a clearly delineated place where our students could easily find the program meetings. We needed a safe space where our participants could share a meal, decompress from the day, and prepare for their postsecondary lives. We bartered a deal with one teacher to use his room on the days our program was scheduled to meet. We also purchased a large sign, with the name of the program, that we placed outside of the classroom before our sessions began. Students became accustomed to seeing the sign and knowing that was an indication of where we were going to meet. In addition, one of the two program directors would stand in the hall after the final bell of the day and greet students who were a part of the program and invite others to join us. Meanwhile, the other program director would be inside the classroom with the students who arrived early preparing the room and setting up lunch for the session. Soon after these rituals were in place, the added greeting of a hug between the directors and students began. These exchanges were not out of obligation, but seemed to be a sign that we were all happy to be there.

There are a couple of aspects of establishing these routines that revealed students' perceptions of care. One of the first things that we noticed is that students would often look for and comment on seeing the program's sign. Well into the first year of the program, after we had established our designated meeting times and place, various students would comment that they would "look for the sign to know [we] were there." This seemed very important to them since we were not staffed at the school and they wanted some assurance of our presence.

Another indication of the perception of care for the program was the students' mere participation. As previously noted, we offered a volunteer program on the days our partner school had early dismissal. Many students in the school used that time to participate in "fun" afterschool events, seek employment opportunities, or simply enjoy some leisure time; yet, thirteen students were consistently commitment to the program over time. Further, students were not shy in mentioning that they were sharing this valuable time with us. Additionally, they would periodically question why we did not meet more regularly or for longer periods of time. When the school would observe school or holiday breaks, we would give the students a week to re-acclimate themselves to the school schedule before we resumed our program activities. By the second year of the program, we would receive light-hearted, electronic messages regarding when we would return, when the program would resume, and why it was taking so long.

Beyond our determination to secure a meeting space and create a warm and welcoming atmosphere, our care for our participants and program was reflected in the time we dedicated to creating a female empowering, culturally relevant curriculum that reflected our knowledge of the students (Evans-Winters & Esposito, 2010; Ladson-Billings, 1994; Noddings, 1988; Pratt-Clarke, 2013; Valenzuela, 1999; Wilder, 1999; Yosso, 2005). At the beginning of each school year, we developed a syllabus based on the college preparatory content that we wanted to cover. Yet, at the end of every session we learned something new about the students, their families, or some experiences they had in school and we identified some way to tweak the curriculum to more closely align with our students' experiences. For instance, when a few young women in the program indicated that they were interested in learning more about social work, we identified an African American, female, social worker to come to a session and speak to our students. However, this experience was not unique. As a matter of fact, the bulk of the first-year curriculum included inviting professional women of color to share their academic and professional trajectories with our participants. In addition to our invited guests, students in the program were expected to learn about successful historical and contemporary African American women in the professions they wanted to pursue. Beyond, the culturally relevant aspects of the curriculum, we also were responsive to the students' college preparatory needs. For instance, when students informed us that they did not get enough time to prepare their personal statements or study for the ACT, we incorporated those activities into subsequent sessions or extended the time that we allocated for those activities.

As program directors we also began to sense what our students needed, even when they did not ask. We would recognize when experiences within the school or activities associated with the program were becoming too overwhelming. We would either slow down the pace or explicitly ask the students what they needed. During our sessions we had "sister circle" time wherein students could share anything they wanted, in any way they wanted. The only criteria that we had were that, as a group, we would respectfully and constructively brainstorm about how to address the issues presented. However, sometimes our students were not able to clearly identify their concerns, but based on our knowledge of the students' lives, both in and outside of school, we were able to address various issues. An example of this occurred during the second year of the program when we noticed "collective burnout." We decided to have a session on time management and how to address multiple responsibilities.

We believe that our students' responses to the program curriculum revealed their recognition of the care we took to provide meaningful, culturally relevant and empowering opportunities. For instance, students were often shy when they met the professional career women of color who we invited to our sessions; however, once the guests would leave the students would reflect on what they learned and how it related to aspects of our program. It was not uncommon for students to ask if our invited guests could serve as their mentors or be members of their dream teams. In addition, we recognized that our students were committed to learning about information and skills that would prepare them for postsecondary life; however, it was their application of the information and skills that exemplified their appreciation for the work of the program. For instance, during the students' senior year we would offer them advice about how to organize and present their personal statements. We frequently required many revisions of their work (beyond what our partner school required). One student jokingly exclaimed that we were making them work too hard, but she said that she knew it was because we loved them. It was during these types of moments that we knew that the students recognized the care with which our program was administered.

CONCLUSION

As researcher-practitioners, we were very clear why Martin Luther King (1967) said there is a possibility for "freedom and famine at the same time." In other words, our *college for all* era suggests that all students are free to traverse their educational pathways of their own free will. However, per the metaphor, there are so many postsecondary preparatory and planning experiences that can keep students from the opportunity to fully participate in the *college for all* era. As university faculty and postsecondary preparation researchers, we shared our experiences because we were uniquely positioned with a purview into what postsecondary planning and support could become.

Our partner school was a *100 percent college acceptance*-leaning school. The school used tools such as a set number of mandatory college applications for all graduating seniors. These sort of *checklist* methods are benign in many ways. For example, yes, it is valuable for students to complete a college application and, yes, completing a college application may lead students to apply to and enroll in college. However, we wanted to explore a fuller extent of how social capital could expended. We wanted to construct a context where students were having cumulative conversations and resourceful interactions linking college knowledge to students' career aspirations and choices. The inherent assumption is that students have these conversations. The reality is that students do not often receive timely information and resources—at home or at school—that is fully integrated into postsecondary planning in meaningful or cumulative ways.

For this chapter, we wanted to share how utilizing social capital as a frame led to instances of navigational capital and an ethic of care. As African American female professors who have spent many years conducting research on college and career preparation, we were aware of the postsecondary preparatory content that needed to be shared while acknowledging the contexts that systematically alienate, marginalize, or ignore underrepresented college-going populations (Conley, 2005, 2010; Holland, 2017; Yosso, 2005). Therefore, we used care and navigational capital to disrupt the archetypal influences and socio-structural inequalities that can impact transitions for young women who are/were navigating their own postsecondary pathways. Our program is on-going; we will continue to help our students until they matriculate through their sophomore year in college. Yet, the lessons we have learned thus far are important for the college for all era and include: constructing networks of support to guide students through inconsistent messaging and systemic barriers; using time, space, and relationship-building toward individualized supports and vision-setting; and demystifying the archetype of social mobility where supports systems are masked and hidden.

NOTE

1. We are aware that most care theorists require some acknowledgment from the "cared for" to determine the impact of the context of care. Although we never explicitly asked our students to reflect on the degree to which they believed we cared for them, we took notice of their words and behaviors as they related to us and the program. These responses were often recorded in our field notes and/or addressed in the directors' program/project meetings and discussions; thus, this analysis includes the program directors' interpretations of the program participants' words and behaviors as they relate to a context of care.

ACKNOWLEDGEMENT

This work was supported by the Hymen Milgrom Supporting Organization (HMSO), which funds Successful Pathways from School to Work research.

REFERENCES

Adelman, C. (2006). *The toolbox revisited: Paths to degree completion from high school through college.* U.S. Department of Education. Washington, DC: Office of Educational Research and Improvement.

Allensworth, E. M., Nomi, T., Montgomery, N., & Lee, V.E. (2009). College preparatory curriculum for all: Academic consequences of requiring Algebra and English I for ninth graders in Chicago. *Educational Evaluation and Policy Analysis, 31*(4), 367–391.

Antrop-González, R., & DeJesús, A. (2006). Toward a theory of critical care in urban small school reform: Examining structures and pedagogies of caring in two Latino community-based schools. *International Journal of Qualitative Studies in Education (QSE), 19*(4), 409–433.

Armstrong, C. F. (1990). On the making of good men: Character-building in the New England boarding schools. In P. W. Kingston & L. S. Lewis (Eds.), *The high status track: Studies of elite schools and stratification* (pp. 3–24). Albany, NY: SUNY Press.

Berg, B. L. (2001). *Qualitative research methods for the social sciences.* New York, NY: Allyn and Bacon.

Burris, C. C., & Welner, K. G. (2005). Closing the achievement gap by detracking. *Phi Delta Kappan, 86*(8), 594–598.

Burris, C. C., Wiley, E., Welner, K. G. & Murphy, J. (2008). Accountability, rigor, and detracking: Achievement effects of embracing a challenging curriculum as a universal good for all students. *Teachers College Record, 110*(3), 571–608.

Cabrera, A. F., & La Nasa, S. M. (2000a). Understanding the college-choice process. In A. F. Cabrera & S. M. La Nasa (Eds.), *Understanding the college choice of disadvantaged students* (pp. 5–22). San Francisco, CA: Jossey-Bass Publishers.

Cabrera, A. F., & La Nasa, S. M. (2000b). Three critical tasks America's disadvantaged face on their path to college. In A. F. Cabrera & S. M. La Nasa (Eds.), *Understanding the college choice of disadvantaged students* (pp. 23–43). San Francisco, CA: Jossey-Bass Publishers.

Cassidy, W., & Bates, A. (2005). "Drop-outs" and "push-outs": Finding hope at a school that actualizes the ethic of care. *American Journal of Education, 112*(1), 66–102.

Chicago Public Schools (n.d.). *Learn. Plan. Succeed.* Retrieved from https://cps.edu/careers/Pages/learnplansucceed.aspx

Coleman, J. S. (1988). Social capital in the creation of human capital. *American Journal of Sociology, 94*, S95–120.

Collins, P. H. (2000). *Black feminist thought.* New York, NY: Routlege.

Conley, D. T. (2005). *College knowledge: What it really takes for students to succeed and what we can do to get them ready.* San Francisco, CA: Jossey-Bass.

Conley, D. T. (2007). *Redefining college readiness, Volume 3.* Eugene, OR: Educational Policy Improvement Center.

Conley, D. T. (2011). Building on the common core. *Educational Leadership, 68*(6), 16–20.

Cookson, P. W., & Persell, C. H. (1985). *Preparing for power: America's elite boarding schools.* New York, NY: Basic Books.

Crenshaw, K. (1991). Mapping the margins: Intersectionality, identity politics, and violence against women of color. *Stanford Law Review, 43*(6), 1241–1299.

Crenshaw, K., Ocen, P., & Nanda, J. (2015). *Black girls matter: Pushed out, overpoliced, and unprotected.* New York, NY: Center for Intersectionality and Social Policy Studies.

Dee, T. S. & Penner, E. K., 2017. The causal effects of cultural relevance evidence from an ethnic studies curriculum. *American Educational Research Journal, 54*(1), 127–166.

Delpit, L. D. (1988). *Other people's children: Cultural conflict in the classroom.* New York, NY: New Press.

Dillard, C. B. (2016). Turning the ships around: A case study of (re)membering as transnational endarkened feminist inquiry and praxis for Black teachers. *Educational Studies, 52*(5), 406–423.

Doughtery, C., & Zavadsky, H. (2007). Giving all students the keys to college and skilled careers: One district's approach. *Phi Delta Kappan, 89*,194–199.

Duffy, H., & Darwin, M. (2013). *The district role in supporting college and career readiness for students: Perspectives from Long Beach, Albuquerque, and Philadelphia.* Washington, DC: American Institutes for Research.

Enriquez, L. E. (2011). "Because we feel the pressure and we also feel the support": Examining the educational success of undocumented immigrant Latina/o students, *Harvard Educational Review, 81*(3), 476–500.

Evans-Winters, V., & Esposito, J. (2010). Other people's daughters: Critical race feminism and Black girls' education. *Educational Foundations,* (Winter-Spring), 11–24.

Farrington, C. A. (2014). *Failing at school: Lessons for redesigning urban high schools.* New York, NY: Teachers College Press.

Farmer-Hinton, R. (2002). The Chicago context: Understanding the consequences of urban processes on school capacity. *Journal of Negro Education, 71*(4), 313–330.

Farmer-Hinton, R. (2008). Social capital and college planning: Students of color using school networks for support and guidance. *Education and Urban Society, 41*(1), 127–157.

Farmer-Hinton, R. (2011a). On being college prep: Examining the implementation of a "college for all" mission in an urban charter school. *The Urban Review, 43*(5), 567–596.

Farmer-Hinton, R. (2011b). Service and scholarship: How opportunities to "give back" foster culturally responsive and respectful research projects. In K. Scott & W. Blanchett (Eds.), *Research in urban educational settings: Lessons learned and implications for future practice* (pp. 145–162). Charlotte, NC: Information Age Publishing.

Farmer-Hinton, R. (2017). Going to college: Why Black Lives Matter too. *Journal of Educational Controversy, 12*(1), 9.

Farmer-Hinton, R. L., & Holland, N. E. (2008). The influence of high school size on access to postsecondary information, conversations, and activities. *American Secondary Education*, 41–61.

Farmer-Hinton R., & Rifelj K. K. (2018). Clearing clogs in the pipeline: College readiness for all in Chicago and Milwaukee. In C. Alfeld, B. Smerdon, & K. Kim (Eds.), *Career and college readiness and success for all students: What do we know and how do we measure it?* (pp. 5–31). Charlotte, NC: Information Age Publishing.

Freeman, K. (2005). *African Americans and college choice: The influence of family and school.* New York, NY: State University of New York Press.

Gast, M. J. (2016). 'You're supposed to help me' The perils of mass counseling norms for working-class black students. *Urban Education,* 1–27.

Griffin, K. A., Allen, W. R., Kimura-Walsh, E., & Yamamura, E. K. (2007). Those who left, those who stayed: Exploring the educational opportunities of high achieving Black and Latino/a students at magnet and nonmagnet Los Angeles high schools (2001–2002). *Educational Studies, 42*(3), 229–247.

Harris, D. (2013). Is traditional college financial aid too little, too late to help youth succeed in college? An introduction to The Degree Project promise scholarship experiment. *New Directions in Youth Development, 140*, 99–116.

Hill, L. (2008). School strategies and the "college-linking" process: Reconsidering the effects of high schools on college enrollment. *Sociology of Education, 81*, 53–76.

Holland, M. M. (2019). *Divergent paths to college: Race, class, and inequality in high schools.* New Brunswick, NJ: Rutgers University Press.

Holland, N. E. (2010). Postsecondary education preparation of traditionally underrepresented college students: A social capital perspective. *Journal of Diversity in Higher Education, 3*(2), 111–125.

Holland, N. E. (2011). The power of peers: Influences on postsecondary education planning and experiences of African American students. *Urban Education, 46*(5), 1029–1055.

Holland, N. E. (2014). Partnering with a higher power: Academic engagement, religiosity, and spirituality of African American urban youth. *Education and Urban Society.* First published on April 15, 2014, doi:10.1177/0013124514530153

Holland, N. E., (2017). Beyond conventional wisdom: Community cultural wealth and the college knowledge of African American youth in the United States. *Race, Ethnicity, and Education, 20*(6), 796–810.

Holland, N. E., & Farmer-Hinton, R. (2009). Leave no schools behind: The importance of a college culture in urban public high schools. *The High School Journal, 92*(3), 24–43.

Hooker, S., & Brand. B. (2009). *Success at every step: How 23 programs support youth on the path to college and beyond.* Washington, DC: American Youth Policy Forum.

Hossler, D., Schmit, J., & Vesper, N. (1999). *Going to college: How social, economic, and educational factors influence the decisions students make.* Baltimore, MD: The Johns Hopkins University Press.

Kelchen, R., & Goldrick-Rab, S. (2014). *Accelerating college knowledge: A fiscal analysis of a targeted early commitment Pell Grant program.* Retrieved July 1, 2014 from http://www.finaidstudy.org/documents/Accelerating%20College%20Knowledge%20Accepted%20Version%20Kelchen%20Goldrick-Rab.pdf

Kerby, S. (2012). *The state of Women of Color in the United States: Although they've made it this far, many barriers remain for this growing population.* Washington, DC: Center for American Progress.

Khan, S. R. (2012). *Privilege: The making of an adolescent elite at St. Paul's School.* Princeton, NJ: Princeton University Press.

Kiyama, J.M. (2010). College aspirations and limitations: The role of educational ideologies and funds of knowledge in Mexican American families. *American Educational Research Journal, 47*(2), 330–356.

Knight-Diop, M. G. (2010). Closing the gap: Enacting care and facilitating Black students' educational access in the creation of a high school college-going culture. *Journal of Education for Students Placed at Risk, 15*(1–2), 158–172.

Knight, M. G. (2003). Through urban youth's eyes: Negotiating K–16 policies, practices, and their futures. *Educational Policy, 17*(5), 531–557.

Knight, M. G., & Marciano, J. E. (2013). *College-ready: Preparing Black and Latina/o youth for higher education—A culturally relevant approach.* New York, NY: Teachers College Press.

Ladson-Billings, G. (1994). *The dreamkeepers: Successful teachers of African American children.* San Francisco, CA: Jossey-Bass.

Ladson-Billings, G. J. (2006). From the achievement gap to the education debt: Understanding achievement in U.S. schools. *Educational Researcher, 35*(7), 3–12.

Lin, N. (2001). *Social capital: A theory of social structure and action.* Cambridge, UK: Cambridge University Press.

Lobosco, K. (September 18, 2015). *Tennessee is picking up the tab for community college students.* Retrieved from http://money.cnn.com/2015/09/18/pf/college/free-community-collegetennessee/?iid=EL

Lobosco, K. (May 11, 2017). *Tennessee makes community college free for all adults.* Retrieved from http://money.cnn.com/2017/05/11/pf/college/tennessee-free-community-college/index.html

Lowery, G., & Hoyler, M. (2009). *Expanding college access and success: The Chicago model*. Washington, DC: Council for Opportunity in Education.

McClafferty, K. A., McDonough, P. M., & Nunez, A. M. (2002, April). *What is a college culture? Facilitating college preparation through organizational change*. Paper presented at the Annual Meeting of the American Educational Research Association, New Orleans, LA.

McDonough, P. M. (1997). *Choosing colleges: How social class and schools structure opportunity*. Albany, NY: State University of New York Press.

Miller-Adams, M. (2009). *The Power of a Promise*. Kalamazoo, MI: W.E. Upjohn Institute.

Miller-Adams, M. (2015). *Promise nation: Transforming communities through place-based scholarships*. Kalamazoo, MI: W.E. Upjohn Institute.

Milner, H. R. (2007). Race, culture, and researcher positionality: Working through dangers seen, unseen, and unforeseen. *Educational Researcher, 36*(7), 388–400.

Morris, E. W. (2007). "Ladies" or "loudies"? Perceptions and experiences of Black girls in classrooms. *Youth & Society, 38*(4), 490–515.

Mulhere, K. (July 5, 2017). *All the places in the U.S. where you can go to college for free*. Retrieved from http://time.com/money/4830367/free-college-tuition-promise-programs/

Nagaoka, J., Farrington, C. A., Roderick, M., Allensworth, E., Keyes, T. S., Johnson, D. W., & Beechum, N. O. (2013). *Readiness for college: The role of noncognitive factors and context*. Chicago, IL: Consortium on Chicago School Research.

New York City Department of Education (2016). *Chancellor Farina announces first 100 high schools to implement college access for all in 2016–17*. Retrieved October 15, 2016 from http://schools.nyc.gov/Offices/mediarelations/NewsandSpeeches/2015-2016/College+Access+for+All+-+High+School.htm

Noddings, N. (1988). An ethic of caring and its implications for instructional arrangements. *American Journal of Education, 96*(2), 215–30.

O'Connor, C. (2000). Dreamkeeping in the inner city: Diminishing the divide between aspirations and expectations. In S. Danziger & A. C. Lin (Eds.), *Coping with poverty: The social contexts of neighborhood, work, and family in the African American community* (pp. 105–140). Ann Arbor, MI: University of Michigan Press.

Patton, L. D. (2009). My sister's keeper: A qualitative examination of mentoring experiences among African American women in graduate and professional schools. *Journal of Higher Education, 80*(5), 510–537.

Perna, L. W., & Leigh, E. W. (2018). Understanding the promise: A typology of state and local college promise programs. *Educational Researcher, 47*(3),155–180.

Perez, P. A. and McDonough, P. M. (2008). Understanding Latina and Latino college choice: A social capital and chain migration analysis, *Journal of Hispanic Higher Education 7*(3), 249–265.

Peshkin, A. (2001). *Permissible advantage? The moral consequences of elite schooling*. Mahwah, NJ: Lawrence Erlbaum Associates.

Portes, A. (1998). Social capital: Its origins and applications in modern sociology. *Annual Review of Sociology, 24*, 1–24.

Powell, A. G. (1996). *Lessons from privilege: The American prep school tradition*. Cambridge, MA: Harvard University Press.

Pratt-Clarke, M. (2013). A radical reconstruction of resistance strategies: Black girls and Black women reclaiming our power using Transdisciplinary Applied Social Justice©, ma'at, and rites of passage. *Journal of African American Studies, 17*(1), 99–114.

Roderick, M., Coca, V., & Nagaoka, J. (2011). Potholes on the road to college: High school effects in shaping urban students' participation in college application, four-year college enrollment, and college match. *Sociology of Education, 84*(3), 178–211.

Roderick, M., Nagaoka, J., & Allensworth, E. (2006). *From high school to the future: A first look at Chicago Public School graduates' college enrollment, college preparation, and graduation from four-year colleges.* Chicago, IL: Consortium on Chicago School Research.

Roderick, M., Nagaoka, J. , Coca, V., & Moeller, E. With Roddie, K., Gilliam, J. & Patton, D. (2008). *From high school to the future: Potholes on the road to college.* Chicago, IL: Consortium on Chicago School Research.

Savitz-Romer, M., & Bouffard, S. M. (2013). *Ready, willing, and able: Developmental approach to college access and success.* Cambridge, MA: Harvard Education Press.

Savitz-Romer, M., Bouffard, S., Schussler, D. L., & Collins, A. (2006). An empirical exploration of the who, what, and how of school care. *Teachers College Record, 108*(7), 1460–1495.

Schneider, B. & Stevenson, D. (1999). *The ambitious generation: America's teenagers motivated but directionless.* New Haven, CT: Yale University Press.

Stanton-Salazar, R. (2011). A social capital framework for the study of institutional agents and their role in the empowerment of low status students and youth. *Youth and Society, 43*(3), 1066–1109.

Stillisano, J., Brown, D. B., Alford, B. L., & Waxman, H. C. (2013). The effects of GO Centers on creating a college culture in urban high schools in Texas. *High School Journal, 96*(4), 283–301.

Stipek, D. (2006). Relationships matter. *Educational Leadership, 64*(1), 46–49.

Tierney, W. G., Bailey, T., Constantine, J., Finkelstein, N., & Hurd, N. F. (2009). *Helping students navigate the path to college: What high schools can do: A practice guide* (NCEE #2009-4066). Washington, DC: U.S. Department of Education.

Tillman, L. C. (2002). Culturally sensitive research approaches: An African-American perspective. *Educational Researcher, 31*(9), 3–12.

Valenzuela, A. (1999). *Subtractive schooling: U.S.—Mexican Youth and the politics of caring.* Albany, NY: State University of New York Press.

Welton, A. D., & Martinez, M. A. (2014). Coloring the college pathway: A more culturally responsive approach to college readiness and access for students of color in secondary schools. *Urban Review, 46*(2), 197–223.

Wilder, M. (1999). Culture, race, and schooling: Toward a non-color-blind ethic of care. *The Educational Forum, 63*(4), 356–362.

Vargas, J. H. (2004). *College knowledge: Addressing information barriers to college.* Boston, MA: The Education Resource Institute (TERI).

Yamamura, E. K., Martinez, M. A., & Saenz, V. B. (2010). Moving beyond high school expectations: Examining stakeholders' responsibility for increasing Latina/o students' college readiness. *The High School Journal, 93*(3), 126–148.

Yosso, T. (2005). Whose culture has capital?: A critical race theory discussion of community cultural wealth. *Race, Ethnicity and Education, 8*(1), 69–91.

Yun, J. T. & Moreno, J. F. (2006). College access, K–12 concentrated disadvantage, and the next 25 years of education research. *Educational Researcher, 35*(1), 12–19.

CHAPTER 9

NÓS POR NÓS (US FOR US)

Black Brazilian University
Students and Social Capital

Jeana E. Morrison

INTRODUCTION

The face of students attending higher education is rapidly changing as access to institutions has increased all over the world (Altbach, 2010). Research aptly shows that the massification of post-secondary systems brings with it the necessity to cater to diverse populations who have varying needs and may require support that differs from traditional attendees (Delgado Bernal, 2002; Heringer, 2013; Penha-Lopes, 2008; Perna, 2007; Schwartzman, 2008, 2009; Trow, 1973). Despite global expansion and internationalization of higher education, it is still an elite system that reproduces challenges for students from marginalized or underrepresented segments of society (Schwartzman, 2004). Brazil in particular is characterized by its extreme exclusion of Black, Brown, and Indigenous[1] students

---

[1] I capitalize racial terms to signify their importance as whole group identifiers that signify particular cultural norms, traditions, and ways of being. I use Black interchangeably with Afro-Brazilian. The Institute of Brazilian Geography and Statistics considers Indigenous an official category of race.

Contemporary Perspectives on Social Capital in Educational Contexts,
pages 145–157.

and a more recent use of affirmative action to increase access to these populations (Heringer, 2015). Despite the uptick in the number of underrepresented students, there is room for improvement especially because African descendants make up 50.7% of the population (IBGE, 2010). As such, students feel unsupported, distanced from white students in terms of knowledge and understanding of the post-secondary environment, and left to their own devices to gain information and pass it along to each other.

Paying attention to minoritized students can be telling for policy analysis, faculty and administrators. It can give keen insight on what is needed for marginalized populations to succeed academically, socially, and emotionally in predominately White spaces such as higher education. Furthermore, examining students with the mindset that they have something to teach us and possess skills that are transferable to academic settings alters the discourse on students of color from deficient to empowered (Delgado Bernal, 2002; Ladson-Billings, 1995; Strayhorn, 2010). While this view has been studied and applied to the North American university context (Birani & Lehman, 2013; Strayhorn, 2010), less empirical research on Brazilian higher education is viewed through a social capital lens.

To challenge and expand Bordieu's idea, this chapter will apply the social capital theory to less dominant actors and illuminate how mainstream ideas about value associated with high status and formal education are problematic in education contexts generally and for underrepresented students in particular. This argument is guided by Delgado Bernal's (2002) assertion that students of color are "creators and holders of knowledge" to demonstrate how these students exemplify and disrupt mainstream understandings of social capital as a linear theoretical concept (p. 106). In doing so, the following questions become important: Is Bordieu's social capital theory an appropriate lens with which to view marginalized groups? If so, how does the positionality of these actors influence the conversation about how we understand and discuss social capital?

To fulfill its purpose, the chapter consists of a background of the Brazilian case detailing the initiation of affirmative action policy in university admissions followed by a brief overview of literature that situates social capital as a framework to examine marginalized groups. Next, it examines the use of social capital theory as a lens to view Afro-Brazilian students' navigation of the university as an elite space. Three examples of social capital in practice are then explored. Finally, the paper concludes with implications for using a social capital perspective to improve the practice of institutions that serve underrepresented students

BACKGROUND

When examining Brazil, one cannot separate its present state from a past that has been so crucial in the formation of its culture, traditions, language and national identity (Fry, 2000; Goncalves e Silva & Araujo-Olivera, 2009; Pazich & Teranishi, 2012; Somers, Morosini, Pan, & Cofer, 2013). As the largest country in South America, Brazil was exploited as a Portuguese colony for its natural resources. The indigenous people of the land suffered at the hand of colonizers, while the largest number of enslaved Africans of any colony in the world were brought against their will. This historical reality serves as the setting for a racially mixed society where no one is completely Indigenous, Portuguese, or African (Telles, 2004). Brazilian people have come to pride themselves on this mixture as evidence of Brazil's "racial democracy" (Fry, 2000; Pazich & Teranishi, 2012; Somers et al., 2013; Schwartzman, 2008, 2009; Torres & Schugurensky, 2002).

Racial democracy as an ideology has roots in the work on Brazilian race relations by sociologist Gilberto Freyre (Brochier, 2014; Fry, 2000). Prior to the publishing of Freyre's writings in the 1930s, race in Brazil was viewed and discussed in terms of the downfall of race mixing and the necessity to lessen the influence of African and Indigenous characteristics in Brazilian people through a process known as *embranquecimento* or whitening (Fry, 2000; Somers et al., 2013; Telles, 2004; Torres & Schugurensky, 2002). Freyre parted ways with traditional thought of the time to embrace miscegenation as Brazil's source of distinction and pride. He used words such as equilibrium, harmony, and fraternization to describe the social intermingling between the races that was very unique to Brazil (Fry, 2000). These ideas provided the fuel that created a national discourse that Brazil was and is race-less and therefore void of racism and inequality (Fry, 2000; Somers et al., 2013). Alongside this dominant discourse exists the voices of activists and scholars who have always expressed the realities of race and the subjugation of Black, Brown, and Indigenous people in Brazil (Gonzalez, 1982; Hansebalg, 1996; Munanga, 1999; Pereira, 2013).

Inequality in Brazil is reflected in multiple areas of social, economic, and political life, including education (Telles, 2004). The experience of Whites and non-Whites in education in general and higher education in particular has not been a universal one. The advantages of higher quality schools stick with White students through the tertiary years as they prepare for and take the national entrance exams, which are the key to university admission. White students are more likely to have access to first-rate preparatory resources that assist with studying for the entrance exams because more often than not, their families can afford it (Heringer, 2013; Schwartzman, 2004). Thus, increasing their chances of getting in to the prestigious and federally subsidized public universities.

To address the enrollment gap in higher education, the Brazilian government turned to affirmative action and implemented the quota system in 2002, which allotted 40 percent of undergraduate enrollment in state universities to be reserved for Blacks and Browns[2]. This legislation was amended in 2003 to include 20 percent of seats to students from public schools, 20 percent for Blacks, and 5 percent for students with disabilities, who are indigenous, or the children of slain police officers who died in service (Somers et al., 2013). In 2012, the Supreme Court

---

[2] Brazil has numerous race categories that include variations of skin color where Black is different from Brown. This distinction becomes important in the context of quotas. See Schwartzman (2008, 2009) for a thorough explanation.

voted to give legal sanction to the use of affirmative action policies in conjunction with new legislation passed by Congress (Heringer, 2015). Thus, the most recent amendments include greater emphasis on students' social class while race is considered a sub-quota (Dietrich, 2015; Mitchell-Walthour, 2015).

SOCIAL CAPITAL AND MARGINALIZED GROUPS

Social capital is the amount of power, privilege, or valued currency that accrues as the result of membership in a group (Bourdieu, 1986). Each individual contributes value that increases when added to the total value of the group. Bourdieu's concept of capital was created to analyze the reproduction of social inequity in French society with an emphasis on ruling class norms and ideals as the societal standard to which all other groups are measured (Lamont & Lareau, 1988).

Although Bordieu has been critiqued for his lack of explanation of the agency of marginalized actors (Birani & Lehmann, 2013) within the social capital framework, the theory has been taken up by other scholars to show its utility when examining less privileged groups. This work demonstrates the challenge in defining social capital for use in specific fields (Carpiano, 2006; Edgarton & Roberts, 2014; Kao, 2004) and commonly presents disadvantaged groups as powerless (McDonald & Day, 2010; Spires & Cox, 2016). Despite these difficulties, there is evidence of scholarship that disrupts deficit thinking to illuminate areas where social capital of minorities can be leveraged as benefits and sources of power. Humphreys (2007) begins to address deficit thinking when she explains how dominant understandings of social capital in the policy sector at times are not sufficient enough to explain the status of under-resourced neighborhoods in Ireland and the residents who live there. She posits that increased social capital vis-à-vis linking residents to state agencies, will not address neighborhood issues without "understanding how [social capital] is influenced by characteristics of people and place" (p. 73). In so doing, she offers a more nuanced understanding of social capital that considers agency and power dynamics. Gamarnikow and Green (1999), earlier contributors to this conversation, critique education policy in the United Kingdom during the Blair administration. They conclude that a social capital perspective elucidates weaknesses of the Education Action Zone agenda that promotes cultural deficit thinking and ignores systemic social inequality.

Additional research has also applied social capital theory to the specific context of higher education to examine the influence of social capital "reservoirs" on the achievement of African American and Latino males (Strayhorn, 2010); how the strength of relationships with institutional agents, families and friends contribute to racial stratification within college opportunity and choice (Teranishi & Briscoe, 2006); and to exemplify how ethnic-minority status can serve as a source of social capital for first generation students in a Canadian university (Birani & Lehman, 2013). All of these studies contribute to our understanding of the social capital of underrepresented students' post-secondary experiences and acknowledges their agency in this process; however, scant research applies this framework to the Afro-Brazilian students explored here.

To address this gap, I turn to Delgado Bernal's (2002) critical raced-gendered epistemologies as a guide to recognize the strengths and valuable experience that Black students bring with them to their predominately White Brazilian institutions. She challenges the assumption that certain ways of knowing are privileged over others and advocates the centering of marginalized experiences using a critical race theory and Latino critical theory orientation. Drawing from interviews conducted with Chicana/Chicano college students, Delgado Bernal identifies her students' responses as counter stories that disrupt dominant Eurocentric perspectives of what constitutes knowledge in educational contexts. Correspondingly, critical raced-gendered epistemologies offer a space to situate the Black students that I interviewed as creators and holders of knowledge as they self-actualize in groups to maximize their social capital.

VIEWING AFRO-BRAZILIAN STUDENTS
THROUGH A SOCIAL CAPITAL LENS

Social capital is an ideological stance that relies on hegemonic relationships based on socioeconomic status and does not account for the ways in which race impacts this relationship. Bordieu (1986) has looked to family ties to make points about how social capital is created and reproduced; however, others have translated this perspective to educational contexts with a focus on inequality (Strayhorn, 2010). Despite Bordieu's emphasis on class and less on race or ethnicity, social capital still is a viable way to examine group networks arranged by race and can help shed light on how this capital is created, cultivated, and reproduced. For instance, the joining together in groups by Black students reflects the necessity to survive within predominately White spaces. So, if this is the case, then who determines the value of this group? What is the currency that is being exchanged? Is this organization into groups temporary?

In addressing these questions, it is important to look at the internal and external forces at work in this context. The groups of Black students at the ground level are created by one person or more; however, the shared identity is somewhat imparted by the larger affirmative action policy process to create access to higher education. The students who take advantage of this benefit are called *cotistas*, a derivative of the word for quotas, and are already grouped by that status regardless of which category of the quota they have applied for. From this perspective, it may seem that students have no part in how they are grouped but this is not the case. This process calls into question the issue of power relations and the designation of value in society by larger forces that are beyond this group's control. Bordieu's explanation of social capital theory places emphasis on high class values and the capital that comes with groups that have affluent backgrounds (Lamont & Lareau, 1988); however, when applied to groups from the lower classes that are deemed by society as having less capital, then in some ways the theory does not adequately fit.

For the purposes of this chapter, currency takes the form of Bordieu's social capital (1986). I situate race, a social and cultural construct, as currency. Currency has value and according to Bordieu, mainstream currency accrues value based on dominant social, cultural, and economic norms. From this point of view dominant group(s) give currency it's meaning and value. This is only one view. I would like to introduce another point of view where the value of currency is decided by those who possess currency, which in this case are Afro-Brazilian university students. In this context, currency is accrued, negotiated, and assigned value. I use the word negotiate because entering the realm of post-secondary education, for un-derrepresented groups who are often from low socioeconomic backgrounds and first-generation, is a negotiation of identity, thought, culture, and of worldview. This standpoint recognizes negotiation as a multi-faceted transaction that has the ability to yield negative and positive returns. What follows is my interpretation of daily transactions and negotiations that students make on a daily basis to cultivate a social capital that simultaneously considers their marginalization as well as their valuable contribution to the university environment.

SOCIAL CAPITAL IN PRACTICE

The idea of social capital in practice differs for varying actors according to how value is placed on them by dominant societal influences. However, what happens when marginalized actors are viewed as possessing agency to ascribe value? To illustrate this, the following discussion will center the collective social capital accrued by self-identified Black Brazilian university students where they create and utilize social capital on their own terms. Data for this chapter is drawn from interviews with 39 students and observations conducted over the course of seven months at The State University of Rio de Janeiro and one of its branch campuses. Students represented nine different universities located in the states of Rio de Ja-neiro and São Paulo. Even though all students self-identified as Black, all of them were not admitted through the race-based quota. Some utilized the public-school quota and others were admitted traditionally without using the quota benefit. It is important to keep in mind that the capital that students exhibited may or may not be seen as valuable to the university, which in this case is an institutional reflec-tion of dominant ideals that are sometimes at odds with student ideals. As such, the social capital they created for themselves by themselves disrupts mainstream understandings making space for an alternative interpretation.

Student Collectives

It was common for students to mention their involvement in a collective—an informal or formal group—that is organized around shared interests, where knowledge and resources are exchanged, events are planned and implemented, and communication between faculty and administration is facilitated in the group's interest.

One such group is the *Filhas de Dandara* or Daughters of Dandara, which will be referred to hereinafter as the Daughters. Dandara was the wife of Zumbi, the infamous Qilombo leader during the 17th century. The Quilombos were a group of escaped slaves who created their own communities in the mountains and hills of Brazil where they fought to maintain their freedom from Portuguese enslavers. Dandara was described as "living proof that woman is not a gender of fragility" exemplified in her ability to harvest crops, plan and make decisions with her powerful husband, and practice capoeira, the Brazilian martial art (Palmares Cultural Foundation, 2014, p. 1). Thus, the name of the collective is in recognition of this strong historical figure. The reference to daughters signifies members' descendant status with the sentiment that Dandara is in their DNA, as well as, their commitment to the continuation of the work of what Dandara represents for the resistance to enslavement and the oppression of Afro-Brazilians. In using Dandara as a model, the Filhas are guided by Black feminism and emphasize the importance of advocating for Black women's standpoint not just in the university but also in every aspect of their lives (Hill Collins, 2000).

The Daughters were an important part of the campus. They regularly put on events that highlighted the Black experience and offered a space for the university community to address issues of race, class, and gender locally and globally. Additionally, these young women stayed connected to their communities by offering workshops and classes for youth that centered Afro-Brazilian history and assisting prospective university students, who could not afford expensive preparatory courses, with studying for the national college entrance exams.

10 out of the 39 interviews were with individual members of the Daughters. All of them mentioned their participation in the collective as monumental to shaping their identities as Black women inside the university. Some with great emotion, expressed the significance of the collective to opening their minds to blackness and accepting themselves as both black and female. Dali explains,

> My identity ... I managed to rescue it through the university, the university that brought me this, because I did not see myself as black, I did not accept my hair, as it was ... And the collective that I am part of now has also helped me a lot, which is the collective Daughters of Dandara. It is a collective of women who help one another so that we can strengthen ourselves and face this university, that we know that this university is elitist and that most of them are white and in this we are seeking to find strength. We also study, we do readings, we have done activities in schools to see if you can expand, beyond the university, expand the black culture, expand so that other people can return, get their identity, because it was something that happened with me here.

It is clear that the Daughters of Dandara as a group galvanized a strength for the young ladies that was not available to them as Black female individuals within the confines of the elite institution. Together they used their prior knowledge and accrued value to respond to the university's discourse of exclusion and its failure to recognize that only giving access to the institution is not enough. The Daughters innately knew that they would have to become their own source of support for each other to not just exist but to persist within the university and see it through to degree completion. Dali references studying beyond the university curriculum and taking what is learned back to their communities to educate the youth so that they can "expand." Here is where the group is making it a responsibility to save and invest what they are accruing to ensure that what they have started will continue. It is recognition of the possibility that the opportunity of a post-secondary education is not guaranteed; therefore, they must do what they can to keep the path to university reproducible for themselves and people like them thus creating social capital on their own terms.

Art/Media Expression

To combat the reality of the university as exclusive spaces closed off to minoritized groups, some Black students at a prestigious private university leveraged their social capital to create a newsletter called *Nuvem Negra* or Black Cloud. The newsletter focuses on topics and information that they would not otherwise find in the mainstream university news. The content, production, and dissemination of Nuvem Negra is an independent effort by the students who recognize the necessity of expressing a collective Black student voice on campus. Although this voice is of utmost importance and highly valued by the students who create and read the newsletter, it is not a priority for the campus at large. Students are responsible for every aspect of producing the newsletter and receive no institutional support. This could be seen as a challenge; however, students recognize it as an opportunity to create and share exactly what they want without input or censorship from faculty or administration. As such, issues of the newsletter include items such as a pictorial for putting on a head wrap, which has roots in African traditional dress, personal poetry that engages the reader in issues of Black identity, a list of quick facts about how the university includes (or not) African and Afro-Brazilian history in course offerings and an ongoing project to find out how many Black professors exist at the university.

Nuvem Negra is a physical product of Black university student social capital. Since the institution did not support the students' efforts in telling their own stories from their perspectives, they decided to do it themselves. The group gathered writers and artists, chose topics of interest for their audience, and negotiated a relationship with a printing company who prints the newsletter on recycled paper for a discounted fee. The newsletter is in response to the silencing of Black students on campus specifically and the invalidation of the Black Brazilian experience nationally. Furthermore, it provides tangible skill building that has great potential for translating to their professional lives post graduation. Some examples are, the ability to collaborate with others, writing for the public, negotiating and interacting with leadership, and conducting research/fact checking. Therefore, accruing social capital that could result in economic gain later on. The skills of negotiation and interaction carry over to the current university experience, particularly in student ties with faculty and staff, which is discussed below.

Faculty/Staff Allies

The lack of Black bodies in university spaces does not end with the students as it also extends to the faculty and administration. It is rare to find more than one Black professor at any institution at a given time; however, there exists a rare case at a small satellite campus of the State University of Rio de Janeiro (UERJ). This campus is located in the northern periphery of the city of Rio in a municipality that is majority Black and working class. As a result, its student body reflects the demographic of the area. At one point, the campus included five adjunct professors and an Academic Coordinator, all of whom self-identified as Black and whose backgrounds and research interests centered issues of race and inequality in Brazil. In addition to this, a large portion of the White faculty were also sensitive to the realities of their Black students, which resulted in an environment that welcomed the discussion of sensitive topics in class or in school wide events. Concurrently, students gravitated toward these potential mentors when they felt that the faculty or staff was supportive in the struggle for equality on and off campus.

Students were very aware of how unique their access to Black and open-minded White faculty was. Ana shares, "You have the potential to have representativeness, because here at...there are many blacks. So, you end up saying, "Oh my God, that's good!" Because where I was studying, I did not have it, so I think it would have helped me there too and a lot...Teachers. There are black teachers here, there were not many of them in my schools, so I've been building myself, you know? Ana's connection with the Black student body and Black faculty is an example of how these ties provided students with confidence and assurance that they deserved to be there and that they could persevere in the exclusive university space.

To further elaborate on the difference between campuses, Rafaela, a student leader involved with the aforementioned Daughters collective, makes the distinction between faculty and staff at the main campus and the branch campus where she attends when she states,

> ..if I had gone to Maracanã [the main campus] I would have given up, because I would not have found Nita, who is my counselor. Suddenly I would have given up, because from what we see there, talking to my friends who are from there ... There you do not create those ties with the teacher. You know? The teacher comes in, teaches and leaves. Not here, we sit and talk to the teacher. You know? We struggle together, we go to the demonstrations together. So it's a different thing, because I know it's not [like this at the main campus]. So if I had been there, in my first semes-

ter when I went into a fit, I would have given up, because there might not have been anyone to say: "No! Stay a little longer, try another semester."

Rafaela points out the approachability of the faculty and their commitment to building connections to the students. She references the struggles and demonstrations that are on-going to combat government budget cuts and the push to privatize UERJ, a well-known public university credited as an early adopter of the quota system to implement affirmative action.

The satellite campus was not the only place where students cultivated relationships with faculty and staff. Students from other campuses were also able to connect with Black faculty in ways that were rewarding and added value to their sense of identity. Leo, a current teacher who recently graduated, remembers,

> It was only at the end of the course of Philosophy, that ... I forgot that there were black writers, that I met a professor of Philosophy, a PhD and a black man. In fact he was a doctoral student, he was finishing up. And he was black, and then I started to contact him, he worked in a state school, which is where I work today. He used to teach teenagers and I did internship with him, I went to talk to him and that has changed a lot because I saw that there were doctors, or black doctoral students. So that to me was another evolution, to see an Afro-descendant being black. And then he goes through a university, a federal university. And then I come to seek, to follow, to join his research groups, and I remember that he said that there was African Philosophy...And then I did not believe in him because [I had] seven years of Greek Philosophy, seven years of German Philosophy and seven years hearing that Philosophy is born in Greece and I was skeptical, but that had already stirred me. I said, "Gee, if he's saying it, then there must be something." But in summary, during graduation ... My identity was greatly weakened due to these contradictions, because of these problems that I just mentioned, but in the end, I was rescued by the teacher who was a PhD and he managed to rescue something [in me].

Through this connection, Leo was able to see something greater for himself as a Black man. He realized that there are Black philosophers who are contributing to this field of study. The relationship he forged with his instructor expounded upon the academic knowledge that he was receiving and encouraged him to think critically about it. Additionally, Leo met other like-minded researchers further building his social capital and making an impact that lasted beyond his post-secondary tenure.

CONCLUSION

Drawing on data from 39 interviews and seven months of observation, the purpose of this chapter was to demonstrate how the lack of institutional support, provides the impetus for creating networks and developing social capital as a way to process marginalization in general and critique students' university experiences in particular. I argue that as creators and holders of knowledge, students place their own wealth and value in their social groups that accrues and is also used to negotiate. Therefore, situating social capital as a pliable framework that is dynamic and at times complex. While the students are a part of a larger social and political happening that is the university implementation of affirmative action policy, they are asserting agency to focus on what is significant to them—a strong black identity, acknowledgement of their marginalized status within the university, and communal support.

Although the university may not be the perfect place to help level playing fields for marginalized students, it is a rich site to explore refocusing intentions of inclusion in exclusionary places. Thus, providing alternative ways to expand social capital as a way to explain contemporary educational contexts.

REFERENCES

Altbach, P. G. (2006). Globalization and the university: Realities in an unequal world. In J. F. Forest & P. G. Altbach, (Eds.), *International handbook of higher education* (pp. 121–139). Dordrecht, Netherlands: Springer.

Altbach, P. G. (2010). Preface. In G. Goastellec (Ed.), *Understanding inequalities in, through, and by higher education* (pp. vii–x). Rotterdam, Netherlands: Sense Publishers.

Birani, A., & Lehmann, W. (2013). Ethnicity as social capital: an examination of first-generation, ethnic-minority students at a Canadian university. *International Studies in Sociology of Education*, 1–17.

Bourdieu, P. (1986). The forms of capital. In J. Richardson (Ed.), *Handbook of theory and research for the sociology of education* (pp. 241–258). New York, NY: Greenwood.

Brochier, C. (2014). The concept of racial democracy in Brazilian intellectual history. *Revue de synthèse/Centre international de synthèse, 135*(1), 123–150.

Carpiano, R. M. (2006). Toward a neighborhood resource-based theory of social capital for health: Can Bourdieu and sociology help? *Social science & medicine, 62*(1), 165–175.

Deitrich, E. (2015). Ambition with resistance: Affirmative action in Brazil's public universities. In O. A. Johnson III & R. Heringer (Eds.), *Race, politics, and education in Brazil: Affirmative action in higher education* (pp. 155–178). New York, NY: Palgrave Macmillan.

Delgado Bernal, D. (2002). Critical race theory, Latino critical theory, and critical raced-gendered epistemologies: Recognizing students of color as holders and creators of knowledge. *Qualitative Inquiry, 8*(1), 105–126.

Edgerton, J. D., & Roberts, L. W. (2014). Cultural capital or habitus? Bourdieu and beyond in the explanation of enduring educational inequality. *School Field, 12*(2), 193–220.

Fry, P. (2000). Politics, nationality, and the meanings of "race" in Brazil. *Daedalus, 129*(2), 83–118.

Gamarnikow, E., & Green, A. G. (1999). The third way and social capital: Education action zones and a new agenda for education, parents and community? *International Studies in Sociology of Education, 9*(1), 3–22.

Goncalves e Silva, P. B., & Araujo-Olivera, S. S. (2009). Achieving quality education for indigenous peoples and blacks in Brazil. In *Routledge international handbooks of education: The Routledge international Companion to multicultural education* (pp.

526–539). Retrieved from http://search.credoreference.com.ezproxy2.library.drex-el.edu/content/entry/routmced/achieving_quality_education_for_indigenous_peo-ples_and_blacks_in_brazil/0

Gonzalez, L. (1982). O Movimento Negro na última década. [The Black Movement in the last decade] In L. Gonzalez & C. Hasenbalg (Eds.), *Lugar de negro* [*The place of the Black*] (pp. 48–50). Rio de Janeiro, Brazil: Marco Zero.

Hasenbalg, C. (1996). Entre o mito e os fatos: racismo e relações raciais no Brasil [Between the myth and the facts: Racism and racial relations in Brazil]. In M. Chor Maio & R. Ventura Santos (Eds.), *Raça, ciência e sociedade* [*Race, Science and Society*] (pp. 235–249). Rio de Janeiro, Brazil: FIOCRUZ/CCBB.

Heringer, R. (2013). O próximo passo: As políticas de permanência na Universidade Pública [The next step: Permanence policies in public university]. In A. Randolpho Paiva (Ed.), *Ação afirmativa em questao: Brasil, Estados Unidos, África do Sul e França* [*Affirmative action in question: Brazil, United States, South Africa and France*] (pp. 74–99). Rio de Janeiro, Brazil: Pallas.

Heringer, R. (2015). Affirmative action and the expansion of higher education in Brazil. In O. A. Johnson III & R. Heringer (Eds.), *Race, politics, and education in Brazil: Affirmative action in higher education* (pp. 111–131). New York, NY: Palgrave Macmillan.

Hill Collins, P. (2000). *Black feminist thought: Knowledge, consciousness, and the politics of empowerment* (2nd ed.). New York, NY: Routledge.

Humphreys, E. (2007). Social capital in disadvantaged neighbourhoods: A diversion from needs or a real contribution to the debate on area-based regeneration? *Irish Journal of Sociology, 16*(2), 50–76.

Instituto Brasileiro de Geografia e Estatíca (IBGE). (2010). *Censo demográfico* [*Demographic census*]. Retrieved from https://ww2.ibge.gov.br/home/estatistica/popu-lacao/censo2010/.

Kao, G. (2004). Social capital and its relevance to minority and immigrant populations. *Sociology of Education, 77*(2), 172–175.

Ladson-Billings, G. (1995). Toward a theory of culturally relevant pedagogy. *American Educational Research Journal, 32*(3), 465–491.

Lamont, M., & Lareau, A. (1988). Cultural capital: Allusions, gaps and glissandos in recent theoretical developments. *Sociological Theory, 6*(2), 153–168.

McDonald, S., & Day, J. C. (2010). Race, gender, and the invisible hand of social capital. *Sociology Compass, 4*(7), 532–543.

Mitchell-Walthour, G. (2015). Afro-Brazilian support for affirmative action. In O. A. Johnson III & R. Heringer (Eds.), *Race, politics, and education in Brazil: Affirmative action in higher education* (pp. 133–154). New York, NY: Palgrave Macmillan.

Munanga, K. (1999). *Superando o racismo na escola* (2nd ed.) [Overcoming racism in school]. Brasília, Brazil: Ministério da Educação/Secretaria de Educação Funda-mental.

Palmares Cultural Foundation. (2014). *Personalidades Negras* [*Black personalities*]. Re-treived from http://www.palmares.gov.br/archives/33387.

Pazich, L. B., & Teranishi, R. T. (2012). Comparing access to higher education in Brazil and India using critical race theory. In W. Allen, M. Bounous-Hammarth, & R.T. Teranishi (Eds.), *As the world turns: Implications of global shifts in higher edu-*

cation for theory, research, and practice (pp. 105–126). Bradley, West Yorkshire: Emerald Group Publishing Limited.

Penha-Lopes, V. (2008). Universitarios cotistas: De alunos a bacharéis [University quota students: From students to graduates]. In J. Zoninsein & J. Feres Junior (Eds.), *Ação afirmativa no ensino superior Brasileiro [Affirmative action in Brazilian higher education]* (pp. 105–133). Rio de Janeiro, Brazil: IUPERJ.

Pereira, A. (2013). *O mundo negro* [The Black world]. Rio de Janeiro, Brazil: Pallas.

Perna, L. W. (2007). The sources of racial-ethnic group differences in college enrollment: A critical examination. *New Directions for Institutional Research*, (133), 51–66.

Schwartzman, L. F. (2008). Who are the blacks? The question of racial classification in Brazilian affirmative action policies in higher education. *Cahiers De La Recherche Sur l'Éducation Et Les Savoirs*, 7.

Schwartzman, L. F. (2009). Seeing like citizens: Unofficial understandings of official racial categories in a Brazilian university. *Journal of Latin American Studies, 41*(2), 221–250.

Schwartzman, S. (2004). Equity, quality and relevance in higher education in Brazil. *Anais Da Academia Brasileira De Ciências, 76*(1), 173–188.

Somers, P., Morosini, M., Pan, M., & Cofer, J. E. Sr. (2013). Brazil's radical approach to expanding access for underrepresented college students. In H. D. Meyer, E. St. John, M. Chankseliani, & L. Uribe (Eds.), *Fairness in access to higher education in a global perspective: Reconciling excellence, efficiency, and justice* (pp. 203–221). Rotterdam, Netherlands: Sense Publishers.

Spires, R., & Cox, J. T. (2016). Addressing social capital for disadvantaged youth: Youth and teacher perceptions of a youth development program in Hong Kong. *Cogent Social Sciences, 2*(1), 1191105.

Strayhorn, T. L. (2010). When race and gender collide: Social and cultural capital's influence on the academic achievement of African American and Latino males. *Review of Higher Education, 33*(3), 307.

Telles, E. E. (2004). *Race in another America: The significance of skin color in Brazil.* Princeton, NJ: Princeton University Press.

Teranishi, R., & Briscoe, K. (2006). Social capital and the racial stratification of college opportunity. In J. C. Smart (Ed.), *Higher education: Handbook of theory and research* (pp. 591–614). Dordrecht, Netherlands: Springer Netherlands.

Torres, C. A., & Schugurensky, D. (2002). The political economy of higher education in the era of neoliberal globalization: Latin America in comparative perspective. *Higher Education, 43*(4), 429–455.

Trow, M. (1973). *Problems in the transition from elite to mass higher education.* Paris, France: Carnegie Commission on Higher Education.

PART II.B

PARTNERSHIPS AND EDUCATIONAL ATTAINMENT

CHAPTER 10

SOCIAL CAPITAL RESOURCES IN SCHOOLS

Explaining Effective School Community

Heather E. Price

Many quantitative studies limit analyses of teachers' influence on student learning to associations with teachers' gender, race, ethnicity, teaching tenure/experience, and university prestige (Nye, Konstantopoulos, & Hedges, 2004; Wayne & Youngs, 2003). If we subscribe to the idea that teachers and the school environments create student learning environments (Waller, 1932), we need to better understand how certain schools produce more effective learning environments than schools with otherwise similar human capital resources. Thus, this study uses teacher network data of the ego, alter, and organization to understand the social capital resources that differentiate aspects of school communities. It is important to understand how various social capital aspects compose school communities so that we can then think about how to create and sustain effective school communities for student learning.

SOCIAL CAPITAL IN SCHOOLS

There is a longstanding sociological idea that schools are primary social spaces where many disparate individuals come together and, through shared experienc-

Contemporary Perspectives on Social Capital in Educational Contexts,
pages 161–180.

es, individuals transform their personal perspectives to take on a more globally centered social being (Durkheim, 1944). Although these social spaces have been described in ethnographic and other descriptive qualitative studies as school communities (see such works as Bryk, Lee, & Holland, 1993; Coleman, 1961; McCloskey, 2008; Powell, 1985), there are few quantitative analyses that describe the variation in school community as outlined by social capital theorists. Indeed, there is burgeoning research, as discussed in the following sections, on how to quantify social capital of teachers and how these measures correlate with teacher and student outcomes, but there is sparse research linking the different facets of social capital to different aspects of school community.

Ideas related to school community about social capital come from two distinct theoretical strains: social closure and common good theories. Both of these notions of school community surfaced in light of findings related to a 'Catholic school effect' found in the US Department of Education's High School and Beyond (HS&B) database of the 1980s. Research with this dataset consistently finds students —of otherwise equal ability and backgrounds—performing better in Catholic high schools. The findings are solid and not swayed by class or school size, material resources, or locale. Researchers credit the difference in Catholic high schools to the closeness of the social ties between families and teachers which were more prevalent than ties found in traditional public schools.

The first strain of school community theory originates with work by Coleman and Hoffer (Hoffer, Greeley, & Coleman, 1985; Coleman & Hoffer, 1987). In this line of research, school community is defined through a social closure mechanism. Social closure centers around the idea that a school community (its school staff, students, and parents) tightly binds its members through uniform values, beliefs, and shared behavioral expectations that members had before entering the school. Within the school, normative sanctioning enforces social control and reinforces the shared values, beliefs, and expectations associated with pro-school behaviors, attitudes, and achievement. "This structural consistency between generations creates what can be described as a functional community, a community in which social norms and sanctions, including those that cross generations, arise out of the social structure itself, and both reinforce and perpetuate that structure" (Coleman & Hoffer, 1987, p. 7).

This social closure definition tightly aligns with traditional social capital where it is "defined by its function. It is not a single entity but a variety of different entities, with two elements in common: they all consist of some aspect of social structure, and they facilitate certain actions of actors—whether persons or corporate actors—within the structure" and what is considered valuable is dependent on the social group (Coleman, 1988, p. S98). This social structure can be captured by the dyadic ties as the object of interest: only certain persons with certain characteristic values and beliefs enter into relationships with others in the shared space community (Portes, 1998). That is, these traits predispose the dyadic interaction. The structural equivalence on these personal actor traits creates the bond by reducing initial levels of mistrust (Borgatti & Everett, 1992). In effect, outcomes related to trust and unity are more likely in situations where the people initially seem alike; persons are more likely to become close to others who look, act, and otherwise appear like them.

The second strain of school community theory originates with Bryk and colleagues. In this line of research, school community is defined as 'school *as* community' in which "a social organization consisting of cooperative relations among adults who share a common purpose and where daily life for both adults and students is organized in ways that foster commitment among its members" (Bryk & Driscoll, 1988, p. 2). In this definition, the dyadic ties themselves are not the object of interest. Instead, the organization-wide attitudes and behaviors which emerge from relationships bound around a 'common good' are the object of interest. These organizationally emergent shared attitudes and behaviors are the mechanisms which create school community. "Because membership involves an ongoing exercise of free will, individuals are less likely to interpret school life as coercive and more likely feel a sense of identification expressed in the phrase, 'This is *my* school.'" (italics in original, Bryk, Lee, & Holland, 1993, p. 313). Under this theoretical specification, the whole of the community creates an effect greater than the sum of the individual ties (Bryk & Driscoll, 1988).

Under this common good mechanism, it is the participation of school members acting on unified goals, no matter their personal background, that creates the school community impact on learning. In this case, networks of persons who bond over their roles and duties in the organization—a structural isomorphism trait—creates the network bond (Borgatti & Everett, 1992). For example, several studies find that teachers who 'substantively' clique on subject matter or grade level are better at attaining their instructional goals (Coburn, Mata, & Choi, 2013; Coburn & Russell, 2008; Coburn, Russell, Kaufman, & Stein, 2012; Frank & Zhao, 2005; Kim, Youngs, & Frank, 2017; Mooleanaar, 2010; Sun, Garrison, Wilhelm, & Frank, 2014; Sun, Penuel, Frank, Gallagher, & Youngs, 2013). In these cases, the learning climate improves when members of the school clique by their organizational role positions and not their personality traits. This common good definition tightly aligns with Bourdieauian social capital idea where the network of members develops an emergent institutional entity of its own (Bourdieu, 1986 in Szeman & Kaposy, 2011).

Although different in formation, school relationships are central in both the social closure and the common good theoretical notions of school community. Trust develops between members as a result of either social capital mechanism (Bryk & Driscoll, 1988; Bryk, Lee, & Holland, 1993; Bryk & Schneider, 2002; Coleman, Greeley, & Hoffer, 1985; Coleman & Hoffer, 1987). Under the traditional Coleman-type social capital, the strongly enculturated norms and beliefs provide a social fabric where all members are entrusted to care for the others as a group expectation. In the Bourdieauian-type social capital, the shared experiences used to build the community developed and continually reinforced the trusted commitment of members to each other.

In sum, Coleman and colleagues propose that the level of social closure between teachers, students, and family is the key to differentiating more effective schools from less effective ones (Coleman & Hoffer, 1987). Bryk and Driscoll (1988) propose that the key is the environment which emerges from school relations and interactions. Although the distinctions between these two explanations may seem unimportant on first read since the outcomes look nearly the same from either type, they in fact rely on quite different theoretical premises. Coleman's explanation encompasses ideas linked specifically to the actual ties between people—a pure social capital effect. Bryk and Driscoll's (1988) ideas relate to the effects from the cultural norms and expectations which arise due to the types of interactions and relationships between persons in a self-contained environment— a Bourdieuian social capital effect.

EFFECTIVE SCHOOL COMMUNITY

There are different aspects that comprise a school community: relational trust, shared values and norms, shared activities, and diffuse teacher roles within a school (Bryk & Driscoll, 1988; Bryk et al., 2010). All four of the aspects are foundational to school community. The **relational trust** characteristic related to school community develops out of relationships and interactions between school members (Van Maele, Moolenaar, & Daly, 2015). For teachers, trust in school workplaces provides an organizational culture where teaching risks and innovations can thrive (Brown, Daly, & Liou, 2016; Bryk & Schnieder, 2002; Bryk, Sebring, Allensworth, Luppescu, & Easton, 2010; Moolenaar & Sleegers, 2010). In trusting schools, teachers cite higher incidences of efficacy which translates into more effective classroom lessons and management and improved student learning. Students exhibit more pro-school behaviors in trusting spaces (Goddard, Goddard, & Tschannen-Moran 2007; Goddard, Tschannen-Moran, & Hoy, 2001; Hoy, Hoy, & Kurz, 2008; Tschannen-Moran & Hoy, 2000). Teachers who are integrated into the schools' decision-making leads to **shared values and norms** among school staff (Firestone & Pennell, 1993; Hillard 2003; Leithwood & Jantzi, 1990; Penuel, Frank, & Krause, 2010; Smith & O'Day, 1991; Robinson, Lloyd, & Rowe, 2008; Spillane 2006). This shared set of values and norms improve teacher morale and engagement with their work (Goldring & Pasternack, 1994; Leithwood & Jantzi, 1990; Leithwood, Leonard, & Sharratt, 1998; Louis et al., 2010; Spillane, 2006). **Sharing activities** is another approach that increases interdependence between teachers and necessitates teachers to agree on learning goals. By design, teachers who share activities work in a more integrated school community (Atteberry & Bryk, 2010; Daly, Moolenaar, Bolivar, & Burke, 2010; Daly, Moolenaar, Der-Martirosian, & Liou, 2014; Goddard, Goddard, & Tschannen-Moran, 2007; Struyve et al., 2016). The **diffuse roles** aspect regards teachers who perform multiple roles in the school experience more inter-reliance among themselves. Teachers' commitment levels benefit from their many ties to others and perception of indispensability (Bloom, Thompson, Unterman, Herlihy, & Payne, 2010; Bryk, Lee, & Holland, 1993; Shear et al., 2008). These four aspects are interdependent yet distinct.

These four aspects can be impacted by human and material resources, but social resources are not necessarily dependent on human and material resources. This means, for example, that schools may be able to overcome low personnel resources with more collaborative work. Thus, social resources can vary beyond the bounds of the schools' human and material resources that can stratify student learning (OECD, 2014). As such, these social resources in the school can therefore be seen by policymakers and school leaders as the most malleable space to torque the lever of school effectiveness and student learning.

DATA AND METHODS

This chapter employs a network analysis to explain the web of relationships that undergird schooling organizations under the assumption that "an organization is a system of linked relationships" (Gamoran, Secada, & Marrett, 2000, p. 59). This study analytically links certain social capital ideas to distinct social resources in school organizations using the tangible, structural configurations of relationships among school faculty that compose the teachers' social capital. This chapter addresses the research question: **What is the extent to which the social resources of teachers in schools explain school community?** The conceptual model (see Figure 10.1) shows that there are theoretically two levels of social resources—interpersonal teacher and organization-wide faculty relationships. Distinguishing between these types of social resources should decouple some of the social capital processes associated with the aspects of positive school community.

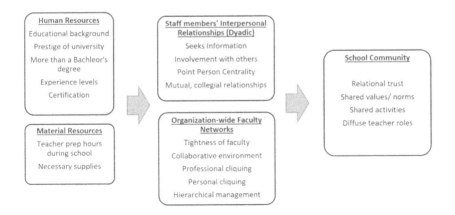

FIGURE 10.1. Social Resources on School Community

This chapter focuses on the following sub-research questions: How do inter-personal and organization-wide social resources relate to school community? To what extent do these social resources explain different aspects of school community?

Data

Charter school networks are chosen because they are expected to experience the least organizational resource constraints of any brick-and-mortar schools (Chubb & Moe, 1990). Theoretically, selecting charter schools as the sample should maximize the width of the lens to test the influence of social resources on the desired school community and effectiveness outcomes. Sociologically, using charter schools to test school community ideas expands the discussion of school community effects from a Catholic versus public school discussion to one that can now include the public charter school sector.

Indianapolis charter schools are particularly ideal to use as the sample schools for several reasons. The consolidation of these schools in one city reduces possible unexplained error due to resource allocation differences from the tax base as well as reduces error from possible spatial and regional differences in normative school culture. Further, the orientation of these schools to the Indianapolis mayoral office levels the playing field with respect to access and information about local resources available to these schools.[1]

In the 2009–2010 school year, 15 of the 18 schools agreed to participate in the study.[2] The schools range in size from serving 50 to 450 students. Corresponding staff at these schools range from ten to 60 persons. The schools serve a range of grade levels: two serve K–5, five serve K–8, three serve middle thru high school grades, and five serve high school students.

This study limits its time frame to within one school year to capture the effects of staff relationships on the school community independent of structural changes that take place between the school years.[3] In all, nearly 900 surveys were collected from teachers, principals, and other school staff members. Response rates averaged 82 percent which surpasses the 70 percent rate recommended as necessary by Wasserman and Faust (1994). This chapter uses 295 of the teachers in the dataset as the analytic sample.

The survey created for this study, the School Staff Network and School Community Survey (SSNSCS), uses respondent reporting to measure school commu-

---

[1] The Mayor's office is the chartering authority in Indianapolis.

[2] See Price (2011) for the statistical discussion about the threat of bias from these three non-participating schools.

[3] Approximately 2/3 of these Indianapolis charter schools are still 'growing,' meaning that these schools are still working toward achieving the building enrollment capacity on size and/or grade levels served. Consequently, the school staff grows every year to accommodate the increases in capacity. Similarly, the year-to-year contract of teachers in charter schools creates an environment where teacher turnover between years could be high.

nity. For validity and comparison, nearly all of these questions mimic the *Schools and Staffing Survey* from the National Center on Educational Statistics. In addition to perception questions, the survey collects two-way social network data on all school staff based on network survey questions by Deal, Purinton, and Waetjen (2009).[4] This method of two-way social network data is seldom done in education research studies, as most social network data only collect one-way data on teachers' out-going ties by naming who a teacher goes to for information and/or help. The SSNSCS questions do ask teachers about who they go to for information (out-going ties) but it also asks teachers who comes to them for information (in-coming ties). Adding the information about who comes *to* the respondent overcomes three limitations of the one-way, unidirectional studies. First, this type of two-way, bi-directional social network data collection allows for the strength or weakness of relationship reciprocity to be analyzed. Second, it increases the validity of the collected data via triangulation. Third, it allows for non-respondents, who are otherwise missing data in unidirectional studies, to be included in the map of the school social network.

Operationalization of Concepts

The network concepts of interest for the social resource analysis align with ideas related to cohesion and unity—features that describe communities, including school communities.

SCHOOL COMMUNITY

School community is defined in the literature (see Bryk & Driscoll, 1988, Bryk et al., 2010, among others) by several key aspects. Relational trust, shared values and norms, diffuse roles, and shared activities, are the most commonly cited key components observed in schools with effective school communities.[5]

Relational trust is a scale, $\alpha=0.92$, that combines the scores from the SSNSCS on the degree to which the respondents feel that the parents, students, administration, teachers, and the overall school community[6] are trustworthy and loyal to the school. The degree to which schools unify around shared values and norms is created from questions gauging the degree to which the administration is supportive and encouraging of staff, backs up teachers with rule enforcement, commu-

---

[4] Qualtrics coding created a school-specific staff name list to appear on each respondents' survey. Name lists increase validity of responses since they increase accuracy of memory and name recognition for a comprehensive answer and reduces respondent burden. To further alleviate respondent burden, respondents are asked to use initials of the staffers as identification in the survey, in lieu of a randomly assigned id number.

[5] A fifth component often cited is high academic standards (Bryk et al., 2010; Phillips, 1997), but due to lack of variation and error associated with social desirability bias, a measure of "high academic standards" is excluded from the analysis..

[6] If applicable, the trustworthiness and loyalty of the charter management organization was also included in the scale score.

TABLE 10.1. Descriptive Statistics

	Obs	Mean	Std. Dev.	Min	Max
School Community Measures					
School Community Overall, wgtd	344	2.215	0.407	0	3.338
Relational Trust	342	7.325	1.387	2.42	9.71
Shared Values and Norms	343	6.192	1.114	2.333	8.994
Shared Activities	343	0.461	0.372	0	3.483
Diffuse Roles	344	0.237	0.450	0	3.715
Dyadic Interpersonal Relationship Characteristics					
Seeks information	490	0.334	0.157	0	0.729
Involvement with others	489	0.250	0.149	0	0.827
Point person centrality	490	0.646	0.351	0	2.105
Mutual collegial relationships	490	0.431	0.496	0	1
Organization-Wide Faculty Relations Characteristics					
Tightness of faculty	489	1.741	1.140	0.261	7.518
Collaborative environment	489	0.467	0.101	0.281	0.895
Professional cliquing	489	0.550		0	1
Personal cliquing	489	0.473		0	1
Hierarchical management	489	0.679		0	1
Human Resources					
Prestige of university	314	0.277		0	1
More than undergrad degree	319	0.370		0	1
Total years of experience	317	4.237	6.818	0	37
Certified in teaching	309	0.702		0	1
Material Resources					
Prep hours during school	342	1.668	2.375	0	20.33
Necessary supplies provided	341	0.724	0.381	0	1

Correlation Matrix of School Community Indicators	1	2	3	4	5
1.School Community Overall, wgtd	1.000				
2.Relational Trust	0.883	1.000			
3.Shared Values and Norms	0.839	0.616	1.000		
4.Shared Activities	0.241	0.176	0.193	1.000	
5.Diffuse Roles	0.110	0.083	0.070	0.020	1.000

Source: SSNSCS, pooled over three spring 2010 surveys

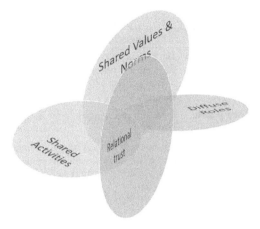

FIGURE 10.2.   Illustration of Dependence of and Independent Contribution from the Four Aspects of School Community

nicates school goals and mission, recognizes staff for good work, and the degree to which teachers consistently enforce rules, share a central mission, are satisfied as a group, and are problematically absent, α=0.83. *Shared activities* aspect is an additive scale of the number of all-faculty and multi-class events at the school, α=0.57. *Diffuse roles* aspect is an index constructed from adding the number of daily hours spent on non-teaching activities of monitoring with pre – and after-school activity participation, α=0.40.

Table 10.1 shows the distribution of these four school community measures. All dependent measures are normally distributed, with the exception of diffuse roles. Due to the positive skew on this count measure, the natural logarithm transformation is used in the modeling specifications. The correlation between these four indicators is relatively low, except for relational trust and shared values and norms that correlate at 0.616. Figure 10.2 illustrates the distinctions and overlap between these four school community aspects.

The school community overall measure is a weighted scale constructed using the standardized factor loadings of the four community indicators (see Price, 2012 for loadings output). Weighting the overall scale is the most appropriate due to the theoretical differences in degree of impact of the four aspects on the overall concept.

Social Capital Resources

To operationalize the social resources, individual social network data produce a school-wide matrix. The network characteristics are measured, coded, and stored to generate quantitative social resource measures. The five network matrices col-

TABLE 10.2. Definitions of Social Resources[a]

Faculty Relations	Organization-Wide Social Resource Concept
Tightness of faculty (Density Cohesion) (Wasserman & Faust, 1994: 164)	The total number of unidirectional ties in the network to the number of possible total ties in the given network. 0 is no cohesion and 1 is total cohesion between all network members.
Collaborative environment (Group Reciprocity)	Density of mutual, two-way ties within the whole school network
Professional or Personal cliquing (Borgatti & Everett, 1992; Bryk & Schneider, 2002, Frank & Zhao, 2005, Mooleanaar, 2010)	*Professional cliquing* (Structural isomorphism): Connection through role position similarity in the network; substantive cliquing on grade level or subject matter taught (Frank & Zhao, 2005) *Personal cliquing* (Structural equivalence): Expressive cliquing on personal, ascriptive, homophily characteristics (Moolenaar, 2010)
Hierarchical management (Rowan, 1990)	Configuration pattern of uni- or bi-directional ties of teachers to principal.
Interpersonal Relationships	**Dyadic social resource concept**
Seeks information (Expansiveness) (Wasserman & Faust, 1994: 175)	Latent construct describing persons with outbound (giving/ sending) ties that reach to others for guidance.
Involvement with others (Wasserman & Faust, 1994: 254–262)	Latent construct describing persons with multiple and diverse groups of people with whom they interact.
Point person (Degree Centrality / Popularity/Prestige) (Wasserman & Faust, 1994: 178–79, 202–10)	Latent construct describing persons with inbound (receiving) ties from other school members.
Mutual, collegial relationships (Ego reciprocity; Mooleanaar, 2010)	Mutual dyads; both in and out degree of i and j with each other.

[a] Calculations of variables can be found at Price (2012) and discussion of latent variable statistics can be found at Price (2013).

lected per survey[7] are added together per survey time point using the consensus structure matrices in UCINET network software (see Krackhardt, 1988). From the school matrix, measures of the interpersonal social resources of the individual school members within the school network and the organization-wide social resources are quantified. In particular, the operationalization of the social resources is described in Table 10.2.

Human and Material Resources

The human and material resources of schools are expected to contextualize social resources within the school (Gamoran, Secada, & Marrett, 2000). Material

---

[7] School staff members were asked to name their outgoing and incoming ties on five areas of need: school information, pedagogical help, discipline help, teaching philosophy, and personal matters.

resources of preparation time and supplying necessary materials intersect with the human resources of the teachers (experience and credentialing) creates a means to facilitate a professional environment (Moolenaar et al., 2014).

Statistical Methods

The quantitative network analysis identifies the patterns which characterize the social resources of the school networks using UCINET 6 software. Regression analyses test the effects of social resources on school community outcomes, controlling for the human and material resources, using Stata 14 software. This chapter uses a fixed effects regression modeling technique to account for the correlated error structure within schools using Stata's 'xtreg' command by using a fixed effect estimator on the school id. *This fixed effect specification focuses the analysis on the impact of social resources to explain variation between school members within schools and not between schools.* Statistical estimates also control for teachers' age, gender, race, and ethnicity.

The regression models test two theoretical ideas in conjunction. First, if social closure is the mechanism creating school community effects, then dyadic ties would associate with school community. Second, if the common good mechanism impacts positive school community, then organization-wide network characteristics would associate with school community.

FINDINGS

As discussed above, the study seeks to investigate the research question from two lenses: 1) to compare the social capital ideas regarding the joint effects of organization-wide faculty relations (the 'sum' of the network 'parts') and the interpersonal relationship characteristics (the 'parts' of the network), and 2) to describe if and how these social resources differentially impact each of the four aspects of school community.

In general, the models in Table 10.3 explain a non-trivial amount of the variation on the outcomes, with the exception of the diffuse roles indicator. Both interpersonal and organization-wide social resources impact overall school community and shared values and norms. Relational trust and shared activities, in comparison, are much more linked to organization-wide social resources than interpersonal ones. When there are similarities between indicators, most of the directions of the coefficients align, with a few notable exceptions.

In particular, Table 10.3 shows that interpersonal relationships—the 'parts' of the network—act similarly on overall school community, albeit to a lesser magnitude, as it does on shared values and norms: the more teachers seek out information, the better the perception of school community and shared values and norms. Teachers who are central point-people also report better school community and shared values and norms. Centrality does differentiate from popular involvement

TABLE 10.3. Social Resources on School Community[a]

	(1)	(2)	(3)	(4)	(5)
	School Community Overall	Relational Trust	Shared Values and Norms	Shared Activities	Diffuse Roles (logged)
Dyadic Interpersonal Relationships					
Seeks information	0.451+	0.730	1.231+	0.431	−0.434
	(0.224)	(0.746)	(0.643)	(0.272)	(1.453)
Involvement with others	−0.331	−0.320	−1.126+	−0.065	−0.658
	(0.288)	(1.045)	(0.624)	(0.405)	(1.635)
Point person centrality	0.113*	0.253	0.326*	0.134	0.628
	(0.052)	(0.192)	(0.139)	(0.113)	(0.586)
Mutual collegial relationships	−0.011	0.117	−0.080	0.026	−0.127
	(0.044)	(0.159)	(0.143)	(0.047)	(0.287)
Organization-Wide Faculty Relations					
Tightness of faculty	0.038+	0.080	0.136*	0.086*	0.166
	(0.019)	(0.069)	(0.054)	(0.037)	(0.236)
Collaborative environment	−0.236	−0.709	−0.769	−0.944*	−2.537
	(0.162)	(0.897)	(0.693)	(0.399)	(1.925)
Professional cliquing	−0.029	0.072	−0.318*	0.024	−0.291
	(0.052)	(0.274)	(0.137)	(0.089)	(0.345)
Personal cliquing	0.059	0.153	0.106	0.031	0.010
	(0.034)	(0.190)	(0.156)	(0.086)	(0.462)
Hierarchical management	0.167*	0.693*	0.222	0.081	0.672
	(0.061)	(0.267)	(0.161)	(0.083)	(0.481)
Human Resources					
Prestige of university	0.008	−0.143	0.108	−0.098*	−0.402
	(0.046)	(0.163)	(0.159)	(0.035)	(0.246)
More than undergrad degree	−0.094+	−0.265	−0.280*	−0.011	−0.219
	(0.047)	(0.204)	(0.100)	(0.051)	(0.246)
Total years of experience	0.004+	0.019+	0.013+	0.000	0.039*
	(0.002)	(0.010)	(0.007)	(0.003)	(0.016)
Certified in teaching	0.085	0.070	0.267	0.134**	0.253
	(0.091)	(0.270)	(0.219)	(0.039)	(0.301)
Material Resources					
Prep hours during school	0.007	0.020	0.013	0.001	0.154**
	(0.005)	(0.020)	(0.011)	(0.007)	(0.052)
Necessary supplies provided	0.257**	0.918***	0.752**	0.095	−0.195
	(0.069)	(0.182)	(0.199)	(0.063)	(0.364)
Constant	1.713***	5.714***	5.126***	0.316	-2.385*
	(0.156)	(0.492)	(0.396)	(0.207)	(0.879)
Observations	295	295	295	295	295
R-squared	0.233	0.199	0.212	0.118	0.066

Robust standard errors in parentheses *** $p<0.001$, ** $p<0.01$, * $p<0.05$, +$p<.10$
a Models run fixed effects for schools and control for teacher age, gender, and race-ethnicity.

with others, as there is a negative relationship of the amount of involvement with others and teachers' perceptions on shared values and norms.

The organization-wide faculty relations—the 'sum' of the network 'parts'— work differently depending on the school community indicators. The density of the faculty network explains better school community overall, shared values and norms, and shared activities. Isomorphic professional cliquing matters little to none on explaining school community while worsening shared values and norms. Higher levels of interdependence reduce shared activities. Hierarchical, one-way directional management of principal to teacher works to heighten relational trust and improve school community overall. To frame the impact of social resources on these outcomes, the models also show the importance of human resources on all components of school community. Moreover, material resources also impact the aspects of school community except shared activities.

In summary, organization-wide faculty relations hold more influence over indicators of school community than dyadic interpersonal characteristics. Yet, both types of social resources matter for the overall school community. The overall school community model shows all four components of school community do uniquely contribute to the school community (as the correlations show in Table 10.2), with shared values and norms perhaps pulling more heavily on the overall concept. These social resources appear to work in concert to describe school community.

DISCUSSION

The models show that school community is a complex phenomenon. It is not a proxy of any one component nor is it defined by one type of resource. Rather, social resources differentially impact the components associated with school community. For the discussion on social capital, it is then imperative to clearly distinguish interpersonal relationship and organization-wide network social resources. With that said, interpersonal relationship social resources appear less impactful on shaping community than the social resources defined by the whole network. For the school community indicator of shared values and norms where dyadic ties did matter more, it makes theoretical sense that it could benefit from preemptively shared ideas among members when forming a community's values and norms. This contrasts to sharing activities and relational trust which largely undergo a shared-experience process to build as community ideals.

In schools, as with other organizations, when members share some underlying structural characteristics, such as working together (structural isomorphism), a network of relationships can generate 'community' (Frank & Zhao, 2005). This community is more likely to form if there exists a shared, productive goal (Lawler, 2001).[8] A shared school mission or pedagogical style, for example, can provide

---

[8] Network theory at the macro level describes how sharing common tasks between individual persons creates tight, bonded communities. Through their social exchanges and shared tasks, the members

this shared, productive goal. Communities can also emerge from a series of relations when individual members share similar traits (structural equivalence), such as similar values and beliefs (Frank & Zhao, 2005). As this study corroborates, communities can also arise from a combination of both of these reasons (Frank & Zhao, 2005). This study did not show that one type of cliquing mattered more or less than the other.

By mapping and measuring the social resources in schools, network analysis provides the theoretical and methodological tools to dig deeply into the social capital processes associated with school community and, ultimately, school effectiveness (Daly & Finnigan, 2010). Some work is currently under development in this area of understanding internal school social resources. Frank and colleagues (Frank & Zhao, 2005; Sun, Penuel, Frank, Gallagher, & Youngs, 2013; Sun, Wilhelm, Larson, & Frank, 2014; Youngs & Frank, 2008) show the influence of strong ties on the diffusion of knowledge among school teachers. Similarly, Nienke Moolenaar and colleagues (Daly et al., 2015; de Jong, Moolenaar, Osagie, & Phielix, 2016; Moolenaar, 2010; Van Meale et al., 2015) find increased levels of trust, democratic decision-making, and innovation in Netherland schools when staff cliques are formally structured into the school by professional characteristics such as formal grade level teams. Other scholars are expanding this research to consider the role of diffusion from the district/board level to the school administrators and teachers (Coburn, Mata, & Choi, 2013; Coburn & Russell, 2008; Coburn, Russell, Kaufman, & Stein, 2012; Daly & Finnigan, 2010; Daly et al., 2015; Finnigan & Daly, 2010).

Further abstracted, these two distinct explanations speak to the classical sociological discussions around *gemeinshaft* versus *gesellschaft* and mechanical versus organic solidarity. Coleman's discussion of the role of social capital in creating positive school outcomes closely aligns with the gesellschaft ideas where school community effects those involved and the actors behave in a manner explained by their mechanical solidarity. Bryk and Driscoll's (1988) discussion of social capital in creating positive school outcomes closely aligns with gemeinschaft notions common to Bourdieu's notion of social capital (1986) where the community itself takes on its own cultural effect greater than the sum of the independent individual actor parts and instead is defined by what organically arises from the contributions of all to the community.

---

of the community develop emotional bonds (Davis, 1963). As the frequency of these emotional experiences increases, the salience of the group context intensifies (Lawler, 2001, pp. 322–323). This process then reinforces collective behaviors within the group, including commitment to the group (Lawler, Thye, & Yoon, 2006). As a result, identities of the group form among committed members (Davis, 1963). Moreover, as they experience more positive emotions, the desire to reproduce positive emotions and share risk increases as uncertainty is reduced (Lawler, Thye, & Yoon, 2006; Uzzi & Spiro, 2005). These results are strongest among groups of structurally bounded persons (Lawler 2001), such as teachers within a school.

FURTHER RESEARCH

Three findings warrant further thought and consideration in relation the existing knowledge about social capital. One, it is curious that persons' involvement with others and collaborative environments decrease many of the desirable school community outcomes. Most theory would postulate that diverse and group-based interactions would improve outcomes related to unity. However, it may be the case that these people who bridge many cliques invoke a saturation response of 'information overload.' Meaning, persons who have high levels of involvement with others may be more acutely aware of the diversity of values and activities within their school thus their perceptions of shared values and norms and shared activities might be a function of a more fine-grained knowledge of the absolute range of persons' attitudes and behaviors in their school, as compared to others' relative perceptions. These persons might therefore be less likely to highly rate perceptions related to unity or sharing on a survey. However, this post-hoc idea cannot be tested with these data.

Secondly, the nearly zero effect of school isomorphic professional clique structure on school community, with the exception of shared values and norms, can be puzzling in light of other evidence that quite strongly shows that school faculty members who congeal around substantive qualities, such as grade level and subject matter, benefit teachers' and students' attitudes. However, I caution readers not to leap to a conclusion of incongruence yet. The models presented in this chapter predict cliquing structure on school community perceptions, not engagement. Extensions of this work from school climate to engagement does show cliquing impacting the direction of teacher engagement (Price, 2012).

Lastly, the strong and positive effect of hierarchical management style on school community may sit uncomfortably with proponents of distributed leadership in organizations. However, fieldwork interviews (see Price, 2015) indicate that teachers appreciate principals who 'take charge' of their schools. Although teachers expressed a desire to be a part of their schools' decisions, they congruently expressed appreciation for principals who initiated these schooling decision processes. As several principals discussed, their style is to press everyone toward a core mission with clear expectations and guidelines to achieve it (Price, 2015). This nuance between distributed leadership opportunities and input in decision-making is corroborated by other research as well (Hulpia, Devos, & Rosseel, 2009).

REFERENCES

Atteberry, A., & Bryk, A. S. (2010). Centrality, connection, and commitment: The role of social networks in a school-based literacy initiative. In A. J. Daly (Ed.), *Social Network Theory and Educational Change* (pp. 51–76). Cambridge, MA: Harvard Education Press.

Bloom, H. S., Thompson, S. L., Unterman, R., Herlihy, C., & Payne, C. F. (2010). *How New York City's new small schools are boosting student achievement and graduation rates*. New York, NY: MDRC.

Borgatti, S. P., & Everett, M. (1992). Notions of Position in Network Analysis. *Sociological Methodology 22*(1), 1–36.

Bourdieu, P. (1986). The forms of capital. In J. E. Richardson (Ed.), *Handbook of theory of research for the sociology of education* (pp. 24–258). Westport, CT: Greenwood Press.

Bourdieu, P. (2011). The forms of capital (1986). In Szeman & T. Kaposy (Eds.), *Cultural theory: An anthology* (pp, 81–93). New York, NY: Wiley and Sons.

Brown, C., Daly, A., & Liou, Y.-H. (2016). Improving trust, improving schools: Findings from a social network analysis of 43 primary schools in England. *Journal of Professional Capital and Community, 1*(1), 69–91.

Bryk, A. S., & Driscoll, M. (1988). *The high school as community: Contextual influences and consequences for students and teachers*. National Center on Effective Secondary Schools, Madison, WI: University of Wisconsin.

Bryk, A. S., Lee, V. E., & Holland, P. (1993). *Catholic schools and the common good*. Cambridge, MA: Harvard University Press.

Bryk, A., & Schneider, B. (2002). *Trust in schools: A core resource for improvement*. New York, NY: Russell Sage Foundation.

Bryk, A. S., Sebring, P. B., Allensworth, E., Luppescu, S., & Easton, J. Q. (2010). *Organizing schools for improvement: Lessons from Chicago*. Chicago, IL: The University of Chicago Press.

Chubb, J. E., & Moe, T. M. (2011). *Politics, markets, and America's schools*. Brookings Institution Press.

Coburn, C. E., Mata, W. S., & Choi, L. (2013). The embeddedness of teachers' social networks: Evidence from a study of mathematics reform. *Sociology of Education, 86*(4), 311–342.

Coburn, C. E., & Russell, J. L. (2008). District policy and teachers' social networks. *Educational Evaluation and Policy Analysis, 30*(3), 203–235.

Coburn, C. E., Russell, J. L., Kaufman, J. H., & Stein, M. K. (2012). Supporting sustainability: Teachers' advice networks and ambitious instructional reform. *American Journal of Education, 119*(1), 137–182.

Coleman, J. S. (1961). *The adolescent society*. Westport, CT: Greenwood Press.

Coleman, J. S. (1988). Social capital in the creation of human capital. *American Journal of Sociology, 94*, S95–S120.

Coleman, J. S., & Hoffer, T. (1987). *Public and private high schools: The impact of communities* (vol. 41). New York: Basic Books.

Daly, A. J. (Ed.). (2010). *Social network theory and educational change* (vol. 8). Cambridge, MA: Harvard Education Press.

Daly, A. J., & Finnigan, K. S. (2010). A bridge between worlds: Understanding network structure to understand change strategy. *Journal of Educational Change, 11*(2), 111–138.

Daly, A. J., Moolenaar, N. M., Bolivar, J. M., & Burke, P. (2010). Relationships in reform: The role of teachers' social networks. *Journal of Educational Administration, 48*(3), 359–391.

Daly, A. J., Moolenaar, N. M., Der-Martirosian, C., & Liou, Y.-H. (2014). Accessing capital resources: Investigating the effects of teacher human and social capital on student achievement. *Teachers College Record*, 116(7), 1–42.

Daly, A. J., Moolenaar, N. M., Liou, Y.-H., Tuytens, M., & Del Fresno, M. (2015). Why so difficult? Exploring negative relationships between educational leaders: The role of trust, climate, and efficacy. *American Journal of Education*, 122(1), 1–38.

Davis, J. A. (1963). Structural balance, mechanical solidarity, and interpersonal-relations. *American Journal of Sociology, 68*(4), 444–462.

Deal, T. E., Purniton, T., & Waetjen, D. C. (2009). *Making sense of social networks in schools*, Thousand Oaks, CA: Corwin Press.

de Jong, K. J., Moolenaar, N. M., Osagie, E., & Phielix, C. (2016). Valuable connections: A social capital perspective on teachers' social networks, commitment and self-efficacy. *Pedagogía Social, 28*, 71–83.

Durkheim, E. (1944). *Education and society*. New York, NY: The Free Press.

Finnigan, K., & Daly, A. J. (2010). Learning at a system level: Ties between principals of low-performing schools and central office leaders. In A. J. Daly (Ed.), *Social Network Theory and Educational Change* (pp. 179–196). Cambridge, MA: Harvard Educational Press.

Firestone, W. A., & Pennell, J. R. (1993). Teacher commitment, working conditions, and differential incentive policies. *Review of Educational Research, 63*(4), 489–525.

Frank, K. A., & Zhao, Y. (2005). Subgroups as meso-level entities in the social organization of schools. In L. V. Hedges & B. Schneider (Eds.), *The social organization of schooling* (pp. 200–224). New York, NY: Russell Sage Foundation.

Gamoran, A., Secada, W. G., & Marrett, C. G. (2000). The organizational context of teaching and learning: Changing theoretical perspectives. In M. T. Hallinan (Ed.), *Handbook of the sociology of education,* (pp. 37–64). New York, NY: Springer Science and Business Media.

Goddard, R. D., Tschannen-Moran, M., & Hoy, W. K. (2001). A multilevel examination of the distribution and effects of teacher trust in students and parents in urban elementary schools. *The Elementary School Journal*, 3–17.

Goddard, Y. L., Goddard, R. D., & Tschannen-Moran, M. (2007). A theoretical and empirical investigation of teacher collaboration for school improvement and student achievement in public elementary schools. *Teachers college record, 109*(4), 877–896.

Goldring, E. B., & Pasternack, R. (1994). Principals' coordinating strategies and school effectiveness. *School Effectiveness and School Improvement, 5*(3), 239–253.

Hilliard, A. (2003). No mystery: Closing the achievement gap between Africans and excellence. In T. Perry, C. Steele & A. Hillard III (Eds.), *Young, gifted, and Black: Promoting high achievement among African American students* (pp. 131–165).

Hoffer, T., Greeley, A. M., & Coleman, J. S. (1985). Achievement growth in public and Catholic schools. *Sociology of Education*, 74–97.

Hoy, A. W., Hoy, W. K., & Kurz, N. M. (2008). Teacher's academic optimism: The development and test of a new construct. *Teaching and teacher education, 24*(4), 821–835.

Hulpia, H., Devos, G., & Rosseel, Y. (2009). The relationship between the perception of distributed leadership in secondary schools and teachers' and teacher leaders' job satisfaction and organizational commitment, *School Effectiveness and School Improvement, 20*, 291–317.

Kim, J., Youngs, P., & Frank, K. (2017). Burnout contagion: Is it due to early career teachers' social networks or organizational exposure? *Teaching and Teacher Education, 66,* 250–260.

Krackhardt, D. (1988). Predicting with networks: Nonparametric multiple regression analysis of dyadic data. *Social Networks, 10,* 359–381.

Lawler, E. J. (2001). An affect theory of social exchange. *American Journal of Sociology, 107*(2), 321–352.

Lawler, E. J., Thye, S. R., & Yoon, J. (2006). Commitment in structurally enabled and induced exchange relations. *Social Psychology Quarterly, 69*(2), 183–200.

Lee, V. E., & Holland, P. B. (1993). *Catholic schools and the common good.* Cambridge: Harvard University Press.

Leithwood, K., & Jantzi, D. (1990). Transformational leadership: How principals can help reform school cultures. *School Effectiveness and School Improvement, 1*(4), 249–280.

Leithwood, K., Leonard, L., & Sharratt, L. (1998). Conditions fostering organizational learning in schools. *Educational Administration Quarterly, 34*(2), 243–276.

Louis, K. S., Leithwood, K., Wahlstrom, K., & Anderson, S. (2010). *Investigating the links to improved student learning: Final report of research findings.* Minneapolis, MN: University of Minnesota.

McCloskey, P. (2008). *The street stops here: A year at a Catholic high school in Harlem.* Berkeley, CA: University of California Press.

Moolenaar, N. M. (2010). *Ties with potential: Nature, antecedents, and consequences of Social Networks in School Teams.* Amsterdam, Netherlands: Ipskamp Drukkers B.V.

Moolenaar, N. M., Daly, A. J., Cornelissen, F., Liou, Y.-H., Caillier, S., Riordan, R., & Cohen, N. A. (2014). Linked to innovation: Shaping an innovative climate through network intentionality and educators' social network position. *Journal of Educational Change, 15*(2), 99–123.

Moolenaar, N. M., & Sleegers, P. J. (2010). Social networks, trust, and innovation: The role of relationships in supporting an innovative climate in Dutch schools. In A. J. Daly (Ed.), *Social Network Theory and Educational Change* (pp. 97–114). Cambridge, MA: Harvard Education Press.

Nye, B., Konstantopoulos, S., & Hedges, L.V. (2004). How large are teacher effects? *Educational Evaluation and Policy Analysis, 26,* 237–257.

OECD. (2014). *TALIS 2013 results: An international perspective on teaching and learning.* TALIS: OECD Publishing. Retrieved from http://dx.doi.org/10.1787/9789264196261-en

Penuel, W., Frank, K. A., & Krause, A. (2010). Between leaders and teachers: using social network analysis to examine the effects of distributed leadership. In A. J. Daly (Ed.), *Social network theory and educational change* (pp. 159–178). Cambridge, MA: Harvard Educational Press.

Phillips, M. (1997). What makes schools effective? A comparison of the relationships of communitarian climate and academic climate to mathematics achievement and attendance during middle school. *American Educational Research Journal, 34*(4), 633–662.

Portes, A. (1998). Social Capital: Its origins and applications in modern sociology. *Annual Review of Sociology, 24,* 1–24.

Powell, A. G. (1985). The shopping mall high school. Winners and losers in the educational marketplace. *NASSP Bulletin, 69*(483), 40–51.

Price, H. E. (2011). *School networks as social resources: The relationship of school resources and school community to school effectiveness.* Doctoral dissertation. Retrieved from Proquest Dissertations & Theses Global. (Order No. 3497151).

Price, H. E. (2013). Connecting network methods to social science research: How to parsimoniously use dyadic measures as independent variables. In F. Depelteau & C. Powell (Eds.), *Applying relational sociology: relations, networks, and society* (pp. 207–225). New York, NY: Palgrave Macmillan US.

Price, H. E. (2015). School leadership in urban schools: How leadership in the social context shapes teacher engagement and school community. In R. H. Milner & K. Lomotey (Eds.), *The handbook of urban educational leadership* (Section 4: Theory and research methodology) (pp. 426–440). New York, NY: Rowan & Littlefield.

Robinson, V. M., Lloyd, C. A., & Rowe, K. J. (2008). The impact of leadership on student outcomes: An analysis of the differential effects of leadership types. *Educational Administration Quarterly, 44*(5), 635–674.

Shear, L., Means, B., Mitchell, K., House, A., Gorges, T., Joshi, A., Smerdon, B., & Shkolnik, J. (2008). Contrasting paths to small-school reform: Results of a 5-year evaluation of the Bill & Melinda Gates Foundation's National High Schools Initiative. *Teachers College Record, 110*(9), 1986–2039.

Smith, M. S. & O'Day, J. (1991). Systematic school reform. In S. H. Fuhrman & B. Malen (Eds.), *The politics of curriculum and testing.* Philadelphia, PA: Falmer Press.

Spillane, J. P. (2006). *Distributed leadership.* San Francisco, CA: Jossey-Bass.

Struyve, C., Daly, A., Vandecandelaere, M., Meredith, C., Hannes, K., & De Fraine, B. (2016). More than a mentor: The role of social connectedness in early career and experienced teachers' intention to leave. *Journal of Professional Capital and Community, 1*(3), 198–218.

Sun, M., Penuel, W. R., Frank, K. A., Gallagher, H. A., & Youngs, P. (2013). Shaping professional development to promote the diffusion of instructional expertise among teachers. *Educational Evaluation and Policy Analysis, 35*(3), 344–369.

Sun, M., Wilhelm, A. G., Larson, C. J., & Frank, K. A. (2014). Exploring colleagues' professional influence on mathematics teachers' learning. *Teachers College Record, 116*(6), 1–30.

Tschannen-Moran, M., & Hoy, W. K. (2000). A multidisciplinary analysis of the nature, meaning, and measurement of trust. *Review of Educational Research, 70*(4), 547–593.

Uzzi, B., & Spiro, J. (2005). Collaboration and creativity: The small world problem. *American Journal of Sociology, 111*(2), 447–504.

Van Maele, D., Moolenaar, N. M., & Daly, A. J. (2015). All for one and one for all: A social network perspective on the effects of social influence on teacher trust. In M. DiPaola & W. K. Hoy (Eds.), *Leadership and school quality* (pp. 171–196). Charlotte, NC: Information Age Publishing, Inc.

Waller, W.W. (1932). *The sociology of teaching.* New York, NY: J. Wiley & sons.

Wasserman, S., & Faust, K. (1994). *Social network analysis: Methods and applications.* Cambridge, MA: Cambridge University Press.

Wayne, A. J., & Youngs, P. (2003). Teacher characteristics and student achievement gains: A review. *Review of Educational Research, 73*, 89–122.

Youngs, P., & Frank, K. (2008). *How mentors, colleagues, and school organizational conditions affect outcomes for beginning teachers and their students.* Paper presented at the Understanding Teacher Effects and Educational Outcomes Conference, University of Notre Dame, Notre Dame, IN.

CHAPTER 11

SOCIAL CAPITAL AND EDUCATIONAL EXPECTATIONS

Exploring Adolescents' Capabilities to Aspire for Postsecondary Education

Chrysa Pui Chi Keung and Esther Sui Chu Ho

FORMATION OF EDUCATIONAL EXPECTATIONS IN ADOLESCENTS

The study of educational expectation has long received attention in the sociology of education (Goyette & Xie, 1999; Hauser & Anderson, 1991; Hossler & Stage, 1992; Kao & Tienda, 1998). Educational expectation refers to a combination of intentions, purposes and plans which an individual expects to achieve at a particular stage of education (Feliciano, 2006; Goyette, 2008). Different from educational aspiration, educational expectation provides more realistic evaluations of personal abilities, financial resources and opportunities for future educational outcomes (Andres, Anisef, Krahn, Looker, & Thiessen, 1999; Feliciano, 2006; Hanson, 1994). The formation of educational expectation, in this view, more realistically reflects an estimation of how far an individual intends to pursue future study (Morgan, 2006).

Contemporary Perspectives on Social Capital in Educational Contexts,
pages 181–199.
Copyright © 2019 by Information Age Publishing
All rights of reproduction in any form reserved.

The formation of educational expectation is prominent in adolescence. In particular, senior years of schooling are seen as the prime exploratory years when adolescents are more active in gathering pathway information and tend to talk with their parents, peers, or teachers about their educational plans. Research suggests adolescents become increasingly aware of their own abilities and more alert to the opportunities in education and the employment market when approaching a major educational transition from secondary education to post-secondary education (Foskett & Helmsley-Brown, 2001; Nurmi, 1991; Wahl & Blackhurst, 2000). Differences in educational expectations also need to consider agency factors. The important differences between those adolescents who aspire to higher education and those who do not may depend on the resources they have at their disposal to act out their agency. Such capacity may be connected to their ability to access post-secondary education information, their level of academic ability, and their degree of preparation for future education and career (Heinz, 2009; Mateju, Smith, Soukup, & Basl, 2007; Plank & Jordan, 2001).

Adolescents' expectations for pursuing post-secondary education are formed by a process, which incorporates various influential inputs from family and educational contexts. Hossler and Gallagher (1987) abstracted the college choice process into three stages: predisposition, search and choice. In the first stage of their model, educational expectation is developed, by which adolescents become predisposed to pursuing post-secondary education. It includes the formation of post-secondary educational goals and plans which are largely influenced by adolescents' family background and their significant others, such as parents, peers and teachers. Adolescents also interact with those who have had first-hand post-secondary education experiences. This predisposition stage is closely linked to the next stage of the process—the search. The Search stage is when adolescents become active in seeking information about higher education opportunities and evaluating options available to them. In the critical process of searching, adolescents might engage in a variety of exploration activities, for example university visits, job placement and other outreach programs. These activities can be very helpful to them in identifying their educational goals and thus formulating pathway choice sets. The Choice is when they make decisions which become their realistic aspirations. As adolescents move from abstract to more concrete education and career plans, their educational expectations tend to become stable and consistent.

BARRIERS TO POSTSECONDARY
EDUCATIONAL EXPECTATIONS

Numerous studies have been conducted with a primary focus on structural and economic barriers as the determinants of post-secondary educational expectations (Goldrick-Rab, 2006; Lynch & O'Riordan, 1998; Reay, David, & Ball, 2005; Teachman, 1987). Those studies generally support the view that adolescents from working class families, due to their social backgrounds and financial status, lag behind their counterparts from upper middle-class families in expectation of and therefore aspirations to pursue post-secondary education.

Parental Background

Status attainment model is a corner-stone of educational expectation research. It suggests that individuals' educational expectations and attainments are primarily driven by parents' background. In the seminal work of Blau and Duncan (1967), their model uses a father's educational background and occupational status to predict a son's educational attainment and first-job status. The model posits that a father's education and occupation affects a son's level of education, which in turn affects a son's eventual occupational attainment. The Wisconsin model of status attainment (Sewell, Haller, & Portes, 1969) extends the Blau-Duncan model by incorporating other variables into the model such as educational and occupational expectations, academic achievement, mental ability, and influence of significant others. The model explains how these factors are combined to shape educational expectation rather than considering only the single impact of parents' background. In their model, it became clear that educational expectation emerged as a mediating variable in the status attainment process (Haller & Portes, 1973).

One of the strongest background factors predicting adolescents' educational expectations is the educational level of their parents. Previous research has clearly shown that adolescents with highly educated parents are more likely to continue education after completing their secondary education (Abada & Tenkorang, 2009; Hossler & Stage, 1992). Those studies reveal that parents with higher levels of education are more likely to have relevant first-hand knowledge about post-secondary education. Therefore, they are able to describe the experiences and benefits of getting higher education to their children. Although working class parents perceive the value of education, most of them have no personal experience of post-secondary education and are often unable to give as much educational support to their children.

Economic Resources

There is a body of research using a primarily economic perspective to explain the differences in educational decisions adolescents make when choosing to attend post-secondary institutions and programs (DesJardins & Toutkoushian, 2005; Ellwood & Kane, 2000; Mangan, Adnett, & Davies, 2001; Manski & Wise, 1983; Paulsen, 2001). The literature has generally taken family resources as the indicator which reflects the economic conditions and financial status of a family. An economic perspective perceives education to be a form of economic investment and is guided by rational calculations of the costs and benefits of education (Becker, 1993; Breen & Goldthorpe, 1997; Manski, 1993; Williams & Gordon, 1981). Parents with higher income are expected to have more resources available to cover the cost of post-secondary education, and thus they are able to invest in their children's education. In contrast, adolescents from low income families with fewer economic resources tend to hold lower expectations than their more advantaged peers. The effect of family structure also becomes an important factor in determining children's educational expectations in today's family context. Children from single parent families lack adequate financial resources and academic support, and they have lower educational expectations than those from two-parent families (Astone & McLanahan, 1991; Han, Huang, & Garfinkel, 2003; Wu, Schimmele, & Hou, 2015). The reduced educational and material resources in single parent families may affect children's opportunities to pursue post-secondary education and achieve higher educational goals.

Subjected to the assumption of utility maximization, working class adolescents may be inclined to lower their expectations of pursuing post-secondary education because they believe continuing education is too costly for them (Goldthorpe, 1996). Economic reasoning plays a significant role in formulating adolescents' final choice sets pertaining to enrollment for post-secondary programs. However, the weakness of economic perspective alone is that it does not explain the extent to which adolescents' educational transitions are influenced by sociocultural and contextual factors (Hatcher, 1998; Hemsley-Brown, 1999; Hossler, Schmit, & Vesper, 1999). One significant sociocultural influence shaping adolescents' educational plans is the accuracy of information they have for informing their potential future study and career choices. Parents and significant others are the sources of information and supports which can increase adolescents' likelihood of expectation of enrolling for a higher-level education (Brooks, 2003; Hossler & Stage, 1992; Kim & Schneider, 2005; McDonough, 1997).

Cultural and Social Resources

Cultural resources. Many studies have applied Bourdieu's cultural capital theory to explain the effects of parents' background and parental influences on their children's educational expectations and choices (for example Aschaffenburg & Maas, 1997; Ball, Maguire & Macrae, 2000; De Graaf, De Graaf, & Kraaykamp, 2000; DiMaggio & Mohr, 1985; Lareau, 2003; Sullivan, 2001). Cultural capital refers to individuals' cultural resources related to cultural background, knowledge and disposition (Bourdieu, 1986). In Bourdieu's (1986) formulation, individuals from the upper middle class are born into a home environment in which there is a homogenous familiarity with school systems and cultural codes that enables such students to adapt to school life and perform well in schools (Bourdieu, 1977; Bourdieu & Passeron, 1977). Bourdieu (1986) distinguishes three other forms of cultural capital: objectified form, embodied form and institutionalized form. Objectified form refers to cultural goods or artifacts, such as books, dictionaries and instruments. Embodied form refers to the appreciation of cultural goods through an individual's mind and body, such as linguistic skill, tastes and attitudes. Finally, the institutionalized form is seen as educational credentials and qualifications, including the school attended and achievements. Bourdieu (1986) observed individuals from upper middle-class families possess more of the first mentioned (i.e., embodied and objectified forms of cultural capital) than their working class counterparts.

It is usual that norms are cultivated primarily in the family context, which means children from upper middle-class families are likely to internalize their parents' educational values (i.e., the attainment of a higher level of education) (Lamont & Lareau, 1988). In a similar vein, schools are driven by middle class values and norms, presenting the argument that students with relevant cultural capital would better fit school culture and thus be more likely to perform better and succeed at school (Bourdieu, 1977; Lareau, 2003; McDonough, 1997). The concept of cultural capital explains cultural background, knowledge and disposition, which may determine levels of educational expectation. Low expectations and attainment levels are most prevalent among working class adolescents as a consequence of their perceived lack of cultural capital. Bourdieu (1986), therefore, sees families and schools as a site for reproducing the unequal access to education. However, plausible as it is, this theory gives comparatively little attention to explaining those exceptional adolescents who lack class-related resources but do have expectations for pursuing post-secondary education.

Social resources. Coleman (1988, 1990) places emphasis on a set of resources individuals can access through their ties with others—which, in turn, facilitate collective actions. He defines social resources and norms that are conducive to the formation of educational expectations as social capital, existing in the structure of relations and available to all individuals. The closed or open nature of social networks is crucial in generating different forms of social capital. Three major forms of social capital include: (a) expectations and obligations people have of and toward each other, (b) the mode of information channels, and (c) the norms within a social group. Coleman (1988) explains obligations and expectations as being a form of exchange when a group member has given favors without receiving reciprocal favors in return. He describes such obligations as effectively governing social relations within networks. The information channels are conceived as obtaining knowledge by interacting with other members of a group or network, either formally or informally.

Social capital is created through interpersonal relationships and social networks in the contexts of family, school and the wider community. It emphasizes the fact that individuals can access the resources which are inherent in the social relationships and connections of social groups. Some studies have found working class adolescents are more in need of educational exposures and experiences because their families and social contacts often hold weaker positions in society (Kim & Schneider, 2005; Perna 2002). For example, Stanton-Salazar and Dornbusch (1995) used social capital theory to investigate the relationship between outside social networks and university-going expectations among Mexican high school adolescents in the San Francisco area. Their findings showed strong networks provide adolescents from low-income families with the guidance regarding university admission which can compensate for the limited social resources and lack of information they would otherwise be able to access.

THEORETICAL PERSPECTIVES

By explaining differential patterns of educational expectations, sociological and economic perspectives help address the structural impact of having or not having economic, cultural and social resources on adolescents' educational expectations. However, utility-based evaluation of cost-benefit analysis and family socioeconomic background are both particularly limited when explaining why economically deprived adolescents still possess goals of pursuing a higher level of education (Unterhalter, 2009). Capability approach offers an alternative view which moves beyond utilitarianism to explain differential educational outcomes and thus differs from the economic perspective which looks at education from the viewpoint solely of being an investment. It can be argued the intergenerational reproduction of socioeconomic milieu is such a strong force that it is inevitable (Heinz, 2009; Jenkins, 1982; Sullivan, 2002). However, there are still knowledge gaps which need to be explored, not the least of which are agency factors that may influence adolescents' levels of educational expectations.

Social Reproduction Theory

In Bourdieu's (1986) account, the domination of education is the most effective means of perpetuating the existing educational resources and environment to the advantage of a privileged class. Social reproduction theory considers social class as a primary determinant for perpetuating existing social structure through the possession and transmission of cultural and social capital across generations (Bourdieu, 1986). Individuals from different class backgrounds have unequal access to educational resources, opportunities and habitus. In Bourdieu's (1993) view, this plays a crucial role in maintaining the existing class pattern. It can be understood as individuals developing their own attitudes and expectations in relation to the sociocultural milieu of their family. They internalize such experience and orientation as "proper" values or actions through a socialization process (Reed-Danahay, 2005, p. 46). *Habitus* is thus constituted as dispositions that one has learned from living in a certain environment. The concept of *habitus* helps explain why upper middle-class adolescents have a more positive disposition toward the pursuit of university study, whereas working class adolescents usually perceive their chance in life is prescribed and they must remain in the working class. This perception leads to their lower educational expectations.

Beyond *habitus*, *field* is another important concept which refers to the site of the unequal distribution of capital (Thomson, 2008). Bourdieu (1993) describes *field* as the power relations among individuals who compete for capital. Bourdieu and Wacquant (1992) use the metaphor of the "game" to imply fields are not fixed but changing in response to the "rules of the game" (Moore, 2008, p. 106). In higher education, Bourdieu (1993) argues working class parents are less familiar with the rules of the game (i.e., about educational settings, values and practices). So, they have relatively less ability to involve their children in the competition for education.

Family also plays a pivotal role in contributing to the reproduction of educational inequality by transmitting cultural capital from parents to their children. Bourdieu and Passeron (1977) argue upper middle-class families possess more financial resources, educational support, knowledge and networks that increase the likelihood of their children achieving educational success. In that sense, the educational attainment levels of individuals are inherited from their parents; thus, adolescents from upper middle class and working-class backgrounds follow different post-secondary transitional routes (Bourdieu, 1986). Upper middle class adolescents acquire cultural capital through their parents' knowledge about the educational system and effective strategies for admission (Bourdieu & Passeron, 1977; Lareau, 2003; Lareau & Weininger, 2003). Conversely, adolescents from working class families lack knowledge about the educational system and, therefore, hold a negative attitude toward continuing to post-secondary education. They lack familiarity with university life and interact with people who hold similar views. For this reason, they develop the attitude that university study is not for them (Bourdieu & Passeron, 1977, Lareau, 2003). Some studies have found working class adolescents have low expectations for the pursuit of university study and low participation rates because of their class-based dispositions (Archer, Hutchings & Ross, 2003; Paulsen & St. John, 2002; Reay, 1998). As such, working class adolescents internalize subjective expectations about the chances and possibility of success in university study, which may exclude them from the realm of post-secondary education.

Bourdieu (1986) places great emphasis on class differentials, which delineates the process making for unequal access to resources and opportunities. This theory can provide an understanding of how persistent educational advantages are maintained by adolescents from privileged backgrounds. However, such an explanation of class-based differences may diminish the importance of individual abilities and experiences and offer limited insight into the channels of developing and enabling an individual's potential to set a higher educational goal.

Capability Approach

Sen's (1985, 1992, 2005) capability approach is another theoretical perspective that addresses the role of agency—which may play a part in explaining different educational transitions. At its core, Sen's (1985, 1992, 2005) capability approach addresses the importance of individuals' well-being by looking at the ability of the person to choose what they value, rather than simply looking at the amount of resources or wealth individuals have (Alkire & Deneulin, 2009; Nussbaum, 2011; Sen, 1999; Walker, 2005). Sen (1985, 1992) argues the assessment of equality should not be limited to resources such as income or utility. It is because possession of these resources or "commodities" (Sen, 1985) does not necessarily lead to an increase in an individual's well-being (Nussbaum, 2011; Saito, 2003; Sen, 1999; Walker, 2005). The notion of well-being, as Sen (1985) suggests, can be evaluated by the extent to which individuals are able to be and do what they value. As Sen (1985) puts it, well-being is essentially "what a person is free to do and achieve in pursuit of whatever goals or values he or she regards as important" (p. 203).

Three core concepts are important to the capability approach, namely *functioning*, *capability* and *agency freedom*. For Sen (1999), the concept of *functioning* denotes "the various things a person may value doing or being" (p. 75). It refers to those things that individuals actually achieved what they have a reason to value. The pursuit of a bachelor degree is regarded as functioning. *Capability* refers to "the various combinations of functions (beings and doings) that the person can achieve" (Sen, 1992, p. 40). It represents the opportunity by which individuals are able to be and to do to achieve their functioning (Sen, 1985, 1997, 2005) or more simply means the ability to achieve. The notion of *agency freedom* can be understood as "one's freedom to bring about the achievements one values and which one attempts to produce" (Sen, 1992, p. 57). The notion of human capability does not refer exclusively to one's abilities, but also means the opportunity to choose freely between different valued possibilities (Alkire, 2005; Sen, 1985). The difference between capability and functioning, as Walker and Unterhalter (2007) said, is the contrast "between an opportunity to achieve and actual achievement, between potential and outcome" (p. 4). An individual's freedom to pursue education depends on the ability to convert those resources into a "functioning" an individual valued (Sen, 1992; Walker, 2005).

Unterhalter (2009) and Walker (2005) point out the distinction between capabilities and functioning is of importance to understand the pursuit of post-secondary education. The barriers to post-secondary education need to be evaluated in order to assess the educational disadvantage (i.e., among those who have limited educational options or alternatives) (Walker & Unterhalter, 2007). A study by Watts and Bridges (2006) found it was important for individuals to have the capability to access the knowledge of higher education which allows them to consider the pursuit of higher education as a possible choice. In their studies, expectations for post-secondary education are informed by the ease of access to various sources of information. They suggested that the expectations for post-secondary education are formed when individuals have information enabling them to visualize future education as possible for them and they have the ability to make such transitions.

Another study by Hart (2014) has combined both social reproduction theory and capability approach to analyze adolescents' choices of schooling and higher education. Hart (2014) studied the nature and formation of educational expectation among adolescents aged between 14 and 19. She provides a critical reflection on Bourdieu's idea about various forms of capital, habitus and field. These concepts can be utilized to explain the influence of family background on adolescents' educational decision to engage with higher education. However, she argues the perspective of social reproduction theory is insufficient to reveal the complexity of adolescents' aspirations. Hart (2014) then applies Sen's capability approach in her study, to explore the factors influencing individual agency which support or constrain the development of adolescents' "capability to aspire" and "capability to realization aspirations" (p. 105). The data, collected through interviews and surveys, suggests the important roles of both "freedom to aspire" and "the functioning of aspiring" in shaping different forms of aspirations. Her term, "capability to aspire" (p. 105) can be seen as a functioning. Hart's study suggests the role of educational settings play in helping adolescents to develop their capabilities and expand their opportunities to choose what they expect to pursue.

SOCIAL CAPITAL AND AGENCY FACTORS ON SHAPING ADOLESCENTS' EDUCATIONAL EXPECTATIONS

The present chapter extends the inquiry by exploring structural and agency factors that influence adolescents' post-secondary educational expectations. It fills the research gap, on the one hand, to examine the social capital which is gained from families and schools shaping adolescents' pursuit of post-secondary education and on the other hand, examining adolescents' own skills and abilities which are formed as important capabilities that influence them in achieving particular educational goal.

Parental Influences

Parents as the primary agent of socialization, exert a great influence on their adolescent children's educational expectations, whether by example as role models or through their own expectations for their children's future paths (Cohen, 1987). Prior research has shown that parental involvement appears as a form of social capital which significantly influences adolescents' educational transitions and outcomes (Catsambis, 2001; Chavkin & Williams, 1989; Coleman, 1988; McNeal, 2001; Plank & Jordan, 2001). Parental involvement and support may include the amount of encouragement and advice that parents give adolescents through discussions with children about future plans and expectations (Reynolds & Burge, 2008). Some studies have found that parents with higher socioeconomic status tend to be more involved in children's education, and therefore indirectly influence children to aim high in their education (Cabrera & LaNasa, 2001; Hill, Casellino, Lansford, Nowlin, Dodge, Bates & Pettit, 2004; Rowan-Kenyon, Bell & Perna, 2008).

Two forms of parental involvement are identified from the literature: home-based involvement (e.g. monitoring children's performance and communicating with children about academic and socio-cultural topics) and school-based involvement (e.g. participating in Parent Teacher Association activities, being volunteers in school events) (McNeal, 2001; Singh, Bickley, Trivette, Keith, Keith & Anderson, 1995; Trusty, 1999). Those studies have shown that parent involvement in children's education is strongly correlated to children's academic performance and expectations. However, while many parental involvement studies have been done on young children. Less study has been done to examine the effect of the specific form of parental involvement referring to parents' provision of emotional support and career information to adolescents, in shaping adolescents' plans for future educational pathway. This type of involvement may include activities such as discussing future careers with their children, providing children with career information, helping children to identify and set career goals, and so forth.

Expectations from parents have been recognized as one of the most important factors affecting children's educational expectation. Higher levels of parental expectation are associated with higher educational expectation levels of their children (Bodovski, 2014; Goyette & Xie, 1999; Hossler & Stage, 1992; Kirk, Lewis-Moss, Nilsen, & Colvin, 2011; Wood, Kaplan, & McLoyd, 2007). Those studies generally supported that adolescents from higher socioeconomic status families are more likely to be encouraged by parents in their post-secondary educational expectations. Some studies show the indirect effect of parental expectation on children's educational expectation through parental education (Hao & Bostead-Burns, 1998; Spera, Wentzel, & Matto, 2009). It is also equally important to examine how exactly parental expectation is perceived by adolescents. Research found that adolescents' perceptions of parental educational expectation are positively associated with adolescents' future education plans and orientations. However, the existing research paid somewhat less attention to investigate how adolescents' educational expectations differed from perceived parental expectation (Hao & Bostead-Burns, 1998; Wang & Benner, 2014; Zhang, Hadded, & Torres, 2011).

External Familial Influences

In addition to parental influences, adolescents' interactions with others outside the family are also significant in shaping their educational plans and expectations. These influences include the views of significant others such as peers and school teachers, as well as activities related to exploring future pathways. There is no doubt that peers are one of the sources of influence, in which expectations, feedback and support of social circles contribute to shape individual's value and disposition towards the pursuit of post-secondary education (Brooks, 2003; Cheng & Starks, 2002; Hossler, Schmit & Vesper, 1999; Tierney & Venegas, 2006). Adolescents reporting having peers with post-secondary education plans are more likely to consider going to university because fellow students and friends are of importance in spurring one another on with encouragement. Brooks (2005) in her longitudinal study of adolescents found that friends play a significant role in shaping adolescents' perceptions of different transitional options. Other studies also found that friends from the same social circle share common language, norms, values and cultures. They tend to hold similar expectations which may reinforce each other's goals and plans.

Another major factor bearing on adolescents' post-secondary educational expectations is the quality of relationships with their school teachers (Muller, 2001). The interaction between teachers and students not only provide useful information, but also transmit values, attitudes and expectations towards education. These may help adolescents to formulate their educational plans. Teachers and counselors provide students the access to resources and opportunities, including higher education information on admissions and requirements. This increases adolescents' likelihood of continuing education (Cheng & Starks, 2002; Hossler, Schmit, & Vesper, 1999; Schuchart, 2003).

Substantial research has looked at how social capital can be gained through social connections and networks formed from participation in extracurricular activities and other exposures. Adolescents' involvements in school activities can strengthen social support, which increase their educational expectation and attainment (Feldman & Matjasko, 2005; Hossler & Stage, 1992; Mahoney, Carins, & Farmer, 2003; Swail & Perna, 2002; Zaff, Moore, Papillo, & Williams, 2003). Some studies have outlined the positive effects of participating in academic activities. This highlights the benefits to pre-university programs of having a network and obtaining related post-secondary educational programs information. Such social support may refer to the availability of information and people who provide them with feedback and educational advice. The qualitative study of Rosenbaum, Rafiullah and Scott (1996) has interviewed high school counselors about their views on providing counseling advice on future educational plan for their students. They found that the extent to which kinds of information are made available to adolescents is mostly dependent on teachers and career advisors. Their analyses showing teachers are seen as the gatekeepers of knowledge and information about post-secondary education.

Influences of Skills and Abilities

Information search is an important skill which may reinforce an orientation towards post-secondary education. Adolescents tend to become certain about going on to pursue further education when they gather more information regarding requirements of post-secondary programs, costs of tuition and financial aid, either grants or scholarships (Hossler, Schmit & Vesper, 199; Perna, 2006; Tierney & Venegas, 2006). The study of Plank and Jordan (2001) using data drawn from the *National Educational Longitudinal Survey (NELS:88)* found that adolescents are able to access financial information about post-secondary education during high school years, thus increasing their likelihood of enrollment in post-secondary education programs when high school achievement are taken into account. Other studies have pointed out that the access to information is closely related to family background. It has been seen that adolescents and parents from disadvantaged families with no knowledge and accessible information about different educational options available to them may defer the pursuit of post-secondary education.

Disadvantaged adolescents and parents may overestimate educational cost as they are lacking accurate information about financial assistance.

Other than background characteristics and parental factors, academic ability is found as a strong predictor of educational expectation. Adolescents with higher academic performance are more likely to expect a higher educational level (Cabrera & LaNasa, 2001; Hegna, 2014; Hossler & Stage, 1992; Sewell, Haller, & Portes, 1969; Spera, Wentzel, & Matto, 2009). Differences in educational expectations are not simply the result of academic ability but follow a process of self-selection by adolescents and their parents. Research has showed that students having the same level of academic achievement make different educational plans according to their class backgrounds (Erikson & Jonsson, 1996; Goldthorpe, 1996; Manski & Wise, 1983).

CONCLUSION

Economists and social reproduction theorists offer explanations of how parents' background and possession of economic, cultural and social resources, in shaping levels of educational expectation. Studies have consistently shown that adolescents from advantaged families with greater material and financial resources are more likely to continue in education. From an economic perspective, the choice of pursuing future education only if individuals' economic conditions meet the cost of education, and they believe the higher level of education can increase future income.

For reproduction theorists, education is regarded as an effective means of maintaining the status quo and class pattern, therefore post-secondary education is reserved for the privileged class. Social reproduction theory provides an explanation of how educational advantages are produced and reproduced by social class backgrounds. In light of class-based habitus described in the previous part, Bourdieu (1993) explains beliefs, dispositions, values and social norms which are embedded in individuals' mindsets and thus influence their perceptions of pursuing post-secondary education. It provides an explanation for the extent to which the upper middle class maintain the structure whereas working class adolescents remain in low class status. However, this perspective limits the analysis of class differentiation and fails to account for those disadvantaged adolescents who have increased their participation in post-secondary education.

Drawing on Bourdieu's cultural capital and Coleman's social capital, the concept of "capital" is useful to account for differential educational expectations through the possession of various forms of capital. It clearly indicates that structural barriers related to the lack of cultural and social capitals may restrict adolescents' access to higher education. Those disadvantaged social groups are able to achieve higher levels of education. The associations with class effect provide only a partial explanation for adolescents continue their study at post-secondary education level. It remains necessary to look beyond how adolescents are conditioned by structural regularities in forming their educational goals.

Sen's capability approach sees the importance of expanding capabilities for developing individuals' potentials to achieve what they value doing and being. That is, both the ability to do and to be is important capacities to achieve what they value rather than just what resources they have access to (Alkire & Deneulin, 2009; Nussbaum, 2011; Sen, 1999; Unterhalter, 2009; Walker, 2005). The important point is to look at whether individuals are able to convert resources into capabilities, and thereafter potentially into functioning (i.e. the pursuit of a bachelor degree). This approach contributes to restate the role of human agency plays in the educational process. The notion of agency is understood as the capacity to act and bring about change through developing human capability.

Existing research is less to examine the relationships among various forms of capital, individual capabilities and adolescents' post-secondary educational expectations. This chapter synthesizes two theoretical perspectives by arguing a single view is insufficient to explain the differential patterns of educational expectation. These two perspectives are not mutually exclusive but may complement each other in explaining the determinants of educational expectation. The work of Bourdieu on social reproduction provides a framework for understanding how the possession and transmission of cultural and social capital shape adolescents' post-secondary educational expectations. However, some limitations suggest that the formation of educational expectation may not be seen in a straightforward and deterministic way. In assessing such impacts, adolescents appear to reproduce forms of capital, but at the same time their acquired capabilities also importantly shape educational expectations. For this reason, the integration of the two theoretical perspectives can provide a comprehensive analytical framework for uncovering the mechanisms of differential post-secondary educational expectations.

REFERENCES

Abada, T., & Tenkorang, E. Y. (2009). Pursuit of university education among the children of immigrants in Canada: The roles of parental human capital and social capital. *Journal of Youth Studies, 12*(2), 185–207.

Alkire, S. (2005). Why the capability approach? *Journal of Human Development, 6*(1), 115–133.

Alkire, S., & Deneulin, S. (2009). The human development and capability approach: Freedom and agency. In S. Deneulin & L. Shahani (Eds.), *An introduction to the human development and capability approach* (pp. 22–48). London, UK: Earthscan.

Andres, A., Anisef, P., Krahn, H., Looker, D., & Thiessen, V. (1999). The persistence of social structure: Cohort, class and gender effects on the occupational aspirations and expectations of Canadian Youth. *Journal of Youth Studies, 2*(3), 261–282.

Archer, L., Hutchings, M., & Ross, A. (2003). Higher education and social class: Issues of exclusion and inclusion. In K. Topping & S. Maloney (Eds.), *The Routledge Falmer Reader in inclusive education* (pp. 5–20). New York, NY: Routledge Falmer.

Aschaffenburg, K., & Maas, I. (1997). Cultural and educational careers: The dynamics of social reproduction. *American Sociological Review, 62*(4), 573–587.

Astone, N. M., & McLanahan, S. S. (1991). Family structure, parental practices and high school completion. *American Sociological Review, 56*(3), 309–320.

Ball, S. J., Maguire, M., & Macrae, S. (2000). *Choice, pathways and transitions post-16: New youth, new economies in the global city.* London, UK: Routledge.

Becker, G. S. (1993). *Human capital: A theoretical and empirical analysis, with special reference to education* (2nd ed.). Chicago, IL: University of Chicago Press.

Blau, P. M., & Duncan, O.D. (1967). *American occupational structure.* New York, NY: Wiley.

Bodovski, K. (2014). Adolescents' emerging habitus: The role of early parental expectations and practices. *British Journal of Sociology of Education, 35*(3), 389–412.

Bourdieu, P. (1977). Cultural reproduction and social reproduction. In J. Karabel & A. H. Halsey (Eds.), *Power and ideology in education* (pp.487–511). New York, NY: Oxford University Press.

Bourdieu, P. (1986). The forms of capital. In J. Richardson (Ed.), *Handbook of theory and research for the sociology of education* (pp. 46–58). New York, NY: Greenwood.

Bourdieu, P. (1993). *The field of cultural production: Essays on art and literature.* New York, NY: Columbia University Press.

Bourdieu, P., & Passeron, J. C. (1977). *Reproduction in education, society and culture.* London, UK: Sage.

Bourdieu, P., & Wacquant, L. J. D. (1992). *An invitation to reflexive sociology.* Chicago, IL: The University of Chicago Press.

Breen, R., & Goldthorpe, J. H. (1997). Explaining educational differentials: Towards a formal rational action theory. *Rationality and Society, 9*(3), 275–305.

Brooks, R. (2003). Young people's higher education choices: The role of family and friends. *British Journal of Sociology of Education, 24*(3), 283–297.

Brooks, R. (2005). *Friendship and educational choice: Peer influence and planning for the future.* London, UK: Palgrave Macmillan.

Cabrera, A. F., & LaNasa, S. M. (2001). On the path to college: Three critical tasks facing America's disadvantaged. *Research in Higher Education, 42*(2), 119–149.

Catsambis, S. (2001). Expanding knowledge of parental involvement in children's secondary education: Connections with high school seniors' academic success. *Social Psychology of Education, 5*(2), 149–77.

Chavkin, N. F., & Williams, D. L. (1989). Low-income parents' attitudes toward parent involvement in education. *Journal of Sociology & Social Welfare, 16*(3), 17–28.

Cheng, S., & Starks, B. (2002). Racial differences in the effects of significant others on students' educational expectations. *Sociology of Education, 75*(4), 306–327.

Cohen, J. (1987). Parents as educational models and definers. *Journal of Marriage and Family, 49*(2), 339–351.

Coleman, J. S. (1988). Social capital in the creation of human capital. *American Journal of Sociology, 94* (Suppl.), 95–120.

Coleman, J. S. (1990). *Foundations of social theory.* Cambridge, MA: Harvard University Press.

De Graaf, N. D., De Graaf, P. M., & Kraaykamp, G. (2000). Parental cultural capital and educational attainment in the Netherlands: A refinement of the cultural capital perspective. *Sociology of Education, 73*(2), 92–111.

DesJardins, S., & Toutkoushian, R. (2005). Are students really rational? The development of rational thought and its application to student choice. In J. C. Smart (Ed.),

Higher education: Handbook of theory and research (pp.191–240). New York, NY: Springer.

DiMaggio, P., & Mohr, J. (1985). Cultural capital, educational attainment, and marital selection. *Journal of Sociology, 90*(6), 1231–1261.

Dumais, S. A. (2002). Cultural capital, gender, and school success: The role of habitus. *Sociology of Education, 75*(1), 44–68.

Ellwood, D. T., & Kane, T. J. (2000). Who is getting a college education? Family background and the growing gaps in enrollment. In S. Danziger & J. Waldfogel (Eds.), *Securing the future: Investing in children from birth to college* (pp. 283–324). New York, NY: Russell Sage Foundation.

Erikson, R., & Jonsson, J.O. (1996). Explaining class inequality in education: The Swedish text case. In R. Erikson & J. O. Jonsson (Eds.), *Can education be equalized? The Swedish case in comparative perspective* (pp. 1–63). Boulder, CO: Westview Press.

Feldman, A. F., & Matjasko, J. L. (2005). The role of school-based extracurricular activities in adolescent development: A comprehensive review and future directions. *Review of Educational Research, 75*(2), 159–210.

Feliciano, C. (2006). Beyond the family: The influence of pre migration group status on the educational expectations of immigrants' children. *Sociology of Education, 79*(4), 281–303.

Foskett, N., & Hemsley-Brown, J. (2001). *Choosing futures: Young people's decision-making in education, training and career markets.* London, UK: Routledge Falmer.

Goldrick-Rab, S. (2006). Following their every move: An investigation of social-class differences in college pathways. *Sociology of Education, 79*(1), 61–79.

Goldthorpe, J. H. (1996). Class analysis and the reorientation of class theory: The case of persisting differentials in educational attainment. *British Journal of Sociology, 47*(3), 481–506.

Goyette, K. (2008). College for some to college for all: Social background, occupational expectations and educational expectations over time. *Social Science Research, 37,* 461–484.

Goyette, K., & Xie, Y. (1999). Educational expectations of Asian American youths: Determinants and ethnic differences. *Sociology of Education, 72*(1), 22–36.

Haller, A. O., & Portes, A. (1973). Status attainment processes. *Sociology of Education, 46*(1), 51–91.

Han, W. J., Huang, C. C., & Garfinkel, I. (2003). The importance of family structure and family income on family's educational expenditure and children's college attendance: Empirical evidence from Taiwan. *Journal of Family Issues, 24*(6), 753–786.

Hanson, S. L. (1994). Lost talent: Unrealized educational aspirations and expectations among U.S. youths. *Sociology of Education, 67*(3), 159–183.

Hao, L., & Bonstead-Bruns, M. (1998). Parent-child differences in educational expectations and the academic achievement of immigrant and native students. *Sociology of Education, 71*(3), 175–198.

Hart, C. S. (2014). *Aspirations, education and social justice: Applying Sen and Bourdieu.* London, UK: Bloomsbury Academic.

Hatcher, R. (1998). Class differentiation in education: Rational choices? *British Journal of Educational Studies, 19*(1), 5–24.

Hauser, R. M., & Anderson, D. K. (1991). Post-high school plans and aspirations of Black and White high school seniors: 1976–86. *Sociology of Education, 64*(4), 263–77.

Hegna, K. (2014). Changing educational aspirations in the choice of and transition to post-compulsory schooling: A three-wave longitudinal study of Oslo youth. *Journal of Youth Studies, 17*(5), 592–613.

Heinz, W. R. (2009). Structure and agency in transition research. *Journal of Education and Work, 22*(5), 391–404.

Hemsley-Brown, J. V. (1999). College choice: Perceptions and priorities. *Educational Management and Administration, 27*(1), 85–98.

Hill, N. E., Castellino, D. R., Lansford, J. E., Nowlin, P., Dodge, K. A., Bates, J. E., & Pettit, G. S. (2004). Parent academic involvement as related to school behavior, achievement, and aspirations: Demographic variations across adolescence. *Child Development, 75*(5), 1491–1509.

Hossler, D., & Gallagher, K. S. (1987). Studying student college choice: A three phase model and implications for policy-makers. *College and University, 2*(3), 207–221.

Hossler, D., Schmit, J., & Vesper, N. (1999). *Going to college: How social, economic, and educational factors influence the decisions students make.* Baltimore, MD: The Johns Hopkins University Press.

Hossler, D., & Stage, F. K. (1992). Family and high school experience influences on the postsecondary educational plans of ninth-grade students. *American Educational Research Journal, 29*(2), 425–451.

Jenkins, R. (1982). Pierre Bourdieu and the reproduction of determinism. *Sociology, 16*(2), 270–281.

Kao, G., & Tienda, M. (1998). Educational aspirations of minority youth. *American Journal of Education, 106*(3), 349–384.

Kim, D. H., & Schneider, B. (2005). Social capital in action: Alignment of parental support in adolescents' transition to postsecondary education. *Social Forces, 84*(2), 1181–1206.

Kirk, C. M., Lewis-Moss, R. K., Nilsen, C., & Colvin, D. Q. (2011). The role of parent expectations on adolescent educational aspirations. *Educational Studies, 37*(1), 89–99.

Lamont, M., & Lareau, A. (1988). Cultural capital: Allusions, gaps and glissandos in recent theoretical development. *Sociological Theory, 6*(2), 153–168.

Lareau, A. (2003). *Unequal childhoods: Class, race and family life.* Berkeley, CA: University of California Press.

Lareau, A., & Weininger, E.B. (2003). Cultural capital in educational research: A critical assessment. *Theory and Society, 32*(5/6), 567–606.

Lynch, K., & O'Riordan, C. (1998). Inequality in higher education: A study of class barriers. *British Journal of Sociology of Education, 19*(4), 445–476.

Mahoney, J. L., Cairns, B. D., & Farmer, T. (2003). Promoting interpersonal competence and educational success through extracurricular activity participation. *Journal of Educational Psychology, 95*(2), 409–418.

Mangan, J., Adnett, N., & Davies, P. (2001). Movers and stayers: Determinants of post-16 educational choice. *Research in Post-compulsory Education, 6*(1), 31–50.

Manski, C. (1993). Adolescent econometricians: How do youths infer the returns to schooling? In C.T. Clotfelter & M. Rothschild (Eds.), *Studies of supply and demand in higher education* (pp. 43–57). Chicago, IL: University of Chicago Press.

Manski, C. F., & Wise, D. A. (1983). *College choice in America.* Cambridge, MA: Harvard University Press.

Mateju, P., Smith, M. L., Soukup, P., & Basl, J. (2007). Determination of college expectations in OECD countries: The role of individual and structural factors. *Czech Sociological Review, 43*(6), 1121–1148.

McDonough, P. M. (1997). *Choosing colleges: How social class and schools structure opportunity.* New York, NY: State University of New York.

McNeal, R. B. (2001). Differential effects of parental involvement on cognitive and behavioural outcomes by socioeconomic status. *Journal of Socio-Economics, 30*(2), 171–179.

Moore, R. (2008). Capital. In M. Grenfell (Ed.), *Pierre Bourdieu: Key concepts* (pp. 101–118). Durham, NC: Acumen.

Morgan, S. L. (2006). Expectations and aspirations. In G. Ritzer (Ed.), *The Blackwell encyclopedia of sociology* (pp. 1528–31). Malden, MA: Blackwell.

Muller, C. (2001). The role of caring in the teacher-student relationship for at-risk students. *Sociological Inquiry, 71*(2), 241–255.

Nurmi, J. E. (1991). How do adolescents see their future? A review of the development of future orientation and planning. *Developmental Review, 11*(1), 1–59.

Nussbaum, M. (2011). *Creating capabilities: The human development approach.* Cambridge, MA: Belknap.

Paulsen, M. B. (2001). The economics of human capital and investment in higher education. In M. B. Paulsen & J. C. Smart (Eds.), *The finance of higher education: Theory, research, policy, and practice* (pp. 55–94). New York, NY: Agathon.

Paulsen, M. B., & St. John, E. P. (2002). Social class and college costs: Examining the financial nexus between college choice and persistence. *Journal of Higher Education, 73*(2), 189–236.

Perna, L. W. (2002). Pre-college outreach programs: Characteristics of programs serving historically underrepresented groups of students. *Journal of College Student Development, 43*(1), 64–83.

Perna, L.W. (2006). Understanding the relationship between information about college prices and financial aid and students' college-related behaviors. *American Behavioral Scientist, 49*(12), 1620–1635.

Plank, S. B., & Jordan, W. J. (2001). Effects of information, guidance, and actions on postsecondary destinations: A study of talent loss. *American Educational Research Journal, 38*(4), 947–979.

Reay, D. (1998). 'Always knowing' and 'never being sure': Institutional and familial habituses and higher education choice. *Journal of Education Policy, 13*(4), 519–529.

Reay, D., David, M. E., & Ball, S. J. (2005). *Degrees of choice: Social class, race and gender in higher education.* Stoke-on-Trent, UK: Trentham.

Reed-Danahay, D. (2005). Education. In D. Reed-Danahay (Ed.), *Locating Bourdieu* (pp. 37–68). Bloomington, IN: Indiana University Press.

Reynolds, J. R., & Burge, S. W. (2008). Educational expectations and the rise in women's post-secondary attainments. *Social Science Research, 37*, 485–499.

Rosenbaum, J. E., Rafiullah M. S., & Scott, K. M. (1996). Gatekeeping in an era of more open gates: High school counselors' views of their influence on students' college plans. *American Journal of Education, 104*(4), 257–279.

Rowan-Kenyon, H. T., Bell, A. D., & Perna, L. W. (2008). Contextual influences on parental involvement in college going: Variations by socioeconomic class. *Journal of Higher Education, 79*(5), 564–586.

Saito, M. (2003). Amartya Sen's capability approach to education: A critical exploration. *Journal of Philosophy of Education, 37*(1), 17–33.

Schuchart, C. (2013). School social capital and secondary education plans. *Educational Studies, 39*(1), 29–42.

Sen, A. K. (1985). Welling-being, agency and freedom: The Dewey Lectures 1984. *The Journal of Philosophy, 82*(4), 169–221.

Sen, A. K. (1992). *Inequality re-examined.* Oxford, UK: Clarendon Press.

Sen, A. K. (1999). *Development as freedom.* New York, NY: Knopf.

Sen, A. K. (2005). Human rights and capabilities. *Journal of Human Development, 6*(2), 151–166.

Sewell, W. H., Haller, A. O., & Portes, A. (1969). The educational and early occupational attainment process. *American Sociological Review, 34*(1), 82–92.

Singh, K., Bickley, P.G., Trivette, P. Keith, T. Z., Keith, P. B., & Anderson, E. (1995). The effects of four components of parental involvement on eighth-grade student achievement: structural analysis of NELS-88 Data. *School Psychology Review, 24*(2), 299–317.

Spera, C., Wentzel, K. R., & Matto, H. C. (2009). Parental aspirations for their children's educational attainment: Relations to ethnicity, parental education, children's academic performance, and parental perceptions of school climate. *Journal of Youth and Adolescence, 38*(8), 1140–1152.

Stanton-Salazar, R. D., & Dornbusch, S. M. (1995). Social capital and the social reproduction of inequality: The formation of informational networks among Mexican-origin high school students. *Sociology of Education, 68*(2), 116–135.

Sullivan, A. (2001). Cultural capital and educational attainment. *Sociology, 35*(4), 893–912.

Sullivan, A. (2002). Bourdieu and education: How useful is Bourdieu's theory for researchers? *Netherlands Journal of Social Sciences, 38*(2), 144–166.

Swail, W. S., & Perna, L. M. (2002). Pre-college outreach programs: A national perspective. In W. G. Tierney & L. S. Hagedorn (Eds.*), Increasing access to college: Extending possibilities for all students* (pp. 15–34). Albany, NY: State University of New York Press.

Teachman, J. D. (1987). Family background, educational resources, and educational attainment. *American Sociological Review, 52*(4), 548–57.

Thomson, P. (2008). Field. In M. Grenfell (Ed.), *Pierre Bourdieu: Key concepts* (pp. 67–84). Durham, NC: Acumen.

Tierney, W. G., & Venegas, K. M. (2006). Fictive kin and social capital: The role of peer groups in applying and paying for college. *American Behavioral Scientist, 49*(12), 1687–1702.

Trusty, J. (1999). Effects of eight-grade parental involvement on late adolescents' educational expectations. *Journal of Research and Development in Education, 32*(4), 224–233.

Unterhalter, E. (2009). Education. In S. Deneulin & L. Shahani (Eds.), *An introduction to the human development and capability approach* (pp. 207–227). London, UK: Earthscan.

Wahl, K. H., & Blackhurst, A. (2000). Factors affecting the occupational and educational aspirations of children and adolescents. *Professional School Counseling, 3*(5), 367–374.

Walker, M. (2005). Amartya Sen's capability approach and education. *Educational Action Research, 13*(1), 103–109.

Walker, M., & Unterhalter, E. (2007). The capability approach: Its potential for work in education. In M. Walker & E. Unterhalter (Eds.), *Amartya Sen's capability approach and social justice in education* (pp. 1–23). New York, NY: Palgrave Macmillan.

Wang, Y., & Benner, A. D. (2014). Parent-child discrepancies in educational expectations: Differential effects of actual versus perceived discrepancies. *Child Development, 85*(3), 891–900.

Watts, M., & Bridges, D. (2006). Enhancing students' capabilities? UK higher education and the widening participation agenda. In S. Deneulin & N. Sagovsky (Eds.), *Transforming unjust structures. The capability approach* (pp. 143–160). Dordrecht, Netherlands: Springer.

Williams, G., & Gordon, A. (1981). Perceived earnings functions and ex ante rates of return to post compulsory education in England. *Higher Education, 10,* 199–227.

Wood, D, Kaplan, R., & McLoyd, V. C. (2007). Gender differences in the educational expectations of urban, low-income African American youth: The role of parents and the school. *Journal of Youth and Adolescence, 36(4)*, 417–427.

Wu, Z., Schimmele, C. M., & Hou, F. (2015). Family structure, academic characteristics and postsecondary education. *Interdisciplinary Journal of Applied Family Studies, 64*, 205–220.

Zaff, J. F., Moore, K. A., Papillo, A. R., & Williams, S. (2003). Implications of extracurricular activity participation during adolescence on positive outcomes. *Journal of Adolescent Research, 18*(6), 599–630.

Zhang, Y., Haddad, E., Torres, B., & Chen, C. (2011). The reciprocal relationships among parents' expectations, adolescents' expectations, and adolescents' achievement: A two-wave longitudinal analysis of the NELS data. *Journal of Youth and Adolescence, 40*(4), 479–489.

CHAPTER 12

SOCIAL CAPITAL IN THE RURAL UNITED STATES AND ITS IMPACT ON EDUCATIONAL ATTAINMENT

Ty McNamee

The 2016 United States (U.S.) presidential election, while highly contentious, created a dialogue around a topic not often discussed in the U.S.—rural America. News stories and reports cited a rural public carrying Donald J. Trump all the way to the White House (Morin, 2016; Zitner & Overberg, 2016) and a country divided along a rural-urban continuum (Badger, Bui, & Pearce, 2016; Gamio, 2016). This election and its resulting coverage ignited meaningful and much needed conversations about the current state of rural America. However, the election failed to highlight the nuanced details and historical evolution of marginalized citizens within rural regions. More specifically, the election failed to cast an illuminating light on the very complex, multifaceted, and persistent marginalization which occurs in the dual realms of rural secondary and postsecondary education.

Rural counties cover 72 percent of the U.S. (Cromartie, 2013). According to the 2010 Census, almost 60 million U.S. citizens reside inside these regions (United States Census Bureau, 2010). Out of the 60 million individuals, around

Contemporary Perspectives on Social Capital in Educational Contexts,
pages 201–219.

10 million citizens are students enrolled in secondary or K–12 schools (NCES, 2012, 2013) and many more attend colleges and universities in rural locations. While millions live, work, and (most relative to this chapter) pursue schooling in rural locations, much of the social science-based educational research centered on geographic location focuses on urban, not rural, locales (DeYoung, 1987; Schafft, 2016), thus resulting in a lack of research on rural educational issues facing the nation. Consequently, these matters are often left out of academic circles, further pushing rural populations to the margins.

The same is true for national education policy dedicated to rural areas. DeYoung (1987) detailed the ways in which policy initiatives from the mid-19th century all the way to the 1980s consistently focused on other educational topics and excluded rural education issues. He noted that in 19th century, reforms for education centered around ways in which the U.S. was becoming more urbanized and education more professionalized, with the "notion that rural ways of life were, and would increasingly become, archaic in an emerging urban and cosmopolitan America" (DeYoung, 1987, p. 124). Those ideals, which permeated the nation, cast rural America and rural education out of the fold. This deficit frame was further reiterated in the early 20th century, when beginning "school surveys" stated that rural schools were inferior compared to schools in other areas (DeYoung, 1987, p. 126).

Throughout the 20th century, the aforementioned perception of rural education continually spread from rural secondary schools to rural postsecondary institutions (or colleges and universities). Instead of attempting to increase college access for rural students, the federal government in the 1900s focused on vocational training (DeYoung, 1987), such as Career and Vocational programs, employment training initiatives as part of the Comprehensive Employment and Training Act, and extension programs centered around agriculture and natural resources (Fratoe, 1979). While these programs surely aided individuals in acquiring technical skills, they did not focus on college preparation for rural populations.

Currently, although seemingly helpful resources for national rural education policy exist, such as the U.S. Department of Education *Rural Education Resource Center*, rural areas are often left out of educational policy initiatives. Most of the education policy created for these locations has been "ad hoc" and does not consider the specific characteristics of rural schools and communities (Schafft, 2016, p. 138). For example, President Trump recently signed the *Presidential Executive Order on Promoting Agriculture and Rural Prosperity in America* (The White House, 2017). Most of the executive order includes vague language about increasing "economic prosperity" and "rural educational opportunities," with no specific language describing how these important tasks will be accomplished. Additionally, the *Rural Education Resource Center* website has revealed no new policies, actions, or press releases since President Obama left office in 2017.

The lack of education-based research and effective policy concerning rural America leaves a portion of the U.S. population forgotten and/or overlooked in the current political and economic landscape, with myriad issues facing rural students. While some statistics show rural K–12 students do find success, with high school graduation rates at times higher than those of students in urban areas (Provasnik, et al., 2007; U.S. Department of Education, 2011), children in rural K–12 schools generally find less academic success and attainment than their peers in non-rural areas (Roscigno & Crowle, 2001), particularly those in suburban locales (Provasnik et al., 2007). In the postsecondary education realm, college-going rates versus high school graduation rates significantly decline, with rural students facing the lowest college-going rates in the nation, when compared to their urban and suburban peers (Adelman, 2002; Provasnik et al., 2007). Even if rural students attend college, the educational disparities persist, as they often attend less selective institutions (Byun, Irvin, & Meece, 2012a; Koricich, 2014) and experience hardship adjusting to (a) rigorous academics, (b) social engagement with other students (Ganss, 2016), and (c) degree completion in light socioeconomic obstacles (Byun, Meece, & Irvin, 2012b).

The problems facing rural America have been neglected in education-based intellectual conversations and public policy arenas. This lack of discussion and action, whether purposeful or unintentional, explains why education scholars and policy-makers must aggressively seek to foster innovative ways to highlight the marginalization faced by rural America and the ways in which this marginalization has detrimentally impacted rural citizens' educational access and success. This chapter fuels dialogue on the academic side, dissecting rural education issues through the utilization of the theoretical lens of "social capital" (Bourdieu, 1986). This discussion takes place through three social domains: spatial, relational, and professional. Each domain speaks to embedded social capital and/or the lack thereof and highlights characteristics of rural America that adversely affect educational outcomes for rural citizens.

RURAL AMERICA AND THE
SOCIAL CAPITAL EMBEDDED WITHIN

While it is important to not treat rural America as a monolithic entity with no differences among rural spaces (Koricich, 2012), there are key similarities among rural areas around the nation that may connect these contexts and the experiences of individuals who reside there. According to the 2010 U.S. Census, rural areas are classified as geographic locations that have "sparse populations" and are "less dense" in population per land square mileage (Ratcliffe, Burd, Holder, & Fields, 2016, p. 4). They are "not built up" with buildings and residences and are located "at a distance" from urban areas (Ratcliffe et al, 2016, p. 4). Given these defining rural characteristics, a portrait of isolated spaces in which educational issues pertaining to access and equity becomes even more pronounced. Rural America, once a setting for economic success in agriculture (Johnson, LiBetti Mitchel, & Rotherham, 2014), has faced considerable changes in the 21st century as the world has modernized (e.g., technological advances, increase in transportation) (Wood,

2008). Population declines (Cromartie, 2017) and out-migration (Schafft, 2016), high rates of poverty (Albrecht & Albrecht, 2000; Bowen, Kurzweil, & Tobin, 2005), comparatively lower educational attainment and success (Adelman, 2002; Provasnik et al., 2007; Roscigno & Crowle, 2001), and a lack of white-collar job markets (Antos, 1999; Schafft, 2016) plague rural spaces.

This evolution of the rural U.S. is key to understanding how capital (i.e. social capital) manifests differently in these non-metropolitan spaces. Bourdieu (1986) defines social capital as one's ability to attain resources because of their network of social connections and relationships, "or in other words, to membership in a group" (p. 21). While other forms of capital (e.g. economic, cultural) can be captured by an individual, social capital differs in that it encompasses relations and exchanges among groups (Coleman, 1988), which is an integral aspect of the ways in which social capital is accrued—or not—in rural spaces. Bourdieu (1986) noted that due to social capital occurring through symbolic actions amongst network actors, social capital can be affected by "physical (geographic), economic, or social space" (p. 21). Granger (2014) detailed a similar concept, *spatial-relational mapping*, which outlines how the characteristics of a space and the people inside it can affect which and how relationships exist among those contexts.

Rural America is a model for how social capital can be altered based upon geographic, economic, and/or social factors inside a specific spatial context. With rural locales made up of small tight-knit communities (Hillery, 1955; Nelson, 2016) scattered across vast amounts of land (Ratcliffe et al., 2016; Wilkinson, 1991) affected by widespread poverty and declining economies (Albrecht & Albrecht, 2000; Bowen, et al., 2005; Petrin, Schafft, & Meece, 2014), rural contextual characteristics are sure to affect the ways in which social relations occur inside these settings. However, what does this mean for educational spaces, as rural students attempt to access and succeed in K–12 and higher education? Taking into account what we know about the rural U.S. and the theoretical concept of social capital, the following sections attempt to address this question. Given that spatial, relational, and professional (i.e., economic, occupational) factors are important when accounting for how social relations are exchanged inside certain contexts (i.e. social capital), each section details how social capital in rural areas can be viewed through these three domains.

The Spatial Domain

In general, geographic location can be a determinant for what resources and opportunities are available to individuals (Tate, 2008). This concept of resources by geographic space, for the purposes of this paper referred to as *spatial capital*, can be seen specifically in rural areas. Spatially, rural locales are often isolated (Tieken, 2014), due to large spreads of land with lower populations that are widely dispersed (Wilkinson, 1991). Within rural communities, spaces can further be segregated and isolated along social lines of demarcation pertaining to race and ethnicity (Tieken, 2014).

According to Hillery (1955), rural communities are geographically separated off from areas around them. However, an even more important aspect of rural life is that communities are bound together by a closed social network of individuals and interaction (Hillery, 1955). Hillery's (1955) 20th century characterization of rural interactions extends well into the 21st century, with rural communities still characterized as tight-knit and filled with many family and community interactions (Nelson, 2016). For the purposes of this chapter, those interactions, although closed in nature, generate unique forms of capital that are specific to rural America. As a result of their geographic isolation, rural individuals often engage with others within their immediate community because they lack social options and cannot find individuals and groups (i.e., beyond rural America) to engage socially (Wilkinson, 1991). These social interactions are seemingly forced, which can be construed as prohibitive; however, in the case of rural America and the *spatial capital* embedded within, forced social engagement can and should be viewed as an actualized reality that deeply shapes rural life and living specifically (be it positively or negatively).

In short, it creates meaningful pathways to channel capital resulting from spatial isolation, inevitably influencing the lives of rural citizens. Although isolated, many rural locations serve as communal gathering places for families, children, clergy members, politicians, educators, and other rural citizens who partake in daily schooling, extracurricular activities, entertainment, and community events (Tieken, 2014). It is within these spaces that the creation and exchange of capital—unique to rural life and living—takes place. When interactions inside isolated, rural spaces create a functioning group or network, a by-product is the unique capital that emerges as a result of the group or network interactions. Rural citizens then have access to the *spatial capital*, or ideas, knowledge, resources, and opportunities embedded within the closed social group or network.

Although the capital is confined to the spatialized make-up of the social/rural group or network, it is still capital nonetheless. Within the context of educational opportunities (i.e., along the continuum), rural students also have access to the focused ideas, knowledge, resources, and opportunities for educational attainment embedded within the specific rural context of their social group or network. Through this unique, social lens, rural students have a great deal of *spatial capital*. To clarify, the enclosed acknowledgement of *spatial capital* within rural communities is just that—an acknowledgement of the existence of a spatialized form of social capital that can be uniquely harnessed to improve opportunities for educational access and success for rural students in K–12 and higher education. The challenge for educational researchers and rural policy analysts is discerning just how to utilize the unique and embedded *spatial capital* within rural communities, while recognizing this capital is manifested differently than in other regions of the country. Further, because of the spatial or geographic isolation of rural America, students have little to no choice in whom they can (a) connect, (b) learn from and exchange ideas, and (c) socially engage—which results in isolated and/or closed social networks. How then can the *spatial capital* embedded within those closed networks be accessed and channeled to help rural students realize their educational aspirations and improve educational opportunities for success? Simply put, rural students are tied to those who are physically closest to them. This forced interaction with a smaller and isolated population of individuals by definition limits the capital (needed to improve educational outcomes) that is accessible to rural students. So how then can the existing *spatial capital* be manipulated, expanded, and employed to provide rural students with the requisite knowledge, ideas, resources, and opportunities to improve the quality of their educational pursuits and maximize their educational outcomes?

The Relational Domain

The answers to the aforementioned questions perhaps lie within the relational domain or exchanges of rural residents. Recognizing the limitations and opportunities brought forth via spatial or geographic isolation is a necessity, and so too is the recognition of social capital embedded between and among the relational exchanges and engagement of rural citizens. In short, as rural citizens develop community-based relationships with each other, they inherently create and simultaneously access an embedded form of social capital that exists as a result of their relational exchanges and engagement. This unique capital can be referred to as *relational capital*. *Relational capital* is founded in the idea that social capital is accrued through relations among individuals interacting and bonding with one another in a particular setting (Adler & Kwon, 2002; Coleman, 1988).

The definition of *relational* capital, derived from theorists, such as Coleman (1988) and Adler and Kwon (2002), builds upon Bourdieu's (1986) definition of social capital, emphasizing the importance of interactions among a network of individuals. Based on this definition, it is clear *relational capital* plays a large and defining role in the educational attainment of rural populations. There are numerous empirical studies which support this claim, particularly at the K–12 end of the educational continuum. For example, a study by Israel, Beaulieu, and Hartless (2001) found that social capital in rural students' families and communities were both key factors in their educational success in high school. Another piece by Dyk and Wilson (1999) detailed the importance of "family social capital," with specific concepts—such as a mother's educational and occupational aspirations, as well as the frequency with which a family discusses jobs and schooling—playing a significant role in children's educational attainment. More recently, Byun, Meece, Irvin, & Hutchins' (2012c) study on social capital in rural locations found that expectations both parents and teachers had of students influenced students' educational aspirations. These studies show the relationships that rural students forge with community and family members are integral to their success in educational environments. As rural students form bonds with others around them who have connections, expectations, or knowledge surrounding education, they are able to gain *relational capital*.

The higher education end of the continuum is no different. Relational exchanges and forms of engagement (especially around issues of higher education) are paramount. Parents' and teachers' expectations of students, (Byun, et al., 2012c; Smith, Beaulieu, & Seraphine, 1995), as well as the college discussions parents have with their children (Byun et al., 2012a; Perna & Titus, 2005), assist students in accessing higher education while also developing their appreciation for higher education, hence the notion of *relational capital*. Other studies have utilized Perna's (2006) "*College Choice Model*" as a way to analyze the college choice decisions of rural high school students (Harris, 2013; Means, Clayton, Conzelmann, Baynes, & Umbach, 2016), each specifically referencing social capital playing a positive role in the development of students' college-going knowledge. This chapter furthers that discussion by focusing on the macro-social capital and micro-forms of social capital, in this case *relational capital*.

While these empirical pieces have shown social capital (and more specifically *relational capital*) is integral to the educational attainment of rural students in K–12 and higher education, students in rural communities seem to be missing a key component in their development and/or acquisition of relevant capital. According to Bourdieu (1986), the networks individuals participate in should offer some other or additional form of capital, such as cultural capital. Traditional forms of cultural capital are largely symbolic and refer to the embodied cultural knowledge one can hold in regards to topics, such as art, music, and writing (Bourdieu, 1986). However, modern definitions have expanded cultural capital to include the knowledge individuals possess to navigate contexts Massey, 2007), particularly educational contexts (Ardoin, 2018). In the case of rural students, the contexts in which they find themselves are often closed or very limited due to spatial or geographic isolation. Consequently, rural students' development of and access to varied forms of cultural capital are also limited. Restated, cultural capital is linked very closely to *relational capital. Relational capital* is an important part of any culture, but in rural America, there is a specific culture that shapes and defines relational exchanges and forms of engagement. That culture is, in essence, limited by the frequency, variations, and types of relationship forged due to the closed nature of rural relational networks.

In so being, rural students (i.e., who are limited to their hometowns) may not receive basic and seemingly fundamental information about how to succeed in K–12 and higher education environments. As a result of closed, relational networks, rural families and communities, as well as educators, can often lack the much-needed knowledge and understanding of educational settings. Consequently, they often fail to pass that critical capital along to their children. Rural parents are more likely than non-rural parents to have low educational attainment both in high school and higher education (Provasnik et al., 2007) as well as fewer expectations that their children attend college (Byun et al., 2012b; Provasnik et al., 2007). It is obvious, then, that higher education access is a consistent issue for rural communities (Adelman, 2002; U.S. Department of Education, 2011). Still, a pressing question emerges, "What can and should be done about this?"

In some cases, rural students might turn to local schools and nearby colleges for pertinent college-going knowledge, but unfortunately, it is a real possibility they may find K–12 teachers and guidance counselors as well as college faculty and staff who lack the qualifications, time, and views on student success that rural students require. In the K–12 sector, studies have found teachers in rural schools tend to be less qualified and less highly-trained than in other areas of the country (Ballou & Podgursky, 1995; Monk, 2007), and although guidance counselors in the U.S. generally play a large role in educational aspirations and attainment, study results have varied in how effective these counselors are in rural areas. One study on rural Appalachian Ohio examined rural high school guidance counselors, noting that due to colleges and universities not providing enough information to these staff members, guidance counselors felt they lacked sufficient information about college-going processes (Crowther, Lykins, & Spohn, 1992). Harris (2013) found that rural high school guidance counselors did not provide in-depth college access information to students, instead simply directing students to (a) institutions to which they should apply and (b) financial aid offers they should accept. While one study did show a rural high school counselor was effective at providing students with information that was helpful to them in applying to college, students noted the counselor was often so busy serving in multiple staff roles for the school that it was hard for her to find time to meet with students (Means et al., 2016). This, ironically, is common in rural schools, where counselors may serve in multiple roles and feel overworked (Sutton & Southworth, 1990).

Similarly, if students (i.e., secondary or postsecondary) search for pertinent college-going knowledge and resources at nearby colleges and universities, they are likely to encounter additional issues. There are, in general, fewer colleges and universities in rural areas than in other geographic locations (Turley, 2009). The institutions that do exist often face difficulties in recruiting and retaining academically-qualified faculty (Cejda, 2010; Leist, 2009, Murray, 2007). The administrators working at these rural colleges and universities are often part of small staffs. So, they have varying responsibilities (Fluharty & Scaggs, 2007) which take up time that could be devoted to students. The lack of qualifications and sufficient college-going knowledge among local K–12 and higher education personnel means that, like family members of rural students, these educators may not have the academic credentials or knowledge that would prove useful to rural students seeking to understand (more) and excel in the pursuit of an advanced and quality education.

What is clear here is that rural communities are tight-knit and essentially closed. Relational exchanges (and the embedded *relational capital*) are limited to rural communities. As a key constituency within such communities, rural students primarily have access to closed and very limited networks made-up almost entirely of their family members, local educators, and others around them. Because of these closed, relational exchanges with their rural families, communities, and schools, pertinent knowledge of how to navigate, access, and succeed in both K–12 and higher education contexts is limited.

The Professional Domain

Families, community members, and K–12 educators are greatly connected to rural students. However, because these relational groups may lack the foundational knowledge necessary for rural students to succeed in educational settings, rural students can potentially seek social connections with professionals (i.e., business people, employers, and other workers in their community) who can provide much needed educational information. Unfortunately, students in rural locations may also face very harsh realities regarding these professional connections and the embedded, what this chapter defines as, *professional capital*. This form of capital should not be confused with Hargreaves and Fullan's (2012, p. xvi) concept of professional capital, defined as implementing capital into the teaching profession in order to improve teaching in schools, nor should it be conflated with Noordegraaf and Schinkel's (2011) notion that professional capital is formed when employees engage in professional behaviors to further careers. Instead, *professional capital* in this chapter represents a level of social capital in the connections an individual can make with white-collar professionals inside a specific spatial context that further one's occupational, educational, and economic opportunities.

For decades, rural America has depended on blue-collar jobs and working-class industries (e.g., manufacturing and agriculture) that are no longer as relevant in the 21st century. This is not to say these industries do not exist and are not greatly helpful to the nation. However, as the world has modernized, changes in the industries that support rural communities have caused rural economies to decline (Petrin, et al., 2014). As economies have declined, poverty has become widespread throughout rural locales (Albrecht & Albrecht, 2000; Bowen et al., 2005) with rural areas often having higher levels of poverty than metropolitan locations (Stoll, 2008). This is especially true for rural people of color, who consistently have higher rates of poverty than White, rural citizens (U.S. Department of Agriculture, 2017).

The economic characteristics of rural regions have, in turn, affected educational attainment and success for citizens in these locales. Perhaps due to a desire to make money in order to supplement for lost economic capital, rural citizens in general tend to favor working over pursuing education (Antos, 1999; DeYoung, 1987), with educational aspiration disparities among rural students and non-rural students being attributed to rural students more often coming from lower socioeconomic status families (Haller & Virkler, 1993). The concept of work superseding education is common in rural areas, which fosters communities that are full of individuals and families who work to increase economic capital, not pursue education that may possibly postpone financial gains.

Although one would hope declining economies and industries would encourage rural citizens to create job markets that assist community members in finding work opportunities, this is not often the case. Isolated rural areas mean citizens in these locations are forced to drive long distances just to find hard-labor employment, such as working at factories or warehouses (Tieken, 2014). Even more concerning is the lack of highly-skilled, job markets (Antos, 1999; Schafft, 2016). Due to the lack of jobs meant for white-collar professionals, out-migration of talented, rural youth has occurred (Schafft, 2016), which causes those who hold high-skilled positions (and the requisite skills, knowledge, and *professional capital*) to move to urban areas where there are more job prospects, individuals to serve, and (in relation to the current chapter) students to network with and professionally mentor.

Rural students, as they approach young adulthood, reach out beyond their families to pursue social connections that will presumably help with their career goals educational attainment (Dyk & Wilson, 1999; Nelson, 2016). However, when one combines rural citizens' desires to work (and not to pursue education) with the lack of sustainable jobs in rural areas (e.g., for white-collar professionals) this creates a rural community environment that is not ideal for students to make meaningful social connections and to network with highly-educated professionals. Seeking structured interactions with such skilled and educated individuals may be difficult, as rural families with fewer resources are busy trying to make ends meet and traveling just to find work and, therefore, may not have the requisite time. Furthermore, because rural families are working jobs that require less education and, in turn, may have fewer academic credentials, the knowledge that more skilled and educated professionals could provide might not be immediately helpful to rural students given financial and other resource constraints. Additionally, without rural employment markets that (a) value professional skills, (b) honor the *professional capital* enclosed therein, and (c) provide professional jobs requiring academic degrees, rural students who eventually earn a college degree may not return to their communities because they will have to search for highly-trained and skilled employment elsewhere. When rural citizens who have succeeded in K–12 and higher education choose to leave their hometowns in search of economic prospects, they take their knowledge, connections, and potential to be a role model to rural students with them. In short, they take their *professional capital*, thereby depriving rural communities and students access to such capital. This is not to say rural students cannot learn valuable lessons from those still in their home communities, but it has been established (i.e., within this chapter) that rural communities are largely shaped by closed *spatial*, *relational*, and (now) *professional* networks. As such, rural students are most likely not learning from highly skilled professionals who have successfully navigated secondary and postsecondary, educational environments. Arguably, such professionals could provide pertinent and necessary, college-going knowledge and *professional capital*. Additionally, they could potentially offer rural students even more professional and education-based connections to help with their educational pursuits.

DISCUSSION AND IMPLICATIONS

In modern America, it feels as if rural areas are being left behind, with their population declines (Cromartie, 2017) and economic troubles (Petrin, et al., 2014). Although some policy initiatives match well with rural needs (Johnson et al., 2014), others find that rural areas are left out of thoughtful policy decisions, when compared to those who live in other areas (DeYoung, 1987; Schafft, 2016). However, with millions residing and going to school inside these non-metropolitan locales (NCES 2012, 2013; United States Census Bureau, 2010), researchers, policy makers, and educators must bring to the forefront of educational discussions the issues facing rural America and its citizens' educational success and access. These stakeholders working together can foster strategies to both harness social capital present in rural areas and combat barriers to the creation of social capital in these contexts. The previous sections detailed the ways in which social capital does— or does not—manifest—inside rural contexts, particularly when viewed through spatial, relational, and professional lenses. Using these lenses, the following sections outline recommendations that serve as a starting point for educators and policymakers to make positive changes in rural educational settings.

Recommendations

Utilizing Technology. Isolation and small populations are ever-present realities in rural America. These realities, coupled with the need for greater educational attainment and more robust, local job markets, serve as a great hindrance in the realization of social capital for rural students. Unless changes are made on these noted fronts, relationships forged within rural locales will potentially remain closed and static. Rural educators in K–12 and higher education environments can help modify this seemingly fixed social reality by fostering creative strategies to virtually bring into curricular and co-curricular spaces those social agents in possession of the required social capital for educational access and attainment. One such strategy is the use of 21st century technology. Researchers have long noted the role technology can play in providing online education and connections beyond one's local context (Altbach, Berdahl, & Gumport, 2005; Chen & Koricich, 2014), and both the Trump administration and U.S. Congress have recently started focusing on bringing high-speed Wi-Fi to rural locations. Now, more than ever, it is integral to the educational success of rural citizens that K–12 and college educators utilize technology to assist with such endeavors. For example, having professionals with academic degrees video-conference into classrooms or co-curricular spaces (e.g., afterschool tutoring programs) would provide helpful educational and college-going knowledge to rural students with aspirations of earning their high school diplomas and college degrees. If rural communities could connect with professionals and college representatives outside of their *spatial, relational*, and *professional* networks—especially those who may have grown up in rural areas—this would greatly assist with the development of expansive, social connections extending beyond the confines of rural America, thereby opening up communication pathways for rural students and families to access individuals and social capital they may not have had access to before. These types of initiatives ultimately lead to enhanced opportunities for educational access and success.

Increasing Educational Knowledge in Families and Institutions. It is true that rural families, educators (K–12 and higher education), and communities may lack the education-based and college-going knowledge deemed beneficial for educational access and success. It is also true that reliance solely upon rural connections and communities will likely not enhance the social capital of students seeking to effectively navigate K–12 and higher education settings. In order to make these social connections more useful for rural aspirants, thereby increasing their *relational capital*, schools and colleges must determine ways to increase the educational and college-going knowledge of rural families, educators, and extended communities so they, in turn, can relay important information to students. This may include focused educational and access programming for parents and other family members. For instance, school programs designed to help parents interact effectively with their children, increase children's self- and academic efficacy, and encourage educational goals and attainment would be helpful in creating familial-based, social capital for students (Israel et al., 2001). Furthermore, familial-based programs on the logistics of applying to and enrolling in college have been found to increase parental involvement in these processes (Fann, McClafferty Jarksy, & McDonough, 2009; Tierney, Bailey, Constantine, Finkelstein, & Hurd, 2009). These types of programs offered by K–12 schools and higher education institutions would be beneficial to families and students in need of college knowledge.

Beyond familial outreach, heightened attention to the educational and college-going knowledge of rural K–12 educators and higher education providers is also needed. It is imperative rural teachers, professors, and administrators possess the competencies and know-how to help students with their educational attainment goals. To assist with this endeavor, professionalized training, specifically created with the rural context in mind (Howley & Howley, 2005), can supplement the educational and college-going knowledge rural educators may be missing. Prior research on teacher professional development have cited its benefits for teachers (Borko, Elliott, & Uchiyama, 2002), specifically for rural educators (Glover, et al., 2016). Whether in-person or online, such trainings can and should provide valuable information that educators can then offer students. Additionally, research details the social capital students can get from bonding with their teachers (Crosnoe, 2004), as well as the subject matter and teaching benefits that stem from teachers continuing their education and subject knowledge acquisition (Mollenkopf, 2009; Prusaczyk & Baker, 2011). While it is a more expensive option than smaller-scale professional development opportunities, rural schools and colleges can fully or partially fund advanced schooling/degrees for local educators to refresh and/or extend their knowledge base (i.e., through traditional, blended, or online delivery) (King, 2002; Prusaczyk & Baker, 2011). By extension, the advanced schooling/degrees would also provide rural educators with a heightened sense of pride and accomplishment for having furthered their own education and strengthened their ability to share pertinent educational and college-going knowledge and social capital with their students. It is through these trainings that students' networks, which include bonds with their local school educators (Crosnoe, 2004), will be bolstered, therefore increasing the students' *spatial* and *relational capital*. If students are limited spatially as to with whom they can interact, by educators enhancing their own knowledge and sharing that with students, the social relationships students build with their community's educators will be more beneficial as it pertains to their knowledge on access, success, and attainment in education.

Connecting to and Enhancing the Community. Addressing the technology and knowledge-driven needs of rural students, families, and educators is important. Addressing the expanded needs of the larger, rural community is also of great importance. In the aftermath of the Great Recession, it has admittedly proven to be very difficult for rural America to recover from the demise of its once-thriving, working-class economy (Goldstein, 2017). However, there are effective ways for K–12 and higher education institutions to substantively connect with and enhance the rural communities they serve. For example, while educational attainment is lower in rural communities than in other regions of the country, there is likely (i.e., in each town or area) at least one person who has obtained a college degree. Tapping such individuals and their educational and college-going knowledge (and perhaps inviting them to serve as mentors, teachers, and tutors) would offer rural students and communities valuable resources and capital, which might otherwise remain inaccessible.

Spatially, as this chapter has already noted, schools are prime settings for individuals and families to gather and coalesce (Tieken, 2014). K–12 schools can utilize their *spatial* and social positions within rural communities to intentionally create cultures in which students gain knowledge and increased efficacy from local community members via constant exposure and encouragement to pursue their educational goals. Community members, in turn, can be made to feel empowered and encouraged to continue their active engagement of rural youth—which is a collective win-win. These cultural and community empowerment initiatives might include a variety of strategies and practices (i.e., posting motivational signs and banners, conducting annual awards ceremonies, highlighting student accomplishments at school and community-wide events, profiling students' college selections, etc.). Overall, these types of events and programs could create a *spatial* and *relational* atmosphere that shines a positive light on students' educational achievements while encouraging the development of their educational aspirations and academic- and self-efficacy (Israel et al., 2001).

Professionally, drawing upon local community members and professionals might be just as helpful (if not more so) in higher education settings, particularly when research has shown that rural students take advantage of these professional connections if they are present (Nelson, 2016). Rural colleges and universities may even have more ability than their secondary counterparts to further incentivize students, professionals, and businesses to stay in rural areas and to actively engage in meaningful, *relational* exchanges. Three healthy and arguably welcomed by-products of such exchanges would be (a) student exposure to area professionals with college-going knowledge, (b) the creation of more jobs for rural citizens with college degrees, and (c) the subsequent bolstering of local/rural economies. These types of *professionally* focused programs and initiatives would inevitably help retain successful, educated professionals in rural areas, who can then connect socially with rural students and contribute knowledge of how to navigate and succeed in educational settings.

CONCLUSION

In the Trump era of K–12 and postsecondary education, rural America is discussed both in positive and negative ways. These conversations have placed rural America into academic circles that have not thought about—nor thoroughly and holistically addressed—rural education issues in recent decades. Given the nature and timing of these national discussions, it is now important in the 21st American landscape that K–12 schools and higher education institutions highlight the nuanced experiences of rural student populations and address the marginalization rural citizens have faced throughout the past century and continue to ensure still today. This chapter has begun the process of highlighting these experiences and addressing this marginalization, using the lens of social capital seen specifically through *spatial, relational,* and *professional* domains.

Rural areas are spaces that are isolated and have small populations (Ratcliffe et al., 2016), creating smaller numbers of individuals with whom rural students can connect (Wilkinson, 1991). Inside these rural spaces, families, community members, and educators often have lower rates of educational success and attainment in K–12 and in higher education (Adelman, 2002; Provasnik et al., 2007; Roscigno & Crowle, 2001), less knowledge on how to navigate educational contexts, and diminished educational expectations for rural students (Byun et al., 2012b; Provasnik et al., 2007), versus their non-rural counterparts. Although students in other regions of the country might be able to rely on local professionals in their areas to gain further social capital, rural locations that have been devastated by declining local economies (Albrecht & Albrecht, 2000; Bowen et al., 2005), generally have fewer white-collar, educated professionals from whom they can seek advice or connections.

While exposing and analyzing the lack of useful social capital students in rural locales may possess, it is not enough to simply discuss these issues. K–12 schools, as well as colleges and universities, must make changes to their work and create innovative solutions for rural students to gain social capital. If educational institutions can accomplish these tasks, students in the rural United States can, in turn, increase their educational aspirations and attainment.

REFERENCES

Adelman, C. (2002). The relationship between urbanicity and educational outcomes. In W. G. Tierney & L. S. Hagedorn (Eds.), *Increasing access to college: Extending possibilities for all students* (pp. 53–94). Albany, NY: SUNY Press.

Adler, P. S., & Kwon, S. W. (2002). Social capital: Prospects for a new concept. *Academy of Management Review, 27*(1), 17–40.

Albrecht, D. E., & Albrecht, S. L. (2000). Poverty in nonmetropolitan America: Impacts of industrial, employment, and family structure variables. *Rural Sociology, 65*(1), 87–103.

Altbach, P. G., Berdahl, R. O., & Gumport, P. J. (2005). *American higher education in the twenty-first century: Social, political and economic challenges*. Baltimore, MD: The Johns Hopkins University Press.

Antos, K. (1999). What is none of the hollering about? Rural youth and educational aspirations. *The Vermont Connection, 20*, 15–24.

Ardoin, S. (2018). *College aspirations and access in working-class rural communities: The mixed signals, challenges, and new language first-generation students encounter*. Lanham, MD: Lexington Books.

Badger, E., Bui, Q., & Pearce, A. (2016, November 11). The election highlighted a growing rural-urban split. *The New York Times*. Retrieved from https://www.nytimes.com/2016/11/12/upshot/this-election-highlighted-a-growing-rural-urban-split.html

Ballou, D., & Podgursky, M. (1995). Rural schools: Fewer highly trained teachers and special programs, but better learning environment. *Rural Development Perspectives, 10*(3), 6–16.

Borko, H., Elliott, R., & Uchiyama, K. (2002). Professional development: A key to Kentucky's educational reform effort. *Teaching and Teacher Education, 18*(8), 969–987.

Bourdieu, P. (1986). The forms of capital. In J. G. Richardson (Ed.), *Handbook of theory and research for the sociology of education* (pp. 241–258). Westport, CT: Greenwood Press.

Bowen, W.G., Kurzweil, M.A., & Tobin, E.M (2005) *Equity and excellence in American higher education*. Charlottesville, VA: University of Virgina Press.

Byun, S., Irvin, M.J., & Meece, J.L. (2012a). Predictors of Bachelor's degree completion among rural students at four-year institutions. *The Review of Higher Education, 35*(3), 463–484.

Byun, S., Meece, J.L., & Irvin, M.J. (2012b). Rural-nonrural disparities in postsecondary educational attainment revisited. *American Educational Research Journal, 49*(3), 412–437.

Byun, S., Meece, J.L., Irvin, M.J., & Hutchins, B.C. (2012c). The role of social capital in educational aspirations of rural youth. *Rural sociology, 77*(3), 355–379.

Cejda, B. D. (2010). Faculty issues in rural community colleges. *New Directions for Community Colleges, 2010*(152), 33–40.

Chen, X., & Koricich, A. (2014, October). Reaching out to remote places: A discussion of technology and the future of distance education in rural America. In *E-Learn 2014 proceedings: World conference on e-learning in corporate, government, healthcare, and higher education* (pp. 370–376). Chesapeake, VA: Association for the Advancement of Computing in Education (AACE).

Coleman (1988). Social capital in the creation of human capital. *American Journal of Sociology, 94. Supplement: Organizations and Institutions: Sociological and Economic Approaches to the Analysis of Social Structure*, S95–S120.

Cromartie, J. (2013). *How is rural America changing?* [PowerPoint slides]. Retrieved from http://www.census.gov/newsroom/cspan/rural_america/20130524_rural_america_slides.pdf

Cromartie, J. (2017). *Rural areas show overall population decline and shifting regional patterns of population change.* Retrieved from https://www.ers.usda.gov/amber-waves/2017/september/rural-areas-show-overall-population-decline-and-shifting-regional-patterns-of-population-change/

Crosnoe, R. (2004). Social capital and the interplay of families and schools. *Journal of Marriage and Family, 66*(2), 267–280.

Crowther, T., Lykins, D., & Spohn, K. (1992). *Appalachian access and success: A research project of the Ohio Board of Regents and a consortium of two-and four-year colleges and universities in Appalachian Ohio.* Institute for Local Government Administration and Rural Development, Ohio University/Shawnee State University.

DeYoung, A. J. (1987). The status of American rural education research: An integrated review and commentary. *Review of Educational Research, 57*(2), 123–148.

Dyk, P. H., & Wilson, S. M. (1999). Family-based social capital considerations as predictors of attainments among Appalachian youth. *Sociological Inquiry, 69*(3), 477–503.

Fann, A., McClafferty Jarsky, K., & McDonough, P. M. (2009). Parent involvement in the college planning process: A case study of P–20 collaboration. *Journal of Hispanic Higher Education, 8*(4), 374–393.

Fluharty, C., & Scaggs, B. (2007). The rural differential: Bridging the resource gap. *New Directions for Community Colleges, 2007*(137), 19–26.

Fratoe, F. A. (1979). *Education training programs and rural development.* Washington, D. C.: National Institute of Education (ERIC Document and Reproduction Service No. ED172967).

Gamio, L. (2016, November 17). Urban and rural America are becoming increasingly polarized. *The Washington Post.* Retrieved from https://www.washingtonpost.com/graphics/politics/2016-election/urban-rural-vote-swing/

Ganss, K. M. (2016). The college transition for first-year students from rural Oregon Communities. *Journal of Student Affairs Research and Practice, 53*(3), 269–280.

Glover, T. A., Nugent, G. C., Chumney, F. L., Ihlo, T., Shapiro, E. S., Guard, K., ... & Bovaird, J. (2016). Investigating rural teachers' professional development, instructional knowledge, and classroom practice. *Journal of Research in Rural Education, 31*(3), 1.

Goldstein, A. (2017). *Janesville: An American story.* New York, NY: Simon and Schuster.

Granger, R. C. (2014). Spatial–Relational mapping in socio-institutional perspectives of innovation. *European Planning Studies, 22*(12), 2477–2489.

Haller, E. J., and S. J. Virkler (1993). Another look at rural-nonrural differences in students' educational aspirations. *Journal of Research in Rural Education, 9*(3), 170–178.

Hargreaves, A., & Fullan, M. (2012). *Professional capital: Transforming teaching in every school.* New York, NY: Teachers College Press.

Harris, K. L. (2013). *The college choice process of four students from rural Appalachian Kentucky* (Unpublished doctoral dissertation). University of Maryland, College Park, MD.

Hillery, G. A. (1955). Definitions of community: Areas of agreement. *Rural Sociology, 20,* 111–123.

Howley, A., & Howley, C. B. (2005). High-Quality teaching: Providing for rural teachers' professional development. *Rural Educator, 26*(2), 1–5.

Israel, G. D., Beaulieu, L. J., & Hartless, G. (2001). The influence of family and community social capital on educational achievement. *Rural Sociology, 66*(1), 43–68.

Johnson, L.J., LiBetti Mitchel, A., & Rotherham, A.J. (2014). Federal education policy in rural America. *Rural Opportunities Consortium of Idaho.* Retrieved from http://www.rociidaho.org/wp-content/uploads/2014/12/ROCI_2014FedEdPolicy_Final.pdf

Johnson, J., & Strange, M. (2009). Why rural matters 2007: The realities of rural education growth. *Rural School and Community Trust.* Retrieved from https://files.eric.ed.gov/fulltext/ED498859.pdf

King, K. P. (2002). Identifying success in online teacher education and professional development. *The Internet and Higher Education, 5*(3), 231–246.

Koricich, A. (2012). Seeing "rural" as a differentiated space. *Forum of the American Journal of Education.* Retrieved from http://www.ajeforum.com/seeing-rural-as-a-differentiated-space-by-andrew-koricich/

Koricich, A. (2014). The effects of rurality on college access and choice. *AERA Annual Conference,* Philadelphia, PA. American Educational Research Association.

Leist, J. (2009). Academic rank: The impact on full-time faculty salaries at public rural community colleges. *Academic Leadership, 7*(4), 211–215.

Massey, D. (2007). *Categorically unequal: The American stratification system.* New York, NY: Russell Sage Foundation.

Means, D. R., Clayton, A.B., Conzelmann, J. G., Baynes, P., Umbach, P. D. (2016). Bounded aspirations: Rural, African-American high school students and college access. *The Review of Higher Education, 39*(4), 543–569.

Mollenkopf, D. L. (2009). Creating highly qualified teachers: Maximizing university resources to provide professional development in rural areas. *Rural Educator, 30*(3), 34–39.

Monk, D. (2007). Recruiting and retaining high-quality teachers in rural areas. *The Future of Children, 17*(1), 155–174.

Morin, R. (2016, November 17). Behind Trump's win in rural white America: Women joined men in backing him. *Pew Research Center.* Retrieved from http://www.pewresearch.org/fact-tank/2016/11/17/behind-trumps-win-in-rural-white-america-women-joined-men-in-backing-him/

Murray, J. P. (2007). Recruiting and retaining rural community college faculty. *New Directions for Community Colleges, 2007*(137), 57–64.

National Center for Education Statistics (NCES). (2012). *Number and percentage distribution of private elementary and secondary students, by type of school and urban-centric 12–category locale: 2011–12.* Retrieved from https://nces.ed.gov/surveys/ruraled/tables/b.1.a.-4.asp

National Center for Education Statistics (NCES). (2013). *Number of students enrolled in public elementary and secondary schools, by school urban-centric 12-category lo-*

cale and state or jurisdiction: Fall 2013. Retrieved from https://nces.ed.gov/surveys/ruraled/tables/a.1.a.-3_2.asp

Nelson, I. A. (2016). Rural students' social capital in the college search and application process. *Rural Sociology, 81*(2), 249–281.

Noordegraaf, M., & Schinkel, W. (2011). Professional capital contested: A Bourdieusian analysis of conflicts between professionals and managers. *Comparative Sociology, 10*(1), 97–125.

Perna, L. W. (2006). Studying college choice: A proposed conceptual model. In J. C. Smart (Ed.), *Higher education: Handbook of theory and research* (vol. XXI, pp. 99–157). New York, NY: Springer.

Perna, L. W., & Titus, M. A. (2005). The relationship between parental involvement as social capital and college enrollment: An examination of racial/ethnic group differences. *The Journal of Higher Education, 76*(5), 485–518.

Petrin, R. A., Schafft, K. A., & Meece, J. L. (2014). Educational sorting and residential aspirations among rural high school students. What are the contributions of schools and educators to rural brain drain? *American Educational Research Journal, 51*(2), 294–326.

Provasnik, S., KewalRamani, A., Coleman, M. M., Gilbertson, L., Herring, W., & Xie, Q. (2007). *Status of education in rural America* (NCES 2007–040). Washington, DC: National Center for Education Statistics. Institute of Education Sciences, U.S. Department of Education.

Prusaczyk, J., & Baker, P. J. (2011). Improving teacher quality in southern Illinois: Rural access to mathematics professional development (RAMPD). *Planning and Changing, 42*(1/2), 101–119.

Ratcliffe, M., Burd, C., Holder, K., & Fields, A. (2016) *Defining rural at the U.S. Census Bureau.* (ACSGEO-1) Washington, DC: U.S. Census Bureau, U.S. Department of Commerce, Economics and Statistics Administration. Retrieved from https://www2.census.gov/geo/pdfs/reference/ua/Defining_Rural.pdf

Roscigno, V. J., & Crowle, M. L. (2001). Rurality, institutional disadvantage, and achievement/attainment. *Rural Sociology, 66*(2), 268–292.

Schafft, K. A. (2016). Rural education as rural development: Understanding the rural school–community well-being linkage in a 21st-century policy context. *Peabody Journal of Education, 91*(2), 137–154.

Smith, M. H., Beaulieu, L. J., & Seraphine, A. (1995). Social capital, place of residence, and college attendance. *Rural Sociology, 60*(3), 363.

Stoll, M. A. (2008). Race, place, and poverty revisited. In *The color of poverty.* A. C. Lin and D. Harris, (Eds.). New York, NY: Russell Sage Foundation.

Sutton, J. M., & Southworth, R. S. (1990). The effect of the rural setting on school counselors. *The School Counselor, 37*(3), 173–178.

Tate, W. F. (2008). "Geography of opportunity": Poverty, place, and educational outcomes. *Educational Researcher, 37*(7), 397–411.

The White House (2017). *Presidential Executive Order on Promoting Agriculture and Rural Prosperity in America.* https://www.whitehouse.gov/presidential-actions/presidential-executive-order-promoting-agriculture-rural-prosperity-america/

Tieken, M. C. (2014). *Why rural schools matter.* Chapel Hill, NC: UNC Press.

Tierney, W. G., Bailey, T., Constantine, J., Finkelstein, N., & Hurd, N. F. (2009). *Helping students navigate the path to college: What high schools can do: A practice guide*

(NCEE #2009-4066). Washington, DC: National Center for Education Evaluation and Regional Assistance, Institute of Education Sciences, U.S. Department of Education. Retrieved from http://ies.ed.gov/ncee/wwc/publications/practiceguides/

Turley, R. N. L. (2009). College proximity: Mapping access to opportunity. *Sociology of Education, 82*(2), 126–146.

United States Census Bureau (2010). *Number and percent of population: 2010—United States—urban/rural and inside/outside metropolitan and micropolitan area*. Retrieved from https://factfinder.census.gov/faces/tableservices/jsf/pages/product-view.xhtml?pid=DEC_10_SF1_GCTP1.US26&prodType=table

U.S. Department of Agriculture. (2017). *Poverty demographics*. Washington, D.C.: United States Department of Agriculture, Economic Research Service. Retrieved from https://www.ers.usda.gov/topics/rural-economy-population/rural-poverty-well-being/poverty-demographics/

U.S. Department of Education. (2011). *The state of states in education* [PowerPoint Slides]. Retrieved from https://www2.ed.gov/about/reports/annual/state-of-states/index.html?exp=5

Wilkinson, K. P. (1991). *The community in rural America*. Westport, CT: Greenwood Publishing Group.

Wood, R. E. (2008). *Survival of rural America: Small victories and bitter harvests*. Lawrence, KS: University Press of Kansas.

Zitner, A., & Overberg, P. (2016) Rural vote fuels Trump; Clinton loses urban grip. *The Wall Street Journal*. Retrieved from https://www.wsj.com/articles/rural-vote-helps-donald-trump-as-hillary-clinton-holds-cities-1478664251

AFTERWORD

REDEFINING SOCIAL CAPITAL WITH AN EYE TOWARD CRITICAL PROACTIVENESS

Phillis L. George

Social capital has long been held as a scarce commodity that is highly stratified and inequitably distributed, particularly among ethnically and socioeconomically marginalized individuals. When paired with meaningful considerations of ways in which to experience upward mobility (i.e., be it socially, economically, or educationally), social capital becomes an important means by which individuals and groups are able to literally change their life trajectories. Indeed, even generational trajectories—both inter and intragenerational—can be altered with enough social capital. To clarify, it is not just the sheer access of social capital or the amount that matters but also the points of access. In essence, the timing of access (i.e., along an individual's or group's mobility journey) matters. In addition to access and timing, the mechanisms that are put in place to help ensure timely, equitable, and meaningful access to social capital are also of grave importance. These mechanisms, otherwise known as accountability measures, are consequential because without them, the severity of inequitable distribution and disproportionate access to social capital will only intensify, thus becoming more problematic for individu-

Contemporary Perspectives on Social Capital in Educational Contexts,
pages 221–223.

als and groups who have either historically and / or systematically been pushed to the margins of society.

The 21st century, which is still very much in its infancy, is wrought with societal events and happenings—which speak to a growing divide between those who have and have not. This divide is not novel, given our understanding of societal stratification and social hierarchy, but the level of persistence and the frequency with which the divide increases is a novelty in present day society. Never has there been such a huge divide between individuals and groups with regard to the possession of capital. This occurrence is exacerbated by the global nature in which we currently engage one another. The world of the 21st century is truly global and very much interconnected. As such, the social and economic divisions which have largely shaped the first 20 years of the current century are nearly replicated across continents. There is no continent or country nor macro- or micro-society that is impervious to this egregiously growing divide.

The question that resonates deep within our collective and societal consciousness is, "What can and should be done about this?" The answer is very nuanced, highly complex, and multifaceted. Further, it is not a fixed answer but rather one that is fluid and shaped by societal needs and demands. The current volume, *Contemporary Perspectives on Social Capital in Educational Contexts*, speaks to social capital through the lens of currency conduits regarding access and accountability to education (i.e., along the continuum). In channeling the powerful symbolism of currency, the volume's contributors sought to highlight a pressing need for greater accountability and more equitable access to currency and currency networks which can then be used to improve educational—and by extension, socioeconomic—attainment levels. This volume is largely responsive to the aforementioned divide, as its effects are both heightened and extremely pronounced within secondary, postsecondary, and continuing education arenas.

Bold in its endeavors, the current volume speaks truth to power by reexamining the importance of social capital through contemporary contexts, thus reminding educational leaders and scholars alike of the larger backdrop of a very dynamic and globally competitive world in which today's student must successfully navigate and dare to thrive. Regardless of their social and economic realities, the 21st century student is charged with obtaining and mastering complex funds of social, economic, and academic knowledge that may or may not be immediately accessible. If they fail to do so, they are (by default) penalized by society for not having proper access to requisite forms of social capital, when in fact society should be tasked with wearing the penalty hat for not doing its due diligence in providing proper access when it is needed the most and for failing to put in place permanent mechanisms for monitoring and ensuring all students are afforded sustained access to quality education.

A continuum mindset is required to truly appreciate and grasp the notion of society's responsibility to ensure access and accountability to the aforementioned currency and currency conduits. The referenced societal responsibility exists from conception to departure and beyond—especially regarding generational social mobility. To adopt and fully embody this continuum mindset, we must concentrate our efforts as educational leaders and scholars on being critically proactive (rather than responsive) and ultimately redefining social capital so that it is more inclusive of access and accountability more broadly defined. In short, we must perennially think of ways in which to be more strategic in the timing of access and focused regarding the frequency of access and our accountability efforts.

Admittedly, this is no easy feat. The task is formidable, but it is important to remember no challenge is insurmountable. By adopting a continuum mindset regarding the systems, policies, and practices that must be put in place to ensure sustained access for all, we can (i.e., as individuals and as part of larger societal institutions … like schools, colleges, and universities) be more proactive in our actions, thereby ushering in a new and more expansive era in which social capital is thought of much more fluidly and comprehensively. Instead of being able to access a single door during a single (albeit) critical point in time, the focus shifts to redefining access and the embedded social capital as a series of doors and indeed pathways along an endless trajectory that is not limited to a single person but rather is extended to all persons stemming from a familial lineage. This is where generational wealth and mobility reassert themselves as being integral to any and all change processes related to ensuring sustained access and accountability for all.

What is proposed within the confines of this Afterword is a not so subtle call to action—a call for redefining social capital, a call for critical proactiveness, and (lastly) a call for the development of a continuum mindset that essentially alters our thinking of social capital as fluid, ever changing, and existing along an endless yet powerful life continuum.

BIOGRAPHIES

SERIES EDITORS

RoSusan D. Bartee, Ph.D. is currently serving as Chair of and tenured Professor in the Department of Education Leadership and Higher Education in the College of Community Innovation and Education at the University of Central Florida in Orlando. Dr. Bartee serves on the college's leadership team and is responsible for managing the department's graduate programs, budget, personnel, and other related administrative matter. For twelve years, Dr. Bartee served at the University of Mississippi in the capacities of a tenured Professor and previous Program Coordinator of Educational Leadership at the University of Mississippi. While at the University of Mississippi, during an eighteen-month period while on academic leave, Dr. Bartee served as Interim Vice President in the Office of Access and Success with the Association of Public and Land-grant Universities in Washington, DC.

A nationally recognized scholar and former recipient of the Research Award of the Year at the School of Education at the University of Mississippi, Dr. Bartee is the author or editor of four books, the editor of a book series and the author or coauthor of numerous academic publications on educational leadership, cultural

Contemporary Perspectives on Social Capital in Educational Contexts,
pages 225–238.
Copyright © 2019 by Information Age Publishing

and social capital, and educational and social attainment. Dr. Bartee has garnered financial awards from major higher education organizations and foundations to support degree completion and institutional advancement efforts and has served as a program evaluator for federal, philanthropic, and related student and school success for K–12 and higher education initiatives totaling nearly $8 million.

In July 2012, Dr. Bartee became the first African American to receive Tenure and Promotion to Professor in the Department of Leadership and Counselor Education at the University of Mississippi. Under Dr. Bartee's leadership as Program Coordinator and Professor of Educational Leadership at the University of Mississippi, the program received nationally recognitions with conditions' status with the Educational Leadership Constituent Council (ELCC). Dr. Bartee teaches graduate level courses and, within her twelve-year tenure at the University of Mississippi (including a 16-month academic leave), Dr. Bartee has successfully chaired nearly 20 dissertations. Prior to becoming a faculty member at the University of Mississippi, Dr. Bartee served as the Associate Director at the National Council for Accreditation of Teacher Education (NCATE) in Washington, DC for the Reading First Teacher Education Network (RFTEN) where she provided administrative leadership for campus-based efforts to restructure teacher education programs for minority serving institutions (i.e. Historically Black Colleges and Universities, Hispanic Serving Institutions, Tribal Colleges). Dr. Bartee has also previously served as Interim Executive Director at the Frederick D. Patterson Research Institute of the United Negro College Fund (UNCF) in Washington, DC and Project Coordinator for the Summer Research Opportunities Program at the University of Illinois at Urbana-Champaign.

Dr. Bartee has been recognized as one of the recipients of the Mississippi's Institutions of Higher Learning Excellence in Diversity Award, Mississippi's Education Policy Fellows, Mississippi's Top 40 Under 40, Distinguished Alumni from the College of Education at the University of Illinois at Urbana-Champaign, Who's Who in Black Mississippi, Who's Who of American Women, Who's Who Among Executives and Professionals, and Who's Who in America. She is also a former Institute of Governmental Affairs Program Fellow (IGAP) at the University of Illinois at Urbana-Champaign and has previously interned with the Office of Civil Rights at the United States Department of Education and the White House. Other recognitions include Commendation from the office of the Mayor of Coldwater, MS, a Presidential Citation from Tougaloo College in Jackson, MS and former member of Leadership Lafayette. Dr. Bartee has further served as Director of the National Educational Policy Forum, one of the activities adjoining the 2008 Presidential Debate at the University of Mississippi, which convened nationally-recognized educational researchers and public policy advocates.

Dr. Bartee is a member of the American Educational Research Association (AERA), charter task force member with the Boys and Girls Club of America, a Board of Examiners Member for the National Council for Accreditation of Teacher Education (NCATE; now the Council for the Accreditation of Educator

Preparation), and former Chair of the Commission on the Status of Women at the University of Mississippi. Dr. Bartee serves as President and CEO of Academic Pathways, Incorporated, an educational consulting organization focusing on K–12 and higher education, and has also served as grant reviewer for federal agencies (i.e. United States Department of Education, National Science Foundation). A recipient of additional awards and honors and a motivational speaker, Dr. Bartee is a member of The Links, Incorporated, Alpha Kappa Alpha Sorority, Incorporated and she engages further in civic, religious, and community contexts.

Dr. Bartee received a Doctor of Philosophy in Educational Policy Studies from the University of Illinois at Urbana-Champaign, a Master of Arts in Liberal Studies from Northwestern University in Evanston, Illinois and a Bachelor of Arts in English from Tougaloo College in Jackson, Mississippi.

Phillis L. George, Ph.D. is an Assistant Professor and Program Coordinator of Undergraduate Studies in the Department of Higher Education, School of Education at the University of Mississippi. Dr. George conducts focused research on equity and policy issues related to access, affordability, and accountability in higher education. She also specializes in higher education curriculum design, program evaluation, and community-based learning. In addition to research, Dr. George teaches educational policy, theory, and organizational management courses in the residential and online Master's degree programs in Student Personnel in addition to the Ph.D. and Ed.D. programs in Higher Education.

Prior to joining the graduate faculty of the University of Mississippi, Dr. George served in a dual administrative and faculty role as the Quality Enhancement Plan (QEP) Director, Director of Service-Learning, and Assistant Professor of Social Science at the College of Coastal Georgia in Brunswick, GA. In this key role, she was responsible for overseeing the institution's reaffirmation of accreditation through the Southern Association of Colleges and Schools and its Commission on Colleges (SACSCOC). Dr. George worked diligently with the college President and the executive cabinet to develop and implement an institutional QEP designed to seamlessly integrate service-learning and civic engagement into the curriculum. She also worked to oversee the design and establishment of the College's inaugural Center for Service-Learning & Civic Engagement. With her help, the College was added to the U.S. President's Higher Education Community Service Roll. In recognition and appreciation of her outstanding leadership, Dr. George was honored by the Golden Isles (of Georgia) Family YMCA during the 2013 Crystal Anniversary of its Tribute to Women Leaders.

Dr. George's work at the College of Coastal Georgia was preceded by her tenure at Jackson State University (JSU), where she served as the Assistant Director of Service-Learning within the Center for Service & Community Engaged Learning. While there, Dr. George oversaw all service-learning integration and assessment activities for the university's undergraduate and graduate curricula. Her responsibilities included curriculum design, program evaluation, grant-writing, and assessment of the institutional and community impact of service-learning. In addition, she collaborated with department chairs and faculty as well as community liaisons to secure and implement high-impact and community-based, service projects (i.e., regionally, nationally, and internationally). One of her most memorable and cherished experiences includes her co-leadership of the Alternative Breaks & Active Citizenship Program where she and a team of her colleagues led students on service immersion experiences internationally in Shanghai, China and domestically in Mississippi, Georgia, and Louisiana. Invariably, her service at JSU exposed her to the cognitive and affective gains of service-learning. As a result, she developed a keen understanding and deep appreciation of the pedagogy and its uses for promoting holistic student development and academic self-efficacy.

When asked of her most formative and salient experiences in higher education administration, Dr. George is quick to recount her service to the University of Wisconsin-Madison as the assistant director of two nationally competitive, scholarship programs housed within the Office of the Provost & Vice Chancellor for Academic Affairs. The programs were designed to attract and retain academically outstanding, underrepresented and disadvantaged students. Innovative and highly structured in terms of expectations for personal and academic success, the programs boasted of four-year retention and graduation rates which regularly exceeded that of the general campus body. In addition to her appointment as assistant director, Dr. George served as a research and program assistant and facilitated and engaged approximately 450 merit-scholars in illuminating processes of self-discovery, independence, and maturation through academic monitoring, advising, and counseling as well as oversight of service-learning and social activities, leadership seminars, and peer mentoring initiatives.

Dr. George continues to gain inspiration and motivation from these two extraordinary programs in her current attempts to challenge students so that they might push themselves—beyond comfort levels—to unimagined heights of achievement. As a scholar-practitioner, she finds this work to be incredibly rewarding and believes it affords privileged opportunities to empower and prepare students for entry into the global world as socially conscious, critically aware, and civically engaged leaders. Further, it helps structure and contextualize her research along with her efforts to disseminate new and more complex funds of knowledge relating to community-based learning, civic engagement, and student success.

Dr. George earned her Bachelor of Arts (BA) in Sociology and Communicative Disorders from the University of Wisconsin-Madison. She continued her studies at Oxford University in England and earned a Master of Science (MSc) degree in Sociology and later returned to her alma mater, the University of Wisconsin-Madison, to earn her doctor of philosophy degree (Ph.D.) in Educational Leadership & Policy Analysis. With over 15 years of administrative and leadership experience in academic and student affairs, Dr. George is a recognized and respected authority on student achievement and community engagement. She is a member of several national organizations, including the Association for the Study of Higher Education (ASHE), the American Educational Research Association (AERA), and the International Association for Research on Service-Learning and Community Engagement (IARSLCE). Most recently, she has served on the Executive Committee of the Gulf-South Summit on Service-Learning & Civic Engagement through Higher Education and the Board of Directors for the United Way of Coastal Georgia. Dr. George is also a member Alpha Kappa Alpha Sorority, Incorporated; The Links, Incorporated; and the Association of Junior Leagues International, Incorporated.

CONTRIBUTORS

Sarah J. Bailey, Ed.S. is an educational consultant, entrepreneur, and former school leader with over 15 years of service in the field of education. For the past five years, Sarah has served as a school leadership coach and school reviewer for public schools in Mississippi and New York State, including the New York City Schools. She has also served as a charter renewal reviewer for the Cleveland Metropolitan School District. Sarah is currently a doctoral student in The University of Mississippi Educational Leadership program and served as a graduate research assistant from 2015-2017. Her dissertation is entitled, *Gauging Leader Preparedness: Designing a Survey Instrument to Measure the Quality of the Educational Leadership Internship*. As a graduate assistant she co-taught educational leadership courses at the University of Mississippi and served as an adjunct instructor for the Mississippi College School of Education.

Sarah has a published book chapter *entitled If I Only Had More Time: Reflections of a School Turnaround Leader* in *The Principal Reader: Narratives of Experience*. Her research interests include school turnaround and leadership for school improvement.

Passionate about school improvement and committed to providing struggling students with the best education possible, Sarah spent the majority of her career in critical shortage areas in rural Mississippi. During her tenure as the school principal of T.R. Sanders Elementary School, Sarah assumed responsibility for the education of children attending a failing school with Mississippi and US Department of Education school improvement classifications. Within three years, with the support of district leadership and a staff committed to school transformation, the school earned a successful school label and exited state and federal school improvement. During the 2013-14 school term, as a US DOE School Improvement Grant recipient, T.R. Sanders was recognized by the US Department of Education and profiled by the American Institutes for Research for significant growth. She received her formal education in mathematics education, curriculum and instruction, and educational leadership at The University of Mississippi.

Sarah has a son Cameron Bailey who is a member of the United States Armed Services.

Nicole Mittenfelner Carl, Ed.D. is a postdoctoral fellow in the Teaching, Learning, and Leadership division at the University of Pennsylvania Graduate School of Education. She received her doctorate in Educational Leadership from the University of Pennsylvania in 2017. Dr. Carl teaches courses related to qualitative research methods, practitioner research for educational leaders, and mentoring strategies for veteran teachers coaching first-year teachers. Prior to studying at Penn GSE, Dr. Carl taught middle school English in the School District of Philadelphia for five years and was the lead teacher for the middle school. In 2008, Drexel University recognized her as one of three recipients of the Drexel University Make a Difference Award for Outstanding Mentoring and Teaching. During the first two years of her doctoral program at Penn GSE, Dr. Carl coached first-year teachers throughout Philadelphia and supported them as they sought Pennsylvania teacher certification. While at Penn GSE, Dr. Carl received multiple fellowships, including the Korn Fellowship for impact assessment to guide the research initiatives of the Center for the Study of Boys' and Girls' Lives. Dr. Carl's research focuses on three primary strands, including (1) the study of qualitative and applied research methods, (2) ways that practitioners and students can conduct research to improve their schools, and (3) the social and cultural contexts of schooling and its implications on students, teachers, parents, and school leaders. Dr. Carl has been conducting qualitative research for more than a decade beginning in 2005 when she was awarded a Mellon Fellowship. Since then, Dr. Carl has led and participated in multiple qualitative and mixed methods research projects and written a seminal text with Sage about qualitative research methods, *Qualitative Research: Bridging the Conceptual, Theoretical, and Methodological.*

Dr. Carl has worked with school leaders, teachers, and students in a variety of contexts (public and independent) to consider ways to use research to drive school improvement as well as lead a multi-year, multi-site impact evaluation of the way that engaging in these projects influenced the schools and the individuals involved. She continues to research ways that practitioners can conduct and use research in their school contexts as well as support schools in the implementation of these projects. Stemming from her experiences as a teacher, teacher leader, and teacher coach, Dr. Carl's dissertation, a multi-year ethnographic study of a K–8 school in a low-income neighborhood in a large, urban city, investigates the ways that hidden curricula of social reproduction and inequity shape schooling experiences. This research offers implications related to the socialization structures in schools and the role of cultural and social capital as well as about the importance of qualitative research, ways to incorporate student voice, and considerations for how policy is experienced by students and teachers.

Jandel Crutchfield, Ph.D. is an assistant professor of social work at the University of Texas at Arlington where she conducts research on social justice in public schools. Dr .Crutchfield earned her doctor of philosophy at Louisiana State University and recently served as an assistant professor of social work at the University of Mississippi. Dr. Crutchfield served as a school social worker in Louisiana and Mississippi schools prior to earning her doctorate and researchers how school social workers can address institutional as well as individual barriers to positive, biopsychosocial student outcomes. Dr. Crutchfield has offered many presentations and is the author of several publications about her research on schools. She also explores how issues of skin color bias (colorism) influence student outcomes in public schools, including how teachers and staff can increase their knowledge of skin color bias and address it. Dr. Crutchfield believes that social justice in schools is a pressing issue for both the fields of education and social work. Dr. Crutchfield is a wife and mother who is engaged in her local community as a soccer coach to her children's soccer teams, parent teacher organizations at her children's schools, and through activities at her local church.

Johnoson Crutchfield, Ed.D. is a Visiting Assistant Professor of Curriculum Instruction at the University of Texas at Arlington. Dr. Crutchfield recently served as an assistant professor of Educational Leadership at the University of Mississippi. He is passionate about K-12 school climate turnaround efforts with at-risk populations. He also serves as Founder and CEO of Teacher on the MOVE, a consulting firm which supports local and state level teacher and leader professional development efforts. Dr. Crutchfield served as a teacher and instructional coach for 5 years at the middle school level in Baton Rouge, Louisiana. He is a native of Tallahassee, Florida and graduated from Florida State University. He earned his Doctor of Education degree from the University of Louisiana-Monroe conducting research on the relationship between PBIS implementation and perceptions of student motivation. His core focuses of instruction involve efforts to improve school climate and culture through training building administrators and teachers. Dr. Crutchfield believes the most valuable asset in education is the teacher. He believes the teacher is important, so quality teacher retention and recruitment are crucial to his approach. Dr. Crutchfield is also a husband and father of two children, and aims to treat the children and community he serves like his very own. Dr. Crutchfield's core turnaround strategies center on building trusting relationships with students and teachers, positively reinforcing desired behavior, and ensuring consistent school discipline practices.

Raquel Farmer-Hinton, Ph.D. is an Associate Professor in the Department of Educational Policy and Community Studies. She teaches graduate and undergraduate courses on research methods, sociology of education, urban education, and cultural foundations of education. She is a scholar of urban education and, for over 20 years, she has conducted research on urban policies, schools and communities. Noteworthy projects include investigations related to a) college-going cultures in urban high schools, b) social capital toward college planning for urban students, c) best practices used in non-selective college preparatory schools, and d) the role of promise scholarship programs toward college planning.

Dr. Hinton has authored or co-authored publications using both qualitative and quantitative methods. Further, she has received research awards and/or served as the principal investigator on grants from the American Educational Research Association, Educational Testing Service, University of Wisconsin-Milwaukee, and the University of Wisconsin Institute on Race and Ethnicity. Dr. Hinton received her B.S. in Psychology, and her M.S. and Ph.D. in Educational Policy Studies from the University of Illinois at Urbana-Champaign. She previously held positions as a Spencer Postdoctoral Research Fellow at the University of Chicago, a postdoctoral research fellow at the Educational Testing Service in Princeton, New Jersey, and a research associate at Westat in Rockville, Maryland.

Denver J. Fowler, Ed.D. is currently the Chair of the Ed.D. program and Professor of PK–12 Educational Leadership at Franklin University in Columbus, Ohio. Prior to his appointment at Franklin University, he served as a Program Coordinator and Assistant Professor of Educational Leadership and Policy Studies at California State University, Sacramento (CSUS). In addition to this role, Dr. Fowler served as an elected Senator on the Faculty Senate at CSUS. Dr. Fowler is starting his 11th year in Higher Education (6 years part-time & 4 years full-time). Prior to his appointment at CSUS, Dr. Fowler served as an Assistant Professor of Educational Leadership at The University of Mississippi (UM) where he taught within the Ph.D., Ed.D., Ed.S., M.Ed., and Principal Corps programs as well as served on several dissertation committees. In addition, he served as the elected President of the Mississippi Association of Professors of Educational Leadership (2015-2017), a state affiliate of the International Council of Professors of Educational Leadership. Prior to his appointment at UM, Dr. Fowler served as an adjunct faculty member for over six years at The Ohio State University, Bowling Green State University, and University of West Florida, where he was responsible for teaching courses (on-line, hybrid, & face-to-face) in educational leadership, educational technology, and teacher education, at both the undergraduate and graduate levels.

In addition to his experience in the Higher Education setting, Dr. Fowler served as a coach, teacher, athletic director, technology coordinator, and school administrator for over a decade in the PreK-12 educational setting in both the private and public school sectors in the state of Ohio. During this tenure, he was named the Ohio Association of Secondary School Administrators (OASSA) and National Association of Secondary School Principals (NASSP) State *Assistant Principal of the Year* in the State of Ohio, and was nominated for the NASSP *National Assistant Principal of the Year* in the United States. A strong supporter of education and policy reform, Dr. Fowler has spoken on Capitol Hill in order to advocate for educators and school leaders nationwide. He is the author of numerous books and other publications on educational leadership. His research interests include ethics, leadership, educational leadership, and research on the superintendency and principalship. Dr. Fowler has presented his research and served as a keynote speaker both nationally and internationally, including presentations in

China, Italy, Greece, Cuba, Africa, Turkey, England, Japan, Canada, and Puerto Rico. Dr. Fowler received his Doctor of Education (Ed.D.) in Educational Administration from Ohio University, Master of Arts in Education (M.A.) from Mount Vernon Nazarene University, and Bachelor of Science in Education (B.S.) from The Ohio State University. In addition to his degrees, Dr. Fowler completed a School Leadership Institute at Harvard University. Dr. Fowler is a licensed Superintendent, Principal, Teacher, and holds a Private School Administrative and Teaching license.

Catherine Hartman, M.Ed. is a doctoral candidate in the Program in Higher Education Leadership at The University of Texas at Austin. Her research centers around student transitions and success, including: how community college students engage academically and socially on their campuses; how students navigate transfer from community colleges to four-year schools; and how community college English learners and international students access higher education and engage on their campuses.

Esther Sui Chu Ho, Ph.D. is Professor in the Department of Educational Administration and Policy and Director of Hong Kong Centre for International Student Assessment at The Chinese University of Hong Kong. She has been Project Manager of HKPISA from 2000 to 2015. Her research interests include Longitudinal Study of Adolescents, Home School Community Collaboration, Spiritual Education and Mindfulness Practices in School Context. School Improvement and Education Reform, Decentralization and School-based Management, Multilevel Analysis in Educational Research. She has recently started a ten-year longitudinal study of youths to examine the transition process of Hong Kong adolescents from 15 to 25 year old with focus on their development of capability and well beings.

Nicole E. Holland, Ph.D. is a Professor in the Educational Inquiry and Curriculum Studies Department and the African and African American Studies Program at Northeastern Illinois University. Dr. Holland teaches all of the Educational Foundations courses, as well as courses in Research Methods; Schools and Cultural Pluralism: and, Power, Communities, and Change. In 2016 she was the Student Advisory Council's College of Education Finalist for the Teacher of the Year Award. Dr. Holland is a trained social psychologist who has conducted research in the fields of pre-school, elementary, secondary, and higher education. Her areas of interest include educational equity, educational policy, social justice and education advocacy, school reform, teacher training, professional community and professional development in schools, particularly as these areas influence conditions that promote success for populations that have a history of educational disadvantage. Her work is particularly focused on examining how individual factors (e.g. personal characteristics, skills, and abilities) and institutional factors (e.g.

organization, structure, and personnel), as well as the intersection between the two, influence academic success.

Dr. Holland's current research explores the postsecondary preparation, enrollment, and success of students from traditionally underrepresented college-going populations. Her research specifically addresses how students and their families, as well as educational practitioners, gatekeepers and policy makers, can demonstrate more agency in creating circumstances that promote more academic engagement, achievement and success as students embark upon their postsecondary pathways. She has received internal and external funding and awards for her research. Dr. Holland's previous research has been published in various peer-reviewed journals such as Race, Ethnicity, and Education; Education and Urban Society; Urban Education; Illinois Committee on Black Concerns in Higher Education (ICBCHE); Journal of Diversity in Higher Education; and, the High School Journal. She is the recipient of multiple Faculty Excellence Awards, the Dr. Melvin E. Cleveland Terrell Award for Research and Literature, and several other research awards. Dr. Holland earned her Bachelor of Arts from Hamilton College in Clinton, New York; her Master's of Arts from Hunter College of the City University of New York, and her Ph.D. from the Graduate School and University Center of the City University of New York.

Alden Jones, M.A. is a third-year doctoral student at University of Texas at Austin in the Higher Education Leadership and Policy program. They attended Winthrop University for their B.S. in Mass Communications and the University of Louisville for their Master's in Higher Education Administration. They were formerly the Senior Program Coordinator at the University of Louisville's LGBT Center. They have served as a policy analyst and campaign coordinator for a health advocacy non-profit in Kentucky. Alden has held various posts on campus in housing and residence life, Greek life, conduct, off-campus and nontraditional student services, and first-year orientation. Alden has also been a consultant facilitator for trans*gender inclusion training for various schools and nonprofit organizations. As a graduate research assistant they are focused on research inquiry that centers marginalized populations broadly conceived. Alden also researches gender and sexuality systems more broadly with respect to graduate student socialization. They also study gender identity and community making in material and digital spaces as well as policy implications for equity and inclusion. Their personal research interests focus on black trans* gender women and femmes and how they understand their place in and around the institution of higher education.

Chrysa Pui Chi Keung, Ph.D. is currently Post-Doctoral Fellow in the Faculty of Education of the Centre for University and School Partnership at The Chinese University of Hong Kong. Her research interests include the sociology of education, postsecondary transition, university choice and success for disadvantaged students, as well as multilevel analysis in educational research. Her work includes an examination of adolescents' expectation for pursuing higher education, class analysis of higher education enrollment, parental involvement in children's future education and career decision making. She recently involves in early childhood research projects related to teacher beliefs, play-based learning and positive education.

Richard Lofton, Jr., Ph.D. is an assistant professor of education at the Center for Social Organization of Schools and Johns Hopkins School of Education and Associate Director of The Johns Hopkins Urban Health Institute (UHI). He is the co-principal investigator for the national evaluation of the Student Success Mentor Initiative, which is funded by the Arnold Foundation. The initiative aims to reduce chronic absenteeism, develop caring relationships within schools and increase successful outcomes for students. Also, his research explores the Black habitus of African American students and parents and the impact of racism, institutional practices and concentrated poverty on homes, schools, and communities. His research examines the importance of uncovering systemic inequalities, illuminating agency and developing meaningful relationships with students and their parents for academic success. He is a graduate of Teachers College, Columbia University, and completed a two-year postdoctoral fellowship at the Center for Social Organization of Schools.

Carlos R. McCray, Ed.D. is a Professor at Montclair State University in the Department of Educational Leadership. He is the co-author of the books, *Cultural Collision and Collusion: Reflections on Hip-Hop Culture, Values, and Schools* and *School Leadership in a Diverse Society: Helping Schools Prepare all Students for Success. Prior to arriving at Montclair State University, Professor McCray was an associate professor and chair at Fordham University.* Professor McCray has worked with school leaders in the metropolitan areas of Atlanta, New York City, and London, UK. Professor McCray teaches courses on Educational Leadership, Social Justice, and Urban Education.

Ty McNamee, M.A. is a fourth-year doctoral student in Higher and Postsecondary Education at Teachers College, Columbia University. He currently resides in Fort Collins, Colorado, where he is completing his doctoral dissertation and working at Colorado State University as an Academic Success Coordinator in the College of Agricultural Sciences and as an Instructor in the Student Affairs in Higher Education graduate program. Prior to Teachers College, Ty received his Bachelor of Arts in English from University of Wyoming in 2013 and his Master of Arts in Higher Education and Student Affairs from the University of Connecticut in 2015. Throughout his academic career, he has served as a Congressional Intern at the United States Senate and in multiple administrative and teaching positions at Columbia University, Yale University, University of Connecticut, and University of Wyoming. Ty's research and scholarly writing focuses on equity and access for underrepresented students in higher education, particularly students from rural areas; teaching and learning at rural colleges and universities; and the experiences of faculty at rural higher education institutions. Upon graduation from Teachers College, his goal is to pursue the tenure-track faculty route in a Higher Education graduate program.

Jeana E. Morrison, Ph.D. is an inaugural AACTE/Holmes Postdoctoral Associate at the Boston University Wheelock College of Education. She received her Ph.D. in Education from Drexel University. She has several years of experience working as a coordinator and director of college access and success programs serving Philadelphia low-income and first-generation youth. Her research sits at the nexus of higher education, race, and policy in global contexts. As a critical ethnographer, her work centers Black student voices of the African Diaspora to articulate how larger social, political, and economic structures impact their access to and inclusive participation in post-secondary education opportunities. Furthermore, she is equally interested in the role that Black students play in confronting these structures, not only in thought but also in action.

Heather E. Price, Ph.D. is Assistant Professor of Leadership Studies doctoral program with concurrent appointment in the Social, Behavioral, and Forensic Sciences department at Marian University where she teaches graduate sociological methods and statistics. Her sociological research agenda on education includes social network analysis in schools, comparing education and education policies at the international level, and analyzing the unforeseen consequences from educational policies. Price primarily publishes on the sociology of education, including studies on school leadership, school community and climate, teacher commitment, school choice, and social capital among educators. These studies are published in journals such as *American Educational Research Journal, Education Administration Quarterly, Educational Policy, Journal of Educational Administration,* and *Social Science Research* and numerous book chapters on international education and social methods. Price also broadly studies the relational sociology, including her book of *American Generosity: Who Gives and Why?* (2016, Oxford).

Price actively participates and presents in professional organizations of the American Educational Research Association (AERA), American Sociological Association, and the Sociology of Education Association where she regularly serves on executive committees as well as reviews for flagship journals and annual conference submissions. Price actively consults for the Organization for Economic Cooperation and Development (OECD) and the International Association for the Evaluation of Educational Achievement (IEA) for the Teaching and Learning International Survey (TALIS) where she works in multi-nation research-policy-maker collaborations to design studies, analyze international data, and translate findings into policy recommendations. Prior to Marian, Price worked as a senior analyst at the University of Notre Dame and in the private educational policy sector as well as taught for years in Milwaukee Public Schools. While in the private sector, Price worked as a principal investigator for multi-year researcher-practitioner partnerships across public, private, and philanthropic organizations to co-design studies, organize and collect data, analyze results, and interpret findings for practitioners' use.

Phyllis F. Reggio, Ed.D. has served as a local instructional superintendent, principal of both middle and high schools, and assistant principal in New York City public schools. As an assistant professor, adjunct, in the Department of Special Education at Hunter College (CUNY) Graduate School of Education, and a professor at Touro College, Graduate School of Education, she worked as a site supervisor for teacher candidates. Currently, she is a principal in the Diocese of Brooklyn, New York. As a qualitative researcher, her interests include women in educational leadership, urban leadership, teacher training, and mentoring. Dr. Reggio holds a doctorate in Urban Leadership from Fordham University.

Lisa S. Romero, Ph.D. is an Associate Professor in the Doctorate of Educational Leadership Program in College of Education at California State University Sacramento. Her research interests include: school climate, trust and social capital, and education policy/politics, with a focus on how educational institutions can better serve marginalized groups. Her research appears in a variety of journals including the *Educational Administration Quarterly*, *Teachers College Record,* the *Journal of Educational Administration.* Prior to joining the academy, Lisa worked as a public school teacher and administrator. Her experience in public education provides her with particular insight into the nexus of theory and praxis.

Sarah Ryan, Ph.D. is a Research Scientist at the Wisconsin Center for Education Research (WCER) where her research focuses on understanding the sources and consequences of group-level differences in educational processes and outcomes, with a particular focus on English learner students, as well as the role of policy in addressing these disparities. Her work can be found in scholarly journals including the *American Educational Research Journal, Education Policy Analysis Archives*, and *Teachers College Record,* as well as in practitioner- and policymaker-friendly outlets. Before transitioning to a career in education research, Ryan spent six years as a teacher and administrator in K–12 public schools, where she worked primarily with English learners and their families. She holds a Ph.D. in education policy from the University of California-Riverside and a M.S. in English language acquisition from the University of Wisconsin-Madison.

Zachary W. (Z.W.) Taylor, M.A., M.S. is a Ph.D. student studying higher education and linguistics at The University of Texas at Austin. His scholarly interests include examining the intersection of linguistics and informatics as they pertain to pre-enrollment materials meant for prospective and current student audiences, such as admissions application guidelines, financial aid application instructions, and institutional policies governing student conduct, rights, and responsibilities. He is also interested in cross-cultural mentoring in the contexts of professional development in higher education, as well as international student recruitment, enrollment, and retention in U.S. institutions. He has published work in the Journal of College Student Development, Higher Education Quarterly, Philanthropy & Education, and Teachers College Record among others. His scholarly work can be found on Google Scholar at ZW Taylor (2019).

Roberto C. Trigosso, Ed.D. is the Chairperson for World Languages and English as a New Language in Nassau County, New York. He has served as an assistant principal, teacher and Middle School Principal in Suffolk and Westchester counties, New York. He has given several professional development workshops in Project Based Learning and strategies to foster Nurturing Relationships for academic success. His quantitative research interests include parent involvement, classroom instructional strategies and leadership capacity. Dr. Trigosso holds a doctorate in Executive Leadership from Fordham University.